ILLUSTRATED OS/2

J. Emmett Beam

Wordware Publishing, Inc.

Library of Congress Cataloging-in-Publication Data

Beam, J. Emmett.
Illustrated OS/2.

Includes index.
1. OS/2 (Computer operating system). I. Title.
II. Title: Illustrated OS/Two.
QA76.76.063B43 1988 005.4'469 88-14339
ISBN 1-55622-053-7

1506 Capital Ave.
Plano, Texas 75074

Printed in the United States of America

ISBN 1-55622-053-7

10 9 8 7 6 5 4 3 2 1
8805

All inquiries for volume purchases of this book should be addressed to Wordware Publishing, Inc., at the above address. Telephone inquiries may be made by calling:

(214) 423-0090

Contents

Contents (Continued)

Recommended Learning Sequence Checklist

Recommended Learning Sequence (Continued)

Acknowledgements

I want to thank Emily Chavez for her friendship, love, encouragement, and exhortations throughout the writing of this book. Her belief and faith in me made this a better book. I also want to thank Gigi Ash for the encouragement and enthusiastic support at the onset of this book. Thanks to my friend Russ Stultz, the President of Wordware Publishing, his staff, the editors and reviewers for their invaluable assistance in all phases of the creation of this book. This book is dedicated to Impulse.

J. Emmett Beam

Preface

About Illustrated Books As a classroom instructor and writer of books about many kinds of microcomputer software applications, I find myself constantly searching for good, authoritative sources of information. This includes books that can help me learn, and that are ready-made to help me teach others—ones that get at the "heart" of the information fast, and that teach principles through practice.

The alphabetized, modular format of the *Illustrated* Series lets you find the area of interest quickly. A description, applications, and step-by-step examples of typical operations are provided. This combination provides quick answers and contains illustrative models that are used to show you precisely how to apply software commands. For the new user, a recommended learning sequence leads you through each command in a simple-to-complex order.

You will find the *Illustrated* approach goes beyond standard documentation and books that treat software theoretically or in broad and sometimes vague terms. Unlike textbooks which have little value as a reference tool, the *Illustrated* format guarantees the book's usefulness long after you complete the learning sequence.

To the best of my knowledge, Wordware's *Illustrated* books comprise the only true computer book series on the market today. The organizational approach, presentation style, and examples are predictably consistent and reliable. Rigid author guidelines have been constructed for Wordware's *Illustrated* book authors to guarantee a reliable, consistent format for all books in the series. Technical audits are conducted to ensure that operational procedures and source listings work. Screen illustrations are captured during the technical audit process to assure that you see exactly what the software displays.

These extra steps have placed books in the *Illustrated* series in hundreds of universities and colleges around the world. In addition, technical schools, corporate learning centers, and computer dealers are using Illustrated books for training purposes. Many dealers use this book as their standard OS/2 reference manual in place of the one supplied with the software.

Russell A. Stultz
President and C.E.O.
Wordware Publishing, Inc.

Module 1
ABOUT THIS BOOK

INTRODUCTION

This book describes the Microsoft® Operating System/2 (MS OS/2), also called the IBM Operating System/2 (OS/2) by IBM. It describes how you can use the various versions of OS/2 to get the most out of your microcomputer.

But what is OS/2, anyway? In simple terms, a disk operating system provides a predictable linkage (one following established rules) between your computer's electronic circuitry (hardware) and the software programs you use, such as word processors, electronic spreadsheets, database managers, and accounting programs.

In addition to providing the software-to-machine interface, OS/2 features a host of handy "housekeeping tools." For example, there are special utilities for preparing new disks, listing the contents (or filenames) of a magnetic disk on the display screen or to your printer, creating, copying, deleting, and combining files, and much more. These features are described in this book.

This book is designed for a broad range of users. It is for beginners who wish to learn OS/2 from scratch. It provides intermediate and advanced users a quick reference that contains command examples that work and serve as useful examples. And, finally, it serves the classroom instructor as an instructionally designed OS/2 textbook.

The OS/2 program is sophisticated; it often appears intimidating because its commands are cryptic. OS/2 does not display a series of friendly menus from which to make a selection. To the contrary, it displays a rather cryptic letter and blinking *cursor*. Although it is not apparent, this is the OS/2 *prompt*, where a prompt invites you to type a command from the keyboard.

Therefore, it is necessary for you to memorize a few fundamental OS/2 *commands*, where commands are instructions that are recognized by OS/2. English-speaking computer users are fortunate, because most OS/2 commands are English derivatives. For example, the DIR command displays a directory (or list) of filenames on the screen. The FORMAT command is used to format (or prepare) a new magnetic storage diskette for use with your microcomputer.

One nice thing about OS/2 is that it tries to stay out of your way unless you call on it by entering one of its special commands. Of course, you can ignore OS/2 by running packaged applications programs. But learning the ins and outs of OS/2 is strongly recommended if you are to exploit the full power of your microcomputer.

If you are a beginning user who is not afraid to "mess around" with OS/2 commands, you will discover that OS/2 is easy to use within a matter of minutes. You can do useful things by learning a half-dozen or so commands. The more you use OS/2, the richer it becomes. After a brief exposure, you will begin to feel like a veteran computer user, because the utility of OS/2 lets you get down to the nuts and bolts of file creation and management.

To prove to yourself how easy OS/2 can be, you may want to jump over to Module 2 and go through the sample session with your computer. The sample session lets you make OS/2 do useful things, and you quickly see how you can have OS/2 working for you in a matter of minutes. Once you develop an appreciation for the usefulness of OS/2, you should have the incentive to explore OS/2 even further.

ORGANIZATION

This book is organized into compact, easy-to-read, example-packed *modules*. In order to best fit the broad range of users that it addresses, these modules include descriptions, applications, and illustrations that show you how OS/2 is used to solve practical, everyday problems. Literally hundreds of examples are presented in the Description, Applications, and Typical Operation sections of the modules.

Having working examples that let you experiment with OS/2 commands takes the mystery out of what might otherwise be difficult to appreciate. In addition to conducting "hands-on" experimentation, you will probably find yourself having a lot of fun, because learning by doing is a rewarding experience.

WITHIN THE MODULES

This module provides information about the book, and it briefly describes what kind of equipment is used with OS/2. It also tells you what you should know before moving on to subsequent modules.

With the exception of Modules 1 through 3, most of the modules in this book contain information that pertains to specific OS/2 commands, functions, or families of commands or functions.

Module 2 introduces you to OS/2. As you experiment with several of the more commonly used OS/2 utilities, you will see how responsive OS/2 is (as well as being relatively easy to use). If you are the kind of person who likes to "dive in," you will enjoy the sample session in Module 2. You will discover not only how OS/2 commands are used, but how you can follow the sample session on your computer. This is a preview of things to come, because this book is designed to let you follow along on your computer.

Module 3 introduces ways in which OS/2 and your keyboard interact. In addition, you will learn about *internal* and *external* OS/2 commands, *hidden* files, and several important new terms. An OS/2 command summary also is provided as a quick reference.

Modules 4 through 65 describe and illustrate the many OS/2 commands. These commands are arranged in alphabetical order, as in a dictionary, for easy reference.

If you are learning OS/2, be sure to follow the Recommended Learning Sequence at the front of this book. This sequence rearranges the commands, which are alphabetized for easy reference, into a simple-to-complex order. This organization is designed specifically for learning (or teaching) OS/2 commands, and has been used by thousands of self-taught users and classroom teachers. As you work your way through this book, you can check off the modules you have completed.

TERMS AND DEFINITIONS

Appendix A contains a list of terms and definitions that are used in this book. Although many are defined when first encountered, there may be a few that slipped in without explanation. If you encounter such a term, check Appendix A for a definition.

OS/2 PRACTICE EXERCISES

Appendix B is provided for both classroom and self-teaching situations. It contains OS/2 exercises. If you are a classroom instructor, you may wish to include these exercises in student assignments. If you are learning OS/2 on your own, the exercises are a good way to see what you have learned about a command. If you can answer the questions, you are ready to move on to the next module in the learning sequence.

HARDWARE AND SOFTWARE REQUIREMENTS

OS/2 operates with Intel's 80286 and 80386 family of microprocessors. OS/2-based computers are being used around the world by thousands of people for thousands of applications. OS/2 runs on hundreds of computer models, ranging from desktops to laptops from nearly as many manufacturers.

With a growing base of complex software programs, the need for larger amounts of memory is increasing. Today, it is not uncommon to find OS/2-based microcomputers sporting from three to eight megabytes (million characters) of memory. Your ability to take advantage of large amounts of memory depends upon the specific programs you use and the way you configure your computer.

A key to good system usage is your ability to use OS/2. You can set up virtual disks, called *memory* or *RAM* disks, to take advantage of extra memory in your system. You can tailor your system for your particular needs by customizing the config.sys file parameters.

WHAT YOU SHOULD KNOW

As a minimum, you should be familiar with computer connection and turn-on procedures. If you have a printer, you should know how to connect it to your computer, set switches, and load paper and ribbon. You should also be familiar with your system's monitor type, keyboard, available memory, and storage subsystem.

Finally, you should be familiar with your keyboard. If the keys on your keyboard are engraved with special symbols instead of words, use the following table to see how they are named in this book.

Symbol	Key
↵	Return or <cr>
←	Backspace
⇤ ⇥	Tab
⇧	Shift
→	Right Arrow
←	Left Arrow
↑	Up Arrow
↓	Down Arrow

If you have not already done so, move to Module 2 to experience a hands-on sample session with OS/2.

Module 2

A SAMPLE SESSION WITH OS/2

INTRODUCTION

This module provides information about your computer's disk drives, diskette storage and handling, and diskette construction. Then it takes you for a tour through a set of commonly used OS/2 commands. Because the intent of this module is to give you some hands-on experience, you will not find in-depth explanations of the OS/2 commands here. If, while using one of the commands, you become curious, check the module that describes that command in depth. When you finish your tour, move on to Module 3, which reveals additional information about the structure of OS/2, special OS/2 operations, and how your keyboard interacts with OS/2.

YOUR COMPUTER'S DISK DRIVES

Your computer is equipped with one or more diskette drives and a fixed (or hard) disk drive. OS/2 assigns different letter designations to disk drives. If you have a two-disk-drive system, the left-hand disk is normally logical disk A, while the right-hand disk is logical disk B. The first hard disk is disk C, and the second hard disk is disk D.

In this book it is assumed that the disk containing OS/2 is drive C. Although many use the term *diskette* to refer to a removable, flexible (or floppy) diskette, and *disk* to refer to a fixed disk, the term *disk* is used in this book to refer to both disks and diskettes. When a fixed disk is specifically referenced, the terms fixed or hard disk are used.

DISK HANDLING AND STORAGE

Flexible disks are delicate and should be handled accordingly. This is particularly true with the popular 5¼-inch diskette. The 3½-inch diskette configuration, on the other hand, is encased in a hard plastic shell and is less susceptible to physical damage. Some suggestions for handling and storage of flexible disks follow.

1. Never touch the exposed magnetic surfaces; always hold disks by their paper jackets.
2. Never expose disks to:
    a. Magnetic fields (magnets, motors, heavy metal objects)
    b. Extreme heat or cold
    c. Direct sunlight
    d. Moisture or oil
    e. Abrasive materials or dust
3. Take care not to scratch, score, or prick the disk or its protective cover.
4. Never eat, drink, or smoke in areas where disks are in use or being stored.
5. Use a soft felt-tip marker when writing on disk labels, and write lightly; do not use pencils, ball-point or nylon-tip pens.

6. Store disks in a flat diskette case or box to avoid bending or folding.

Following these simple suggestions minimizes the possibility of damage to your valuable programs and stored information (or *data*).

DISK CONSTRUCTION

The various parts of standard 5¼- and 3½-inch disks are contained in Figure 2-1. A description of each part is also provided.

1. Write protect notch—When covered, prevents information from being recorded on the disk; when uncovered, information can be recorded.
2. Temporary label—An adhesive-backed label allowing the contents of a disk to be identified.
3. Permanent label—When used, contains disk manufacturer and capacity information.
4. Exposed recording surface—Metal oxide surface used to magnetically record data. Do not touch!
5. Protective jacket—Houses magnetic disk; provides protective cover.
6. Diskette envelope (sleeve)—Used to store disks; prevents accidental contact with exposed surface.
7. Protective slide—Protects magnetic media surface; slides open when inserted into a diskette drive (only on 3½-inch diskettes).

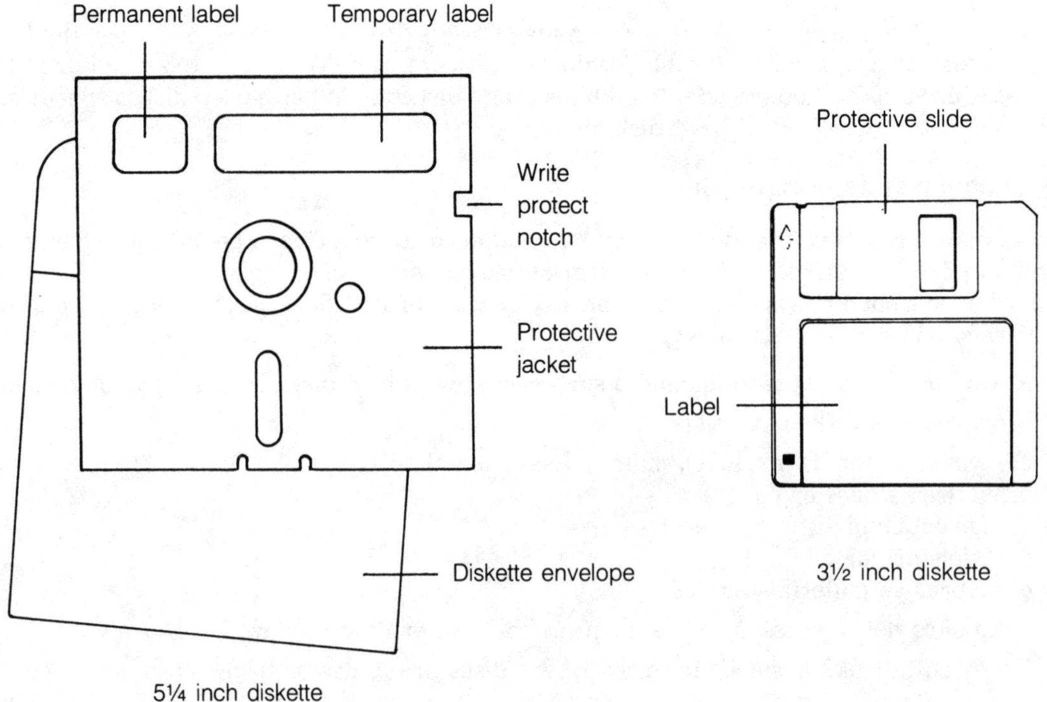

Figure 2-1 The Parts of a Floppy Disk

USING OS/2

Your tour of OS/2 includes formatting a new, blank disk, creating, copying, displaying, and deleting files from the disk. The formatted blank disk is used with the rest of the procedures in this book.

FORMATTING A WORKING DISK Begin your tour by performing the following procedure:

1. Check to see that your computer is connected properly and plugged into a wall outlet.
2. Turn on your computer and allow it to start (boot).
3. Begin at the OS/2 command prompt. If your computer starts and displays a menu titled "Program Selector," then you can get to the OS/2 command prompt with just a few key strokes. First, if not already there, you move the high-lighted line to the window labeled "Switch to a Running Program" by pressing the **Tab** key. Next move down by pressing the **Down Arrow** key, until the high-lighted line is the "OS/2 Command Prompt" (or CMD.EXE). Now press **Return** to select the OS/2 command processor which displays the command prompt.

NOTE

When the Typical Operation section directs you to begin at the OS/2 command prompt, you begin in the directory, C:\ with a prompt of [C:\].

When the Typical Operation section directs you to begin at the DOS command prompt, you can follow the instructions above except select "DOS Command prompt" and press **Return**.

To return to the Session Manager and the Program Selector menu from both OS/2 and DOS, press **Ctrl-Esc**.

4. Insert a blank high-denisty diskette in drive A: and close the load lever as shown in Figure 2-2.

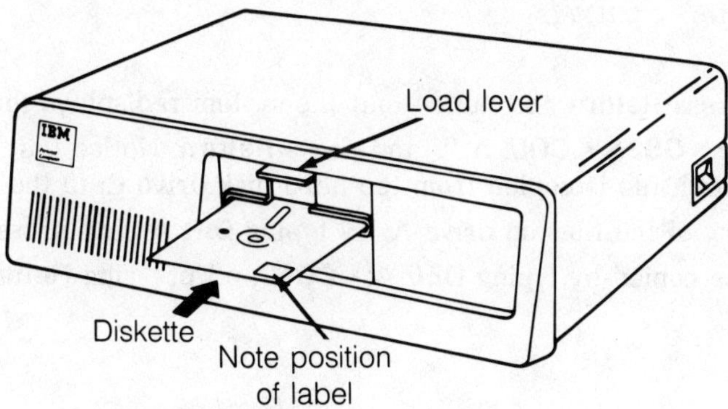

Figure 2-2 Inserting a Flexible Disk into a Disk Drive

NOTE

In steps 5 through 10, the FORMAT and COPY commands are used to format the new disk and then to copy some of the contents of your OS/2 disk to the new diskette.

5. Type **FORMAT A:** and press **Return**; notice the display.

```
[C:\]FORMAT A:

Insert new diskette for drive A:
and strike any key when ready _
```

6. Press any key (like Spacebar) and notice that the display indicates the formatting process. FORMAT displays head and cylinder locations, which identifies defective regions of a disk when encountered. Next FORMAT prompts for the volume label:

```
Enter up to 11 characters for the volume label,
or Press ENTER for no volume label. _
```

7. Enter **SCRATCH** and press **Return**.
8. Upon completion of the formatting process, a message similar to the following is displayed:

```
Formatting is complete.

1213952 bytes total disk space
1213952 bytes available on disk

Format another (Y/N)?_
```

9. Type **N** and press **Return** and notice that the system redisplays the OS/2 prompt.
10. Type **COPY C:\OS2*.COM A:/V** and press **Return**. Notice that a list of filenames is displayed as each file is copied from the hard disk drive C: to the disk in drive A:.
11. List a directory of the files on drive A: by typing **DIR A:** and pressing **Return**.
12. Delete the files copied by typing **DEL A:*.COM** and pressing **Return**.

NOTE

In the following step, you create a new file by copying the contents of the *console* (keyboard and screen), designated CON:, to drive A:. Notice that device names always end with a colon (:). In the case of disk drives, the drive name (A:), followed by a one- to eight-character filename, tells OS/2 where a disk file is located.

13. Create a new file as follows:

NOTE

The notation Ctrl-X designates pressing and holding the Ctrl key while typing a second key (X). This is like pressing and holding the Shift key to type a capital letter. You may type commands in either upper or lower case.

a. Type **COPY CON: A:MYFILE** and press **Return**.
b. Type the following two lines of text, ending each line by pressing **Return**:
   This is my first file.
   I am going to save it.
c. Press **Ctrl-Z** and then press **Return**. Notice the display screen; it should resemble the following illustration.

```
[C:\]COPY CON: A:MYFILE
This is my first file.
I am going to save it.
^Z
        1 File(s) copied

[C:\]_
```

14. Display your new file (MYFILE) on the screen by typing **TYPE A:MYFILE** and pressing **Return**.
15. Make a copy of MYFILE called MYFILE.#2 by typing **COPY A:MYFILE A:MYFILE.#2** and pressing **Return**.
16. Combine the files MYFILE and MYFILE.#2 into a file called MYFILE.#3 by typing **COPY A:MYFILE + A:MYFILE.#2 A:MYFILE.#3** and pressing **Return**.
17. Display a directory of the three new files by typing **DIR A:MYFILE.*** and pressing **Return**.

18. Notice the display screen; it should resemble this illustration:

```
[C:\]DIR A:MYFILE.*
Volume in drive A has no label
Directory of A:\

MYFILE          48   5-09-88    9:38a
MYFILE    #2    48   5-09-88    9:38a
MYFILE    #3    97   5-09-88    9:41a
        3 File(s)  1212416 bytes free

[C:\]_
```

19. Display the file named MYFILE.#3 on the screen by typing **TYPE A:MYFILE.#3** and pressing **Return**.
20. Notice the display screen; it should resemble this illustration:

```
[C:\]TYPE A:MYFILE.#3
This is my first file.
I am going to save it.
This is my first file.
I am going to save it.

[C:\]_
```

21. Rename the file MYFILE.#2 to MYTWO.TXT by typing **REN A:MYFILE.#2 MYTWO.TXT** and pressing **Return**.
22. Display a directory of filenames beginning with "MY" by typing **DIR A:MY*.*** and pressing **Return**.
23. Notice the display screen; it should resemble this illustration:

```
[C:\]DIR A:MY*.*
Volume in drive A has no label
Directory of A:\

MYFILE          48   5-09-88    9:38a
MYTWO     TXT   48   5-09-88    9:38a
MYFILE    #9    97   5-09-88    9:41a
        3 File(s)  1212416 bytes free

[C:\]_
```

24. Delete the file MYFILE by typing **DEL A:MYFILE** and pressing **Return**.
25. Display a directory of filenames beginning with "MY" by typing **DIR A:MY*.*** and pressing **Return**.
26. Notice the display screen; it should resemble this illustration:

```
[C:\]DIR A:MY*.*
Volume in drive A has no label
Directory of A:\

MYTWO     TXT  48   5-09-88    9:38a
MYFILE    #3   97   5-09-88    9:41a
        2 File(s)  1212928 bytes free

[C:\]_
```

27. Open the disk drive load lever, remove your new working disk, put it in its protective envelope, and store it in a safe place for later use.
28. Turn off the power to your computer equipment.

As a result of this practice session, you can now perform the following OS/2 operations:

- Format a blank disk
- Copy some files from one disk to another
- Display a directory of all filenames on a disk
- Display a directory of filenames on the disk in drive A
- Create a file
- Display (type) the new file on the screen
- Make a copy of the new file
- Combine two files to create a third
- Display a directory of selected filenames on the disk in drive A
- Rename a file
- Delete a file

As you can see, OS/2 performs a number of important tasks. However, these are just a few of the OS/2 operations available to you. You will learn many other equally powerful and useful OS/2 operations as you work your way through the rest of this book.

If you are beginning the learning sequence, turn to Module 3. There information about a number of OS/2 characteristics is provided. These include:

- The structure of OS/2
- An OS/2 command summary
- The names that OS/2 uses for different input/output devices
- The way your keyboard interacts with OS/2

Module 3

SYSTEM OVERVIEW

INTRODUCTION

This module provides an overview of OS/2 and the OS/2 commands described in this book, specifically, information about the following subjects:

- The structure of OS/2
- An OS/2 command summary
- The names that OS/2 uses to address the different computer input/output devices
- The way that your keyboard interacts with OS/2

WHAT IS OS/2?

Your disk operating system (OS/2) performs a number of essential jobs. These include:

1. Controlling the way various application programs, like word processors, electronic worksheets, database managers, accounting programs, etc., operate with your computer. OS/2 creates an environment that lets these programs "talk" to your computer and its input and output devices (printers, modems, display screen, keyboard, disk drives, etc.). Keyboard- and program-generated information is read, interpreted by OS/2, and transferred to the selected computer device. Data being returned by your computer is again translated by OS/2 into useful information and written to an output device, such as your display screen, printer, or disk.
2. Providing "housekeeping" and file management utilities that perform useful tasks such as:
   - Disk preparation (formatting, copying, etc.)
   - File operations (creating, displaying, copying, combining, renaming, deleting, etc.)
3. Automating repetitive tasks through automatic execution, or *batch*, files.
4. Controlling the way certain information is displayed on the screen.
5. Controlling the way your computer interprets certain commands.
6. Controlling the execution of multiple programs at the same time. Allows you to switch quickly to any executing program.

This book describes the generic version Microsoft® Operating System/2. Resellers of this operating system, like IBM, rename some of the files to be unique in the personal computer industry. For instance, the files named OS2BIO.COM and OS2DOS.COM by Microsoft are called IBMBIO.COM and IBMDOS.COM respectively by IBM. The author purchased the OS/2 Software Development Kit from Microsoft and therefore uses the Microsoft names in this book.

Figure 3-1 contains a simplified diagram of the way OS/2 interacts between your computer programs and computer (*hardware*). Notice the *BIOS* and *ROM BIOS* (read-only memory basic input/output system.) The OS2BIO.COM is a software module that contains hardware initialization and loads the standard *device drivers*. Hardware initialization includes preparing various parts of the hardware, such as memory, communication ports, etc., for operation. OS2BIO.COM loads the standard device drivers from disk and also loads OS2DOS.COM from the disk and transfers control to the user. Device drivers are small programs that accept calls from OS/2 to perform the appropriate hardware operation. The ROM.BIOS is actually a hardware device that contains a series of unalterable computer control programs (hence the term *read-only*). The ROM BIOS intercepts and processes instructions from OS2BIO.COM. When instructions are received, the ROM BIOS handles the operation of your computer's hardware devices. Returning control, information passes through ROM BIOS, OS2BIO.COM, OS2DOS.COM, and back to the program being used.

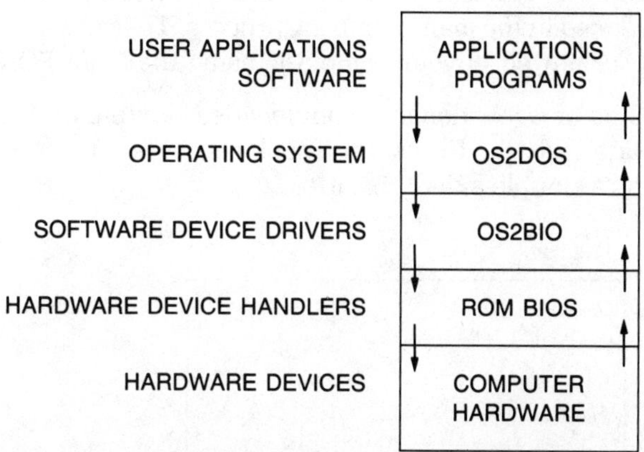

Figure 3-1 OS/2 and Your Computer, Simplified Diagram

OS/2 AND DISKS

The care and storage of disks (or diskettes) is described at the beginning of Module 2. Here a description of the construction and organization of a typical disk is provided.

CONSTRUCTION Almost everyone is familiar with audio recording tape. The tape is a long, flexible acetate or mylar strip coated with ferrous oxide. This coating, which is a powdered iron-like substance, is affected by magnetic fields. Tape recorders are equipped with record and playback heads. The record head places magnetic patterns on the tape. These patterns may be a derivative of voice, music, or even audible computer data. The playback head detects the recorded patterns, which then are amplified several thousand times. The amplified signal is finally reproduced by a speaker.

A disk is similar to a recording tape in substance. Flexible (floppy) disks are also made of ferrous oxide-coated mylar material. Fixed (or hard) disks are made of a more rigid material, but they still have the ferrous oxide coating.

The playback and record heads on a disk drive are called read and write heads, although they perform the same functions as their tape recorder counterparts.

Pre-recorded tape cassettes containing valuable music programming are protected with a plastic tab. This tab prevents tape recorders from recording over (erasing) the audio information. Flexible disks also can be *write protected* to keep you from accidentally writing over valuable programs or stored data. Any time you have a valuable program or data disk, be sure to place an adhesive-backed write protect tab or tape over the write protect notch on the disk sleeve.

ORGANIZATION Figure 3-2 is a diagram of a disk. Because the 5¼-inch double-sided, double-density disk is most common, it is illustrated. Other disk formats vary in tracks, sectors, and data storage density.

Notice that the disk is organized into concentric *tracks* instead of one continuous track (like the groove in a phonograph record). The tracks are further subdivided into wedge-shaped *sectors*. Tracks and sectors are not produced in the manufacturing process. They are created magnetically (*soft sectored*) when a disk is formatted in your computer using the OS/2 FORMAT command.

There are 40 tracks on each side of a low-density, double-sided flexible disk. These tracks are numbered zero though 39 on side zero (the first side). Track numbers 40 through 79 are located on side one (the "flip" side) of a double-sided diskette.

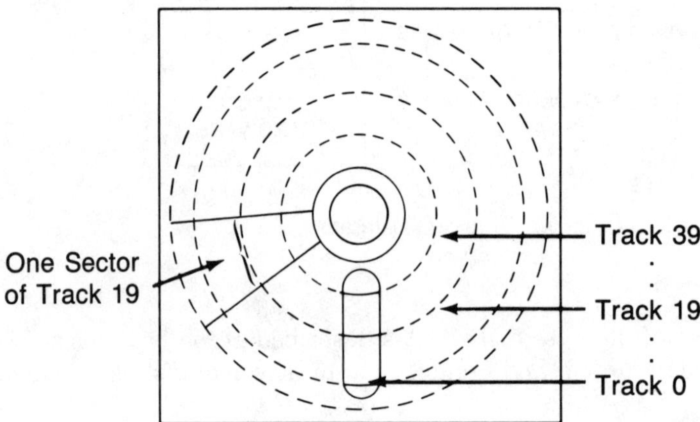

Figure 3-2 Disk Organization

Track number zero is reserved for disk directory information. The other tracks are available for program and file information. You can think of the disk directory like a post office, because it maintains name, address, and other important information about every file stored on the disk. Directory information includes:

- The file address (where a file begins and ends by track and sector location)
- The filename (assigned by programmers and computer users)
- The total size of the file in bytes (or characters)
- The date the file was last saved
- The time the file was last saved

NOTE

Before continuing, a few definitions are in order. The term byte represents a single computer character. A kilobyte (or KB) is 1,000 bytes. A megabyte (or MB) is one million bytes.

Each sector (or *track-sector*) on a standard high-density disk stores 512 bytes of information, with 15 sectors per track. OS/2 also supports the PC/MS-DOS standard disk that contains nine sectors per track.

The 3½-inch diskette format was adopted by a number of laptop computers. This storage device was initially rated at 720KB capacity. With the introduction of the IBM Model 50 Personal System/2, a 1.44MB format was offered. Table 3-1 shows total formatted storage capacities. Unless otherwise noted, diskettes are 5¼-inch.

Table 3-1 Approximate OS/2 Storage Capacities

Description	*Tracks*	*Sectors*	*Bytes/Sector*	*Total Capacity*
2-Sided	80	9	512	368,640 bytes
2-Sided 3½-inch	80	9	1024	737,280 bytes
1-Sided	40	9	512	184,320 bytes
2-Sided	80	9	512	368,640 bytes
High capacity	80	15	1024	1,228,800 bytes
2-Sided 3½ inch	80	9	1024	737,280 bytes
2-Sided 3½ inch	160	9	1024	1,474,560 bytes

OS/2 PROGRAMS

Knowing a few things about OS/2 may help further your understanding of how OS/2 works, making you a more skilled OS/2 user. This section includes information about:

- System control programs
- Internal and external commands
- OS/2 program summary
- Input-output device designations (or names)

SYSTEM CONTROL PROGRAMS There are four essential programs associated with the control of your computer and the way it interacts with: 1) programs; 2) your keyboard and display screen; and 3) attached devices like disk drives, printers, and modems. These programs are:

- Boot Record
- OS2BIO.COM
- OS2DOS.COM
- CMD.EXE

The Boot Record The term *boot* or *bootstrap*, when used with computers, means start or start-up. When you "boot" your computer, you are turning it on and loading the operating system into your computer's memory. This includes reading the *boot record* into memory, which passes control to OS/2. Next, OS/2 checks for the presence of OS2BIO.COM and OS2DOS.COM. If these files are found, the OS/2 prompt is displayed on your screen. This prompt, normally an [A:\] or [C:\], depending on which disk drive is active, invites you to type a command. If OS2BIO.COM and OS2DOS.COM are not found, an error message is displayed.

Your computer will not boot without a *boot record*. Instead, an error message is displayed telling you to insert a system disk. The boot record is located on track 0, sector 1, side 0 of your formatted OS/2 disk. The boot record is located on the first sector of the first cylinder of the OS/2 partition on the fixed disk.

The OS2BIO.COM Program This program interacts between your computer's ROM BIOS (read-only memory basic input/output system) and calls from the OS2DOS.COM program described next. At start-up, OS2BIO.COM resets the disk system and initializes any attached devices. OS2BIO.COM always loads at least five device drivers, which are used to control the operation of your keyboard, screen, printer, disk controller, and system clock. Other device drivers that are often loaded include device drivers to control large, external hard disks, serial communications, joy sticks, and mouse devices.

The final task performed by OS2BIO.COM is to load the command processor program, CMD.EXE. The OS2BIO.COM file is programmed by the manufacturer of your computer system. Therefore, the specific type and number of device drivers vary amoung computers.

The OS2DOS.COM Program This program interacts directly with applications programs and the OS2BIO.COM program described above. You can think of this program as the bridge between applications programs and OS2BIO.COM, as it intercepts program calls for printing, data storage or retrieval, information display, and so on, and routes these calls to the OS2BIO.COM program, which responds to the request with the appropriate reaction.

The CMD.EXE Program The CMD.EXE program is called the *command processor* because it reads commands from the keyboard and executes them. The commands are OS/2 commands or executable command files. The external OS/2 commands have file extentions of .COM or .EXE, and batch files have the extention .CMD. CMD.EXE also produces the OS/2 disk prompt ([C:\]), performs error checking, and displays error messages when system errors are detected.

Protected-mode and Real-mode OS/2 runs in protected mode within the 80286 and 80386 microprocessors. This means that when multiple programs are executing at the same time, one program can not access memory that is not assigned to it. Therefore the name, since programs are protected from a misbehaving program (one with a bug). OS/2 also allows a single PC/MS-DOS program to be running in what is called a compatability box. This allows the migration from PC/MS-DOS to OS/2 as simply and conviently as possible for the user. The PC/MS-DOS program runs in the microprocessor's Real-mode. In this book the programs and commands that run in the microprocessor's Real-mode are referred to as DOS Mode commands and programs.

The commands and programs that run in protected mode are referred to as OS/2 Mode commands and programs. Some OS/2 commands run only in the OS/2 Mode, some only in DOS Mode, but most work in both modes. Likewise, some application programs work in both modes.

INTERNAL AND EXTERNAL COMMANDS There are two kinds of OS/2 commands: *internal* and *external*. The internal commands are loaded into memory when OS/2 is booted. Internal commands are always available for your use, although they are not seen when you display the disk directory of filenames on your screen. Some internal commands are:

COPY	(copies files)
DEL (or ERASE)	(deletes files)
DIR	(lists a directory of filenames on the logged disk)
PROMPT	(changes the form of the system prompt)
REN	(renames files)
TYPE	(displays a named file on the screen)

External commands are conventional program files. These files can be deleted, copied, and even renamed. Their filenames are displayed when DIR lists a directory on the screen. Some examples of frequently used external commands are:

CHDIR	(changes directory)
CHKDSK	(checks the available space on the selected disk)
CLS	(clears screen)
COMP	(compares files)
DISKCOMP	(compares disks)
DISKCOPY	(makes verbatim copies of the source disk)
FORMAT	(organizes new disks for use with OS/2)

OS/2 PROGRAM SUMMARY Table 3-2 is a summary of OS/2 commands. In addition to command names and descriptions, the OS/2 version (D for DOS Mode, O for OS/2 Mode) and the type of command (I for internal, E for external) are listed. The Protected-mode commands are described in the modules of this book that include working examples.

Table 3-2 OS/2 Command Summary

Command	*Version*	*Type*	*Description*
ANSI	O	E	Supports ANSI escape sequences for video and keyboard control.
APPEND	D	E	Searches specified directories for data files not found in current directory.
ASSIGN	D	I	Reassigns the specified disk drive designations.
ATTRIB	O D	E	Sets "read-only" file attribute.
BACKUP	O D	E	Copies files from a fixed disk to flexible disks; produces "insurance" copies of working files and programs.

Table 3-2 OS/2 Command Summary (Continued)

Command	Version	Type	Description
BREAK ON/OFF	O D	I	Instructs OS/2 to check for a Ctrl-Break from the keyboard during program operation.
BUFFERS = nn	D	I	Allocates a number of disk buffers in memory equal to nn, which are activated at system turn-on. The value nn is a number between one and 99. The buffers command is contained in a file named CONFIG.SYS, that is automatically read at turn-on.
CHCP	O D	I	Changes to specified national language code page; NLSFUNC must be run prior to use.
CHKDSK	O D	E	Checks disk space, showing space occupied by files and space remaining for use.
CHDIR	O D	I	Changes OS/2 directory in use; short form is CD.
CLS	O D	E	Clears screen from OS/2 prompt.
CODEVIEW	O D	E	Provides facility for debugging, displaying, and modifying program files.
COMP	O D	E	Compares designated files.
CONFIG	O D	E	Selects communications parameters.
COPY	O D	I	Copies and combines files.
COUNTRY	O D	E	Selects the date and time format in a configuration file used at system turn-on.
CTTY	D	I	Assigns console control to a remote device.
DATE	O D	I	Sets the system date.
DETACH	O	E	Starts a program in the background.
DEVICE	O D	I	Entered as a command line within the CONFIG.SYS file to specify the name of a file containing a device driver. The device driver is loaded upon system turn-on.
DIR	O D	I	Lists a directory of filenames on the designated disk to the display screen.
DISKCOMP	O D	E	Compares the contents of two disks; used to verify that a diskcopy operation has been performed properly.
DISKCOPY	O D	E	Makes a duplicate copy of a disk.
EDLIN	D	E	Used to create and edit files; a simple line editor that is provided as a standard OS/2 utility.
ERASE (or DELETE)	O D	I	Deletes (or erases) files from a disk.
EXE2BIN	?	I	Used to convert program .EXE files into .COM OS/2 programs by programmers.

Table 3-2 OS/2 Command Summary (Continued)

Command	Version	Type	Description
FCBS	D	I	Specifies the number of files that can be open at the same time. Prevents files from being automatically closed by an active program.
FDISK	O D	E	Used to divide a fixed disk into two or more partitions. Allows two or more operating systems to be used on the same fixed disk.
FILES = nn	O D	I	Allows up to 99 files, specified by *nn*, to be simultaneously opened during program operation. The default value is eight.
FIND	O D	E	Finds and displays or writes all lines from a specified filename containing a specified text string.
GRAFTABL	D	E	Enables code page extended graphics characters to be displayed.
HELPMSG	O D	E	Provides help information about OS/2 error and warning messages.
JOIN	D	E	Creates a file path and joins files on a specified disk drive to give access to those files as if they existed in the newly created file path.
KEYB	O D	E	Selects code page keyboard layout to replace the default US keyboard.
LABEL	O D	E	Used to create, change, or delete disk volume name (or *label*).
MKDIR	O D	I	Creates a new directory branch.
MORE	O D	E	Reads data, such as a displayed directory, pauses output to the display screen when a full-screen condition is detected, and displays the message "—More—." Pressing any key resumes output until the next full-screen condition is detected, at which time "—More—" is displayed again.
MODE	O D	E	Sets output parameters to output devices including printers, display units, and asynchronous communications devices (modems).
PATCH	O	E	Make changes to .EXE and .COM programs.
PATH	O D	E	Searches specified directories for executable program (or batch) files that were not found in the main directory.
PRINT	O D	E	Queues from one to ten specified data files for printing. The queued files print from a special memory buffer, allowing you to perform other tasks on your computer during printing. Sometimes called a print spooler.
PROMPT	O D	I	Modifies the form of the OS/2 prompt.

Table 3-2 OS/2 Command Summary (Continued)

Command	Version	Type	Description
RECOVER	O D	E	Recovers defective files.
RENAME	O D	I	Renames an existing disk file.
REPLACE	O D	E	Replaces (or updates) all existing files on a target disk with matching files from a source disk.
RESTORE	O D	E	Reads backup files from flexible disks and writes them to a fixed disk.
RMDIR	O D	I	Removes a directory from a disk. The short form is RD.
SET	O D	I	Displays the computer's environment; lets you enter changes to the setting from the keyboard.
SETCOM40	D	E	Set COM ports so that a DOS program can access the COM port directly.
SHELL	D	I	Used by system programmers to specify the name and location of a command processor to be used in place of the standard DOS command processor (COMMAND.COM) for the DOS Mode.
SORT	O D	E	Sorts designated filenames or disk directories in alphabetical order.
SPOOL	O D	E	Background printer spooler and printing.
START	O	I	Start an OS/2 program from another session.
SUBST	O D	E	Substitutes a disk drive designation in place of a file path name.
SYS	O D	E	Transfers OS/2 to the designated disk.
TIME	O D	I	Sets the system time.
TREE	O D	E	Displays a hierarchy of disk directories.
TYPE	O D	I	Displays a designated file on the screen.
VDISK	O D	E	Establishes a memory disk; added to OS/2 at system turn-on.
VER	O D	I	Displays the version of OS/2 being used.
VERIFY	O D	E	Verifies the integrity of copied data.
VOL	O D	E	Displays the volume name of the designated disk.
XCOPY	O D	E	Copies files selectively.

DEVICE DESIGNATIONS A device designation is a reserved abbreviation followed by a colon, that stands for different computer devices. For example, the device designations for disk drives A and B are A: and B:. The device designation for your keyboard and screen, referred to as the *console*, is CON:. Like OS/2 commands, device designations can be typed in either upper or lower case. So the designation "con:" is interpreted by OS/2 as "CON:." Table 3-3 is a list of OS/2 device designations and their meanings.

Table 3-3 Device Designations

Designation	*Description*
A: through G:	Disk drive designations A through G.
CON:	The *console*, or keyboard and screen, designation. Used when copying keyboard/screen information to a file or other device. Ctrl-Z (or F6) is used to mark the end of a file.
COM1: or AUX:	Communications Port 1 or the serial communications or printer designation.
COM2:	Communications Port 2 or the second serial communications port.
LPT1: or PRN:	First parallel printer port.
LPT2:, LPT3:	The second and third parallel printer ports.
NUL:	A dummy device used when testing a command. Input operations encounter an immediate end-of-file condition. Output operations are simulated without actual data transfer.

OS/2 AND YOUR KEYBOARD

Keyboards vary with the brand of computer. However, almost all computer keyboards have similarities. This section describes the categories of keys used by computer keyboards.

KEYBOARD LAYOUT The keyboard layout of a typical personal computer is shown in Figure 3-3.

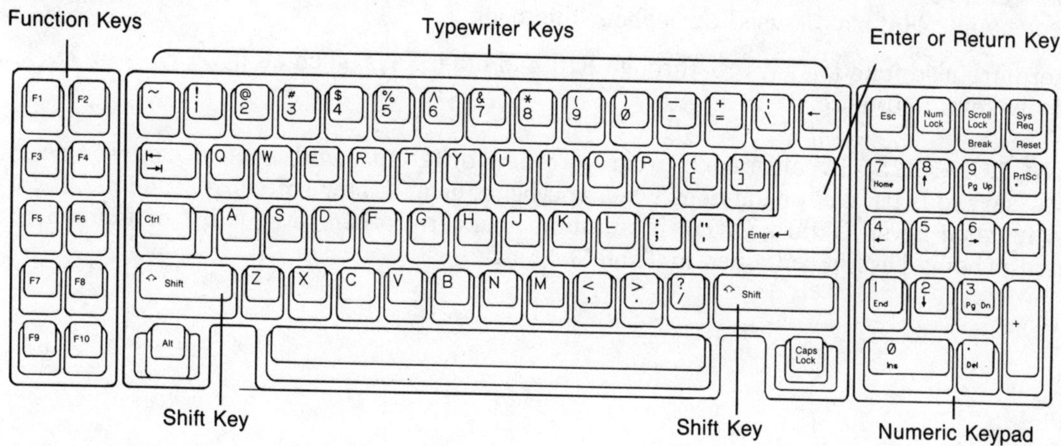

Figure 3-3 Typical Keyboard Layout

STANDARD TYPING KEYS The standard typing keys are the same as those used on a conventional typewriter. These include letter and number keys, the Tab key, and the Shift keys. Your Shift key is used to type upper-case letters and the symbols above the upper row of number keys, just as on a typewriter. The Caps Lock key lets you type in upper case without pressing a Shift key. When the Caps Lock is on, pressing Shift produces lower-case characters. There are also several special character keys available to you on the computer keyboard, such as the vertical bar, back slash, tilde, and grave (accent mark) symbols:

Description	*Symbol*
Vertical Bar	¦
Back Slash	\
Tilde	~
Grave	`
Greater Than	>
Less Than	<
Open Bracket	[
Close Bracket	]
Open Brace	{
Close Brace	}

SPECIAL CONTROL KEYS Special control keys send special codes to your computer. These codes are used frequently to perform special operations. For example, the Arrow keys are used to move the cursor (flashing bar or block) left, right, up, or down. Some programs use the Ins and Del keys to insert and delete characters.

Expressions like Ctrl-X and Alt-X, where X is any keyboard character, indicate that the Ctrl or Alt key is pressed and held while the indicated character key is pressed. This is done in the same way that capital letters are typed using the Shift key. Keystrokes that you press or type in procedures are boldfaced as in **Ctrl-KB** or **Return**.

The ↵ key is used like a carriage return key on a typewriter. It ends a line or completes a command. "Return" is used throughout this book.

There are also function keys F1 through F10 and other keys, such as Ins, Del, Num Lock, the Arrow keys, and more.

FUNCTION KEYS Because each program reacts differently with special control keys, it is necessary to learn what each does when you begin using a new software product. OS/2 uses the function keys, F1 through F6, in addition to several other keys. A list of functions and corresponding keys is contained in Table 3-4.

Table 3-4 OS/2 and the Keyboard

Function	Key(s)
Complete command or end a line	Return or Enter
Move down one line to continue typing	Ctrl-Return
Backup cursor to blank text or retype	Backspace
Discard typed command so you can retype it correctly	Esc
Discontinue or cancel program operation	Ctrl-Break or Ctrl-C
Pause scrolling of text on screen; press any key to resume scrolling	Ctrl-Num Lock or Ctrl-S
Print displayed screen	Shift-PrtSc
Print characters that are typed or displayed on the screen	Ctrl-P or Ctrl-PrtSc
Type capitals	Shift-(letter/number key)
Lock capitals on/off	Caps Lock
Shift numeric keypad between numbers and function keys	Num Lock
Type numbers with Num Lock on, use cursor and special control keys with Num Lock off	Numeric Keypad
Reset (warm boot) your computer	Ctrl-Alt-Del
Used with character keys to perform special operations	Ctrl

NOTE

Previously typed OS/2 commands are stored in a temporary memory location called a *buffer*. The following keys are used to reuse and modify the stored command line. These may vary slightly depending upon your microcomputer.

Function	Key(s)
Copy one character from the buffer	F1
Copy all characters from the buffer up to the character *x*	F2 x
Copy all remaining characters from the buffer, beginning at the present position to the end of the line	F3
Skip all characters up to the character *x*	F4 x
Use the last edited line for further modification	F5
Insert one or more characters in a line	Ins
Delete the next character from the buffer	Del
Cancel this line and start over; does not change contents of the buffer	Esc
Type End-of-file marker	F6 or Ctrl-Z

RESETTING WITH Ctrl-Alt-Del

Pressing the Ctrl, Alt, and Del keys simultaneously restarts your computer system. This process is called a *warm boot*, *reset*, or *re-initialization*. If your computer "hangs" (or *crashes*) for some reason, it may be necessary to reset with Ctrl-Alt-Del to get it going again. You should do this only as a last resort. If the Ctrl-Alt-Del key sequence has no effect, it means that the codes being sent from your keyboard are no longer being received and interpreted by your computer. If this happens, you must turn the power off, wait several seconds, and turn the power back on again to resume operation. If you have a fixed disk, you should wait until disk rotation stops before turning your computer back on.

If you are following the learning sequence, turn to Module 53.

Module 4

ANSI

DESCRIPTION

The ANSI command is an external OS/2 Protected Mode command. This command enables and disables ANSI escape sequences in the protected OS/2 Mode. An ANSI escape sequence is a series of characters beginning with an Escape character that provides application programs with extended screen control features. These sequences were developed by the American National Standards Institue (ANSI) to standardize cursor commands in application programs. The ANSI codes allow application programs to run without modification on many different computer systems.

The form for the ANSI command is

ANSI ON	—enables the extended screen and keyboard control
ANSI OFF	—disables the extended screen and keyboard control
ANSI	—shows the current setting of the ANSI command

The DOS Mode counterpart to this command is a device driver, named ANSI.SYS, and described in Module 22 (Device Drivers). Refer to this module for enabling the ANSI sequences in Real Mode. The OS/2 command and the ANSI.SYS device driver are functionally equivalent.

ANSI ESCAPE SEQUENCES

The ANSI escape sequences are categorized into four categories:

- Cursor Functions
- Erase Functions
- Mode Functions
- Keyboard Functions

In the following definitions, the variables are replaced by values to accomplish the desired result. The other characters within the sequences are constants.

Variable	*Meaning*
Xn	A decimal number specified with ASCII digit(s)
Xs	A decimal number specified with ASCII digit(s) to select a subfunction. You may repeat subfunctions, but separate them with semicolons.
Xr	A decimal number specified with ASCII digit(s) to select a row on the screen
Xc	A decimal number specified with ASCII digit(s) to select a column on the screen
Cursor Functions	Affect on Cursor Positioning
ESC [Xr ; Xc H	— Position cursor to row/column Xr,Xc
ESC [Xr ; Xc F	— Position cursor to row/column Xr,Xc
ESC [F	— Move to upper left corner on screen
ESC [Xn A	— Position cursor up Xn rows, same column
ESC [Xn B	— Position cursor down Xn rows, same column
ESC [Xn C	— Position cursor Xn columns forward, same row
ESC [Xn D	— Position cursor Xn columns backward, same row
ESC [6 n	— Output device status report
ESC [s	— Save cursor position
ESC [u	— Restore cursor to last saved position
Erase Functions	Affect on Screen Display
ESC [2 J	— Erase screen, home cursor to upper left
ESC [0 K	— Erase to end of line from current column
Mode Functions	Affect on Screen Graphics
ESC [Xs m	— Set graphics rendition

where:

Xs	Function	Xs	Function
0	— All attributes off	5	— Blink on
1	— Bold on	6	— Rapid blink on
2	— Faint on	7	— reverse video on
3	— Italic on	8	— Concealed on
30	— Black foreground	40	— Black background
31	— Red foreground	41	— Red background
32	— Green foreground	42	— Green background
33	— Yellow foreground	43	— Yellow background
34	— Blue foreground	44	— Blue background
35	— Magenta foreground	45	— Magenta background
36	— Cyan foreground	46	— Cyan background
37	— White foreground	47	— White background
48	— Subscript	49	— Superscript

Keyboard Functions	
ESC [Xn ; Xn p	— First Xn is redefined to second Xn
ESC [0 ; Xn ; "string" ; 13p	— Redefine a function key Xn to string F1 = 59, F2 = 60, F3 = 61, . . . , F10 = 68

EXAMPLES OF ANSI SEQUENCES In the following examples the capital "E" represents the ESCAPE character. The escape sequences are sent as follows exactly. Spaces are placed in the above descriptions as separators for your easy viewing.

E[5;10H	— Position cursor to row 5 column 10
E[2J	— Erase screen, position cursor to upper left corner
E[5A	— Move cursor down five lines, remains in same column
E[12C	— Move cursor forward 12 columns on the current line
E[0K	— Erase from cursor position to end of current line
E[31;44m	— Set red foreground and blue background

APPLICATIONS

Some programs do not operate properly without the ANSI command turned on. The default setting is ANSI ON, with which almost all programs will operate normally. Most users run with the ANSI command on.

The ANSI sequences make it easy for you to customize and program your keyboard characters and function keys.

The ANSI sequences make it easy for programmers to write portable application programs.

TYPICAL OPERATION

In this activity you use the ANSI command to turn the ANSI escape sequences on and off. Begin at the OS/2 prompt, [C:\].

1. Type **ANSI off** and press **Return**. Notice the following message:

   ```
   The ANSI extended screen and
   keyboard control are off.
   ```

2. Type **ANSI on** and press **Return**. Notice the following message:

   ```
   The ANSI extended screen and
   keyboard control are on.
   ```

3. Turn to Module 6 to continue the learning sequence.

Module 5
APPEND

DESCRIPTION

The APPEND command is an external OS/2 command. It is used to provide access to data files located in other directory paths or other disks. The APPEND command functions in DOS Mode like the DPATH command in OS/2 Mode.

If you wish the APPEND paths to be saved in the DOS environment, the first time you use APPEND include the /E parameter. For example,

```
APPEND /E
```

The general form for the APPEND command is

```
APPEND pathname
```

To illustrate the APPEND command, assume you have a file named GATOR.DAT that is located in a subdirectory. You are not sure if it is on disk C or disk A, so you want to search both disks and TYPE the file when found. To complicate matters, you are not sure if the program is in the SWAMP subdirectory or the MUD subdirectory.

Here is where the APPEND command comes to your rescue. To set up a search for GATOR.DAT, you can specify the disk and directories using the APPEND command. While logged on disk C, assuming that you have a fixed disk system, type

```
APPEND \SWAMP;\MUD;B:\SWAMP;B:\MUD
```

When you enter TYPE GATOR.DAT, OS/2 first searches the C:\SWAMP subdirectory, then the C:\MUD subdirectory. Next, it searches the B:\SWAMP subdirectory. Finally, it searches the B:\MUD subdirectory where GATOR.DAT is found and typed on your monitor.

You can also use the APPEND command to display the data path setup. To do this, type APPEND and press Return. A display similar to the following is displayed:

```
[C:\]APPEND

APPEND=\SWAMP;\MUD;B:\SWAMP;B:\MUD
```

To cancel the data path settings, type

```
APPEND ;
```

and press Return. The semicolon is the critical agent in this APPEND command.

APPLICATIONS

As you may suspect, a primary use of the APPEND command is to provide access to data files located in multiple subdirectories. This provides you with the flexiblity to organize your data files in meaningful ways without having to recompile your application programs.

TYPICAL OPERATION

In this activity you use the APPEND command to establish a directory search and then use it to display the established routing. Finally, the data paths are canceled. Begin at the DOS prompt, [REAL C:\].

1. Type **APPEND /E** and press **Return** to inform APPEND to save the append values in the environment.
2. Type **MD SWAMP** and press **Return**.
3. Type **MD SWAMP\MUD** and press **Return**.
4. Type **APPEND \SWAMP;\SWAMP\MUD** and press **Return**.
5. Type **APPEND**, press **Return**, and notice the following display:

```
[REAL C:\]APPEND

APPEND=\SWAMP;\SWAMP\MUD
```

6. Cancel the path by typing **APPEND;** and pressing **Return**.
7. Type **APPEND** and notice the following display:

```
[REAL C:\]APPEND
APPEND=
```

8. Type **RD SWAMP\MUD** and press **Return**.
9. Type **RD SWAMP** and press **Return**.
10. Press **Ctrl-Esc** to return to Session Manager. Select OS/2 Command Prompt in the SWITCH TO A RUNNING PROGRAM window to return to OS/2 Mode.
11. Turn to Module 47 to continue the learning sequence.

Module 6

ASSIGN, JOIN, SUBST

DESCRIPTION

The ASSIGN, JOIN, and SUBST commands all provide access to files on other disk drives or within other directories. Each is described with clarifying examples. These commands only work in DOS Mode, you cannot use them in an OS/2 session.

ASSIGN The ASSIGN command is an external OS/2 command. It tells OS/2 to look at an assigned disk, rather than on the disk that is normally used by programs. For example, if you have a program on the disk in drive B: and the logged drive is A:, you can type the command ASSIGN A = B. Although you may be logged to drive A:, typing the program name causes it to run. Why? Because the ASSIGN command rerouted the command to the disk in drive B:. To cancel the ASSIGN command, just type ASSIGN and press Return, and everything returns to normal.

If you have a computer with three disk drives, you can use a command like ASSIGN A = C B = C. This tells DOS to look on the disk in drive C: for all programs and files. Even if you type DIR A:, the ASSIGN command causes DOS to list a directory of drive C:.

There are a few commands that ignore ASSIGN. These include DISKCOPY and DISKCOMP. However, most commands honor the ASSIGN setting. Therefore, you should always remember when ASSIGN is in use. Otherwise, unpredictable things may happen when you use common DOS commands. In particular, never use the ASSIGN command when the PRINT command (Module 45) is active.

JOIN The JOIN command is an external command. The JOIN command is used to create a temporary subdirectory and join a designated disk drive and all of its subdirectories to the new subdirectory. The root directory is not a valid directory.

The command JOIN A: C:\TEMP creates a subdirectory named C:\TEMP. You can move to this subdirectory with CD \TEMP. In the new subdirectory, commands are redirected to the "joined" drive, which is A: in this illustration. If you use the DIR command, a list of the files on the diskette in drive A: is displayed as if they were in the TEMP subdirectory.

You can use existing disk subdirectories only if they are empty. Attempting to use a subdirectory having files results in a "Directory not empty" message. Once a JOIN relationship is established, typing JOIN alone displays the relationships. In our example, you see A: = > C:\TEMP. To disconnect a JOIN relationship, use JOIN A: /D.

Here are a few precautions that you should know about:

1. One drive is restricted to one relationship at a time.
2. Avoid joining directories or drives that are involved in ASSIGN or SUBST relationships.
3. JOIN does not allow the use of network drives.

4. Never use BACKUP, DISKCOMP, DISKCOPY, FORMAT, or RESTORE when JOIN is active.
5. The specified path cannot be the current directory.

SUBST The SUBST command is an external OS/2 command. With this command you can have OS/2 substitute a path wherever you use the associated drive letter. The SUBST allows you to abbreviate access to a subdirectory. For example, if you make a lot of references to files with a directory having the path of C:\ACCOUNT\REBECCA, you can, with the following SUBST command, use the drive letter Z: instead of the path specifier:

```
SUBST Z: C:\ACCOUNT\REBECCA
```

Therefore, you can use either Z:BILLS.DAT or C:\ACCOUNT\REBECCA\BILLS.DAT to access the file BILLS.DAT in your directory after you type the above SUBST command.

The Z: represents a virtual drive since you can use the drive letter in commands as if Z: is a real drive.

To cancel the SUBST command enter

```
SUBST Z: /D
```

which deletes the substitution of the virtual drive.

Use the SUBST command with no parameters to display all current substitutions.

APPLICATIONS

Often, programs are written to use two or more disks on a floppy system. In these cases, the program "looks" for files on specific disk drives other than the one on which the program is actually located. This is often the case when a program is put on a hard disk system. Here, you can use ASSIGN to redirect calls to the hard drive. The command ASSIGN B = C does the job.

The JOIN command lets you work with a subdirectory that directs all commands to the joined drive and all of its directories. This lets you operate with a single drive without having to remember which disk drive contains particular files. For example, if your computer has two floppy drives and one hard drive, you can use subdirectory names with the JOIN command that indicate the file types stored on each diskette. For example, if program files are on drive A and data files on B, you can use commands like JOIN A: C:\PROG and JOIN B: C:\DATA. Typing JOIN displays

```
A => C:\PROG
B => C:\DATA
```

Often, the pathnames to OS/2 files become quite long. You can use the SUBST command to shorten your typing. It is quicker and less prone to error to type a drive letter than a 50+ character pathname.

Another use is when you have similar data files with the same name in different directories. Using the SUBST command, you can have one batch file do reporting from the appropriate data file. For example, the files C:\DATA\COMPANY1\CUSTOMER.DAT and D:\DATA\COMPANY2\CUSTOMER.DAT can be accessed with the same batch file depending on which of the two following SUBST commands was last entered:

```
SUBST Z: C:\DATA\COMPANY1
```

or

```
SUBST Z: D:\DATA\COMPANY2
```

Z:\CUSTOMER.DAT can reference either data file, depending on which one of the above two SUBST commands you enter.

TYPICAL OPERATION

In this activity you use the ASSIGN command to temporarily designate drive B as the active drive. Begin at the DOS prompt, [REAL C:\].

1. Insert a formatted data disk containing files into drive A:.
2. Type **ASSIGN B = A** and press **Return**.
3. Now type **DIR B:** and press **Return** to display a file directory. Notice that the file directory is that of the disk in drive A:.
4. Type **ASSIGN** and press **Return** to remove all assignments.

In this activity you use the JOIN command to join the files on drive A: to a subdirectory named C:\TEMP. Start at the DOS prompt, [REAL C:\].

1. Insert a floppy disk in drive A: that contains DOS files.
2. Type **MD C:\TEMP** and press **Return**.
3. Type **JOIN A: C:\TEMP** and press **Return**.
4. Type **DIR C:\TEMP** and press **Return**; notice that the files in drive A are listed.
5. Type **JOIN A:/D** and press **Return** to discontinue the JOIN relationship.
6. Type **CD C:\TEMP** and press **Return**.

In this activity you use the SUBST command to temporarily designate drive Z: for a subdirectory on drive A:. Begin at the DOS prompt, [REAL C:\].

1. Insert a formatted disk into drive A:.
2. Type **MD A:TESTDIR** and press **Return**.
3. Type **COPY COMMAND.COM A:\TESTDIR** and press **Return**.
4. Type **SUBST Z: A:\TESTDIR** and press **Return**.
5. Type **DIR Z:** and press **Return**. Notice that the directory of A:\TESTDIR is displayed:

```
[REAL A:\]DIR Z:

Volume in drive A has no label
Directory of Z:\

.                <DIR>     4-05-88    1:00p
..               <DIR>     4-05-88    1:00p
COMMAND   COM    17792     3-17-87   12:00p
                 3 file(s) 112456 bytes free
```

6. Type **SUBST Z: /D** and press **Return**. This deletes the Z: substitution for the directory A:\TESTDIR.
7. Type **SUBST** and press **Return**. Notice that there are no substitutions active now:

```
[REAL A:\]_
```

8. Press **Ctrl-Esc** to return to Session Manager. Select OS/2 Command Prompt in the SWITCH TO A RUNNING PROGRAM window to return to OS/2 Mode.
9. Turn to Module 14 to continue the learning sequence.

Module 7
ATTRIB

DESCRIPTION

The ATTRIB command is an external command that is used to change the attribute of a file. For example, you can use ATTRIB to make a file "read-only," which prevents the file from being written over (or changed). The ATTRIB command gives you the ability to set the *archive bit*, which is set to one when a file is created or changed. This bit is used by the BACKUP, COPY, and XCOPY commands to determine if new or changed files exist, providing a time-saving option for marking those files that require updating.

ATTRIB uses + R and − R to set and remove the read-only attribute. The + A and − A options give you control over the archive attribute.

You can use wildcards in the pathname to specify a group of files. You can use the /s switch when you want ATTRIB to process all subdirectories as well as the path specified.

Study the following examples.

First, you can use ATTRIB to determine the attribute status of a file by typing ATTRIB, the filename, and pressing Return.

To make MYFILE1.TXT a read-only file, type

```
ATTRIB +R MYFILE1.TXT<cr>
```

To cancel the read-only status, type

```
ATTRIB -R MYFILE1.TXT<cr>
```

To make all payroll programs read-only files, type

```
ATTRIB +R C:\PAYROLL\PAY*.EXE<cr>
```

Similarly, to set the archive attribute (change it to one), type

```
ATTRIB +A MYFILE1.TXT<cr>
```

To reset the archive bit back to zero, type

```
ATTRIB -A MYFILE1.TXT<cr>
```

To reset the archive bit on every file on a disk, type

```
ATTRIB -A a:*.* /s
```

APPLICATIONS

Being able to make a file read-only avoids damage from modifying it accidentally. This is particularly important if your system is in a networking environment, where many users have access to valuable programs. By making the programs read-only, the programs cannot be modified by network users.

Resetting the archive attribute is sometimes desirable when using BACKUP and XCOPY. For example, if you discover that a damaged file was copied to your archive diskette or tape, you can change the file attribute in order to recopy it during the backup process. Refer to the BACKUP, COPY, and XCOPY commands for their specific action based on the archive bit.

TYPICAL OPERATION

In this activity you use ATTRIB to make the CHKDSK.EXE program read-only. Begin at the OS/2 prompt, [C:\].

1. Type **COPY C:\OS2\CHKDSK.COM** and press **Return** to copy CHKDSK.COM to C:\.
2. Type **ATTRIB +R CHKDSK.COM** and press **Return** to make the CHKDSK program read-only.
3. Check the attribute of the file by typing **ATTRIB CHKDSK.COM** and pressing **Return.** Notice the following display:

```
[C:\]ATTRIB CHKDSK.COM

       R      [C:\]CHKDSK.COM
```

4. Type **ATTRIB +A CHKDSK.COM** and press **Return** to set the CHKDSK program archive bit.
5. Check the attribute of the file by typing **ATTRIB CHKDSK.COM** and pressing **Return.** Notice the following display:

```
[C:\]ATTRIB CHKDSK.COM

  A    R      [C:\]CHKDSK.COM
```

6. Type **DEL CHKDSK.COM** and press **Return** to delete the copy that you made.
7. Turn to Module 51 to continue the learning sequence.

Module 8

AUTOMATIC FILE EXECUTION (BATCH COMMANDS)

DESCRIPTION

OS/2 lets you create and store a series of OS/2 commands that are acted upon (or "executed") automatically one line at a time in the order entered. The file containing the series of OS/2 commands is called a *batch file*. These files must have the extension .CMD (.BAT in DOS Mode) and contain legitimate OS/2 commands on each line.

If the batch file is given the special filename STARTUP.CMD (AUTOEXEC.BAT in DOS Mode), it is executed automatically when you first start your computer. If the batch filename is given another name, like LIST.BAT, you must type LIST and press Return for the commands in the batch file to run.

SPECIAL OS/2 BATCH FILES

OS/2 has three special batch files:

- STARTUP.CMD
- AUTOEXEC.BAT
- OS2INIT.CMD

The STARTUP.CMD file is executed one time by OS/2 when the computer is booted.

The OS2INIT.CMD file is executed each time you select the OS/2 Command Prompt through the Session Manager. This allows you to set default values into the environment for each OS/2 session.

The AUTOEXEC.BAT file is executed once, the first time you select the DOS Command Prompt through the Session Manager. This allows you to set the default values into the environment for the one DOS Mode session.

Here is an example of a batch file you might want to use for OS2INIT.CMD and for AUTOEXEC.BAT. It clears the screen and turns Help on. Do not type the remarks.

	Remarks
`CLS`	Clears the screen.
`CALL HELP ON`	Turns the Help line on, sets prompt

You can use EDLIN or the COPY command to create the file. With COPY, the file is created by typing the following lines from the OS/2 prompt. End each line by pressing Return.

```
COPY CON: STARTUP.CMD
CLS
CALL HELP ON
^Z
```
(Use Ctrl-Z or press F6 to insert the ^Z character.)

OS/2 lets you create, save, and use batch files. The following table lists special OS/2 batch commands and summarizes their use.

Batch File Commands

Command	*Description*
Ctrl-Break or Ctrl-C	Stops batch file operation and displays the message: `Terminate batch job (Y/N)?` Type Y to display the OS/2 prompt; N resumes batch file operation.

%0-%9	Lets you substitute from one to ten character strings in a batch file command line. The strings are substituted in the order encountered when the %n (where n is a number from 0 to 9) is encountered in a command line.
	
	Example:
	
	`CD %1`
	`TYPE %2`
	
	If the batch filename is CDSHOW.BAT (for "change directory and show a file"), you can type
	
	`CDSHOW WP MOMS.LTR`
	
	to cause the following commands to be executed.
	
	`CD WP`
	`TYPE MOMS.LTR`
	
	Notice that %1 is replaced with "WP" and %2 is replaced with "MOMS.LTR." If a filename contains a %, use a double % ("%%") to represent a literal percent sign.

REM	Displays remark lines when encountered within a batch file. Remarks can be up to 123 characters long. REM without following text displays a blank line during batch file execution. In this example, the text following the REM statement is displayed when encountered in the batch file. `REM Transferring files ...`

PAUSE	Pauses batch file operation and displays the message "Strike any key when ready. . ." on the next line. You can add a message following the word PAUSE.
	
	`PAUSE Insert your program disk in drive A.`
	`Strike any key when ready...`

ECHO	Turns screen display off and on during batch file operation. If off, the command ECHO, followed by a message, displays that message. This lets you display specified messages even when ECHO is OFF. `ECHO OFF<cr>` (Turns batch file display off.) `ECHO WAIT<cr>` (Displays message.) `ECHO ON<cr>` (Turns batch file display on.)

Batch File Commands (Continued)

Command	*Description*
FOR	Used to perform an operation on a set of filenames that follow the FOR %%variable expression. The entire expression might be `FOR %%f IN (FILE1.TXT FILE2.TXT) DO TYPE %%f` This command line uses the TYPE command (following the DO expression) to type FILE1.TXT and FILE2.TXT automatically.
GOTO	Transfers batch file operation to the line following a label name. The label name is always "flagged" with a preceding colon. For example, :FLAG1 might be used as a label. The expression `GOTO FLAG1` transfers batch file operation to the line following the label :FLAG1.
IF	The IF batch file command lets you set conditions for executing batch file commands. If the following condition is met, the following command (see examples) is executed. If not, batch file operation moves to the next command line. There are two forms of the IF command. You can use either IF or IF NOT to test one of three conditions:

- EXIST filename — Checks to see if the filename exists in the condition string. If the filename exists, the condition is considered "true."

Example:

```
IF EXIST MOMS.LTR GOTO FLAG1
ECHO File not found
CLS
GOTO FLAG2
:FLAG1
TYPE %1
   :
   :
:FLAG2
```

Here, if the file MOMS.LTR exists, the GOTO FLAG1 command is acted upon. If it does not exist, then control moves to the next line, which displays the message "File not found."

- string1 = = string2 — Checks to see if string1 is an exact match with string2, including a match of upper and lower case. If an exact match exists, the condition is met and the following batch file command is executed. If the condition is not met, batch file control moves to the next line.

Batch File Commands (Continued)

Command	Description
	Example:

```
IF NOT %1 == UNCLES.LTR GOTO FLAG2
COPY %1 WP\%1
CD WP
GOTO FLAG1
:FLAG2
CD WP
WP %1
:FLAG1
```

If the first string in the command line does not match "UNCLES.LTR," then the CD WP command (change directory to the WP subdirectory) is executed; otherwise, control skips to the next batch file command line.

- ERRORLEVEL number — Checks to see if the program in use exists with an error number. If the error number is equal to or greater than the one designated, the condition is met, and the command line is executed. If it is not, execution skips to the next command line in the batch file.

Example:

```
IF ERRORLEVEL 1 REM Program failure, check for overlay file.
```

This example "traps" a program error level of one or greater. If an error occurs, the remark "Program failure . . . " is displayed, and batch file operation is discontinued.

SHIFT

This command lets you shift the relationship between character strings and substitution parameters (%0 through %9) one number to the left. For example, assume the following relationships between strings and substitution numbers 0% through 3%:

```
0%   ONE.LTR
1%   TWO.LTR
2%   THREE.LTR
3%   FOUR.LTR
```

Having SHIFT on a line in a batch file changes the relationships as shown.

```
0%   TWO.LTR
1%   THREE.LTR
2%   FOUR.LTR
3%
```

The file ONE.LTR is no longer associated with the command string. This adds space for an additional substitution string.

EXTPROC

This command allows an alternate command processor to execute the commands in this batch file. This must be the first command in the batch file.

Example:

```
EXTPROC NEWCMD.EXE
```

The NEWCMD.EXE is used to process the commands in this batch file, instead of CMD.EXE.

Batch File Commands (Continued)

Command	*Description*

CALL	Calls a batch file from within another batch file. When the called batch file completes running, the calling batch file resumes running.
	Examples:
	`CALL ENDOFDAY`
	`CALL ENDOFDAY EODIN`
	In the first example, ENDOFDAY is the called batch file. When it terminates, the calling batch file continues executing at the command following the CALL ENDOFDAY command.
	In the second example, ENDOFDAY is the called batch file; however, when it terminates, the calling batch file continues executing at the command following the label :EODIN.

SETLOCAL
ENDLOCAL
	Lets you save the drive, directory, and environment settings when this command is executed. ENDLOCAL restores these to their original settings. A typical usage is to place a SETLOCAL command at the beginning of a batch file and then throughout the batch file change the drive, path and environments settings as necessary. At the end of the batch file, the ENDLOCAL command is executed to restore the drive, directory, and environment settings.
	Example:
	`SETLOCAL`
	`D:`
	`CD    D:\GL`
	`DPATH C:\ENDOFDAY\APRIL89`
	`PATH  C:\GL\PROGRAMS;C:\OS2`
	`GL    ENDOFDAY`
	`ENDLOCAL`
	In this example, the drive and environment are restored at the conclusion of this batch file, so the system is preserved and not interferred with by the execution of this batch file.

@	The @ symbol can be placed in front of a command line in a batch file to prevent that line from appearing on the screen. `@ECHO OFF` — does not display this line

The last command line in a batch file is sometimes the name of another batch file. This lets you run multiple batch files. OS/2 "remembers" where it started, and when batch file operation is finished, it takes you back to the original directory.

The balance of this section provides an example of a series of batch files that display menus, execute commonly used programs, return to the top level directory, and automatically redisplay your menu.

By typing the batch file names, you can perform many convenient tasks if:

1. You have a hard disk with ample space for the program files used in the batch file.

2. The following subdirectories exist:
   - a. DB <DIR> — Contains dBASE II; typing DBASE filename starts this program. The filename is optional.
   - b. WS <DIR> — Contains WordStar; typing WS filename starts this program. The filename is optional.
   - c. MP <DIR> — Contains Multiplan; typing MP filename starts this program. The filename is optional.
   - d. LOTUS <DIR> — Contains Lotus 1-2-3; typing LOTUS starts this program.
3. The batch file MENU.BAT is typed as follows using either EDLIN, the COPY command, or a word processor that produces an ASCII text file. Place this file in the root directory of your boot disk drive (assumed to be C:\).

```
echo off<cr>
cls<cr>
path \<cr>
prompt [OS/2 $p]<cr>
echo              *** Program Menu ***<cr>
echo        ===============================<cr>
echo          To Run               Enter<cr>
echo        -------------------------------<cr>
echo        dBASE II ........ DB filename<cr>
echo        Multiplan ....... MP<cr>
echo        WordStar ........ WS filename<cr>
echo        Lotus 1-2-3 ..... LOTUS<cr>
echo        ===============================<cr>
echo        Note: "filename" is optional.<cr>
```

Next, it is necessary to type individual batch files that act on the commands DB, MP, WS and LOTUS. These commands change to the appropriate subdirectory and then start the program. Those commands that can use filenames require substitution characters (%1). The DB.BAT and the LOTUS.BAT batch files are shown. The WS.BAT batch file is similar to the DB.BAT batch file as both programs can use filenames, and the MP.BAT batch file is similar to LOTUS.BAT.DB Batch File DB.BAT:

```
SETLOCAL
CD DB
DBASE %1
ENDLOCAL
C:\MENU
```

LOTUS Batch File LOTUS.BAT:

```
SETLOCAL
CD LOTUS
LOTUS
ENDLOCAL
C:\MENU
```

APPLICATIONS

As you can see by the above examples, batch files are extremely powerful tools. They let you minimize the keystrokes required to perform a series of OS/2 operations. You can pack hundreds of commands into one or more batch files. The batch files can be executed with just a few simple keystrokes, saving time and minimizing the potential for typographical errors.

The STARTUP.CMD batch file is excellent for automatically starting a program when you turn on your system power. This lets inexperienced computer operators use programs without having to know how to use OS/2 commands or program startup sequences.

TYPICAL OPERATION

In this activity you create and use a batch file. Begin at the OS/2 prompt, [C:\].

1. Use the COPY command to create the following DEMO.CMD file. Type the indicated lines, ending each by pressing **Return**.

```
[C:\]COPY CON: DEMO.CMD

PROMPT [demo OS/2 $p]
CLS
^Z
```

Note: Obtain ^Z by pressing **F6** or **Ctrl-Z**.

2. Execute the DEMO.CMD file by typing **DEMO** and pressing **Return**. IT MOVES BY QUICKLY.
3. Notice the display:

```
[C:\]DEMO

[C:\]PROMPT [OS/2 $p]

[demo OS/2 C:\]CLS
```

Notice that CLS clears the screen, giving:

```
[demo OS/2 C:\]
```

4. Type **PROMPT [$P]** and press **Return** to restore the [C:\] prompt.
5. Turn to Module 18 to continue the learning sequence.

Module 9
BACKUP

DESCRIPTION

The BACKUP command is primarily used with fixed disks. BACKUP is an external command used to copy files automatically from a fixed disk to floppy disks. BACKUP lets you copy selected files, all files in a specified directory path, or every file on the fixed disk. It also lets you copy only those files that have been changed or saved after a specified date.

If the files being copied exceed the capacity of the target floppy disk, BACKUP prompts you to change disks and then to continue the process. Files can be divided between floppy disks. The BACKUP command automatically tags each backup disk in the sequence used. Later, you can use the RESTORE command (Module 52) to copy the files back to the fixed disk. Having each disk numbered helps you restore the fixed disk in the right order.

The general form of the BACKUP command is

```
BACKUP C:\path A:
```

The form copies all files in the specified directory path to the disk in drive A. There are a number of parameters available with the BACKUP command. These are:

Parameter	*Description*
/S	Causes all files in subdirectories of the specified path to be copied. `BACKUP C:\ A: /S` This form of the BACKUP command copies all files in all subdirectories from the fixed disk to floppy disks in drive A.
/M	Copies only those files that have been modified since the last backup operation. `BACKUP C:\WP*.TXT A: /M` Copies all files in the WP directory having the filename extension TXT that have been saved since the last time BACKUP was used. The files are copied from drive C to drive A.
/A	Adds files to those that already reside on the target disk. When /A is not used, BACKUP erases all files on the target disk and replaces them with those being copied. `BACKUP C:\DB*.PRN A: /A` Copies all files in drive C with the directory path DB and the extension PRN to the disk in drive A. This does not erase any files that presently exist on the disk in drive A.

NOTE

The /A switch will not be accepted if files exist that were backed up from PC/MS-DOS version 3.2 or earlier.

Parameter	*Description*
/F	Causes an unformatted target diskette to be formatted.
/D	Lets you copy those files saved on or after a specified date (in the DATE command format mm-dd-yy). Note that the date varies according to the country code. `BACKUP C:\ A: /S /D:07-01-88` Copies all files on drive C (in all subdirectories) that have been saved on or after 07-01-88 to the disk(s) in drive A.
/T	Lets you copy those files saved on or after a specified time. `BACKUP C:< A: /S /T:10:4:59` Copies all files on drive C (in all subdirectories) that have been saved on or after 10:4:59 to the disk(s) in drive A.

/L	Causes a log file to be created or appended to the source disk. An entry is made into the log file for each file backed up.
	`BACKUP C:\ A: /L:BU122589.LOG`
	Copies all files in C:\ directory to the floppy in drive A, plus makes a log entry into the file BU122589.LOG for each file backed up. If no filename is given with the /L parameter then the default filename of BACKUP.LOG is used. The log file is created if it does not exist on the source drive.
	Note that the log file is an ASCII file that you may list out with the TYPE command. For example,
	`[A:\]TYPE C:\BU122589.LOG`
	
	`12-25-1989 10:05:22`
	`001 \CMD.EXE`
	`001 \EXE2BIN.EXE`
	
	`[A:\]`
	will list the files backed up in the above example. The log file contains the date and time backed up, the disk number that the file is backed up on, and the filename.

Before using BACKUP, you should format several floppy diskettes or have a tape backup device available. If you are using floppy diskettes, plan on using as many as 28 to 30 360KB floppy diskettes (8 or 9 of the 1.2MB floppy diskettes) for each 10-megabytes of fixed disk capacity. As files are backed up, filenames are displayed on the screen. As each target diskette fills up, you are prompted to insert the next disk. This process continues until the last file is copied.

Although BACKUP tags each disk with a number, you should also write a sequential number on your disks, beginning with 1, as they are removed from the floppy drive. This lets you stack your diskettes in the right order when you must restore files to your fixed disk.

NOTE

You may not be able to restore files that are backed up from assigned, joined, or substituted drives.

APPLICATIONS

Having a backup copy of the files on your hard disk is the best insurance you can have. Although it is not necessary to backup the entire disk, it is always a good idea to backup new files as they are created and stored. For example, you might wish to backup your files or individual directories two or three times a week. In the case of big, irreplaceable files, you should back them up as soon as they are filed.

If you ever encounter a fixed disk failure, you will be very thankful for your backup copies. If you have not backed up, you will likely start talking to yourself in an uncomplimentary way.

TYPICAL OPERATION

In this activity you use the BACKUP command to back up all files on your root directory. The procedure assumes you have a fixed disk designated as drive C:. If the drive is E:, then substitute E: for C:. Begin at the OS/2 prompt, [C:\].

1. Place a formatted scratch disk in drive A:.
2. Type **BACKUP C:*.EXE A:** and press **Return**. Notice a prompt similar to the following:

```
[C:\]BACKUP C:*.EXE A: /L

Insert the backup diskette 01 in drive A:
Warning! The files in the root directory
of target drive A: will be erased.

Press Enter to continue or Ctrl-Break to cancel.
```

3. Press any key and watch the filenames appear on the screen as they are copied.

NOTE
This prodcedure may require more than one disk to backup your root directory.

4. Save your backup disk for use in the Typical Operation activity of Module 52 (RESTORE).
5. Turn to Module 52 to continue the learning sequence.

Module 10

CHCP

DESCRIPTION

The CHCP command is an internal OS/2 command for use with code-page switching. The CHCP command allows you to switch back and forth between two code-pages that have been prepared for your system. The two code-pages that you can switch between are

- Your national language code-page
- The multilingual code-page

The national language code-page is the character set used by your country for the alphabet, the numbers, and the special characters. The multilingual code-page is an international data processing standard character set that includes most of the characters in the languages of most American and European countries.

The form of the CHCP command is

```
CHCP nnn
```

where *nnn* is a code-page number. If the code-page number is not included in the command, the current code-page number is displayed:

```
CHCP<return>
```

```
Active character set:  437
Prepared system character set(s):  437, 850
```

The above is displayed with country = 001 in the config.sys file.

```
CHCP 850<return>
CHCP<return>
```

```
Active character set:  850
Prepared system character set(s):  437, 850
```

The CHCP command above changed to the 850 code-page.

If you select a code-page that has not been prepared then you receive an error message.

The CHCP command only changes the code-page for the session that the CHCP command is issued in. However, any program started within a session inherits that sessions active code-page.

APPLICATIONS

The CHCP command lets you change code-pages for all devices and their corresponding code-pages. However, it is necessary that all devices are properly configured and installed.

TYPICAL OPERATION

There is no activity required for this command, as its use relies on a series of events associated with code-page switching. For more information about associated commands, refer to Modules 14, 18, 22, 38, and 41. These modules describe Code Page Switching, Configuration File, device drivers, and the MODE and KEYB commands.

Turn to Module 35 to continue the learning sequence.

Module 11

CHKDSK

DESCRIPTION

The CHKDSK command checks the status of a selected disk, whether a hard disk or floppy. It is an external OS/2 command, and it displays several important items of information. These include:

- The total disk space
- The total disk space occupied and the number of files
- The total disk space either lost or considered unusable by the system
- The amount of disk space available for use

The general form of the CHKDSK command is

```
CHKDSK D:
```

where D: is the drive letter holding the disk to be checked. For example, the command CHKDSK B: performs a disk check of the disk in drive B:. If no disk drive is specified, the logged disk drive is assumed, as is the case with most OS/2 commands.

THE GENERAL FORM When CHKDSK is typed and the Return key pressed, the following message is displayed:

```
[A:\]CHKDSK

 Volume SCRATCH created  4-4-1988  1:26 pm

362496 bytes total disk space.
 22528 bytes in 2 hidden files.
 10240 bytes in 2 directories.
139264 bytes in 24 user files.
  5120 bytes in bad sectors.
185344 bytes available on disk.

[A:\]
```

The "hidden files" are usually system files. OS/2 commands and "user files" are those that are listed when the DIR command is used.

The amount of available disk space is perhaps the most important line in the report. This tells you if you have enough space on a disk for continued work. If the amount of space is limited, it may be time to use another disk, delete obsolete files to recover disk space, or copy inactive files to another disk and then delete them from the current one.

NOTE

In DOS Mode the CHKDSK command also gives you a report on your computer's memory. The total amount of memory and the amount of free memory is displayed. In the sample report below, the system is using 41,520 bytes (or characters) of memory space. This is often called *system overhead.*

```
[Real A:\]chkdsk

    Volume SCRATCH created  4-4-1988  1:26 pm

   362496 bytes total disk space.
    22528 bytes in 2 hidden files.
   139264 bytes in 24 user files.
   200704 bytes available on disk.

[DOS mode storage report]
   262144 bytes total memory
   220624 bytes free

[Real A:\]
```

CHKDSK PARAMETERS

A /V parameter (you can think of V for View) displays the directories and files as they are checked. If errors are encountered, additional information is displayed.

An /F (for Fix) parameter is also available to recover lost *clusters* within *chains*, which are sections of disk that have been inadvertently misallocated in the directory. If lost clusters are found by the CHKDSK operation, you see a message similar to the following:

```
[A:\]CHKDSK B:

  Volume SCRATCH created  4-4-1988  1:26 pm

Errors found, F parameter not specified.
Corrections will not be written to disk.


1 lost clusters found in 1 chains.
Convert lost chains to files (Y/N)?
```

Type Y and press Return to display information similar to the following:

```
      4096 bytes disk space
           would be freed.

  362496 bytes total disk space.
   22528 bytes in 2 hidden files.
   10240 bytes in 2 directories.
  139264 bytes in 24 user files.
  190464 bytes available on disk.

[A:\]
```

To recover the lost disk space, enter CHKDSK B: /F. The lost data is recovered and placed in a file having the name FILE0000.CHK. You can examine this file by displaying it on the screen with the TYPE command (Module 61), EDLIN (Module 27), or with a text editor. If it is garbage, you can delete it from the disk with the DEL command (Module 28). If it is important data, you may wish to use an editor to perform necessary repairs.

CHECKING FILES WITH CHKDSK

The CHKDSK command also determines how one or more files are scattered across the geography of a disk. For example, when a file occupies adjacent sectors, disk input/output operations are relatively quick. As files are edited, new portions often "leap frog" over other files on the disk to find available disk space. This creates what is called a *non-contiguous* file, that is, one scattered across two or more blocks of space. To check a file named LETTER1.TXT on disk B, you can type CHKDSK B:LETTER1.TXT and press Return. A display similar to the following appears:

```
[A:\]CHKDSK B:LETTER1.TXT

Insert diskette for drive B: and strike
any key when ready
```

Pressing any key displays a message like the following one.

```
Volume SCRATCH created  4-4-1988  1:26 pm

 362496 bytes total disk space.
  22528 bytes in 2 hidden files.
 136192 bytes in 8 user files.
 203776 bytes available on disk.

All specified file(s) are contiguous.
```

If you want to determine if there are files on disk B having discontiguity, you can type CHKDSK B:*.* and press Return. This presents a display similar to the following:

```
[A:\]CHKDSK B:*.*

Insert diskette for drive B: and strike
any key when ready
```

Pressing any key displays a message similar to the following:

```
Volume SCRATCH created  4-4-1988  1:26 pm

 362496 bytes total disk space.
  22528 bytes in 2 hidden files.
 136192 bytes in 8 user files.
 203776 bytes available on disk.

B:\LETTER1.TXT
   Contains 2 non-contiguous blocks.
B:\LETTER2.TXT
   Contains 3 non-contiguous blocks.
```

COMMAND SUMMARY

Because several forms of the CHKDSK command are available, a summary of these command forms is presented for your convenience.

CHKDSK or CHKDSK B:	Checks the total disk space, the amount of disk space occupied by files, the amount of disk space available for use.
CHKDSK /V	Displays each directory and file as it is encountered by the program. Also displays disk error information.
CHKDSK /F	Used to recover (or fix) disk space that has been misallocated in the directory. Places recovered disk space into files and assigns filenames beginning with FILE0000.CHK, FILE0001.CHK, and so on.
CHKDSK *filename*	Checks the designated file for contiguity in the way it is arranged on the disk. Displays a message telling whether the file blocks used are contiguous.
CHKDSK *.*	Checks all files on the designated disk for contiguity. Lists the names and number of non-contiguous blocks for all files having more than one contiguous block.

APPLICATIONS

The CHKDSK command is one of the more frequently used OS/2 utilities. You can use it to determine whether or not there is enough file space available on a disk to continue using it.

The CHKDSK command options let you perform many helpful functions. In particular, the CHKDSK /V option lets you view all directories and all files, helping you quickly find a misplaced file (when you forget which directory contains the file).

If file access time starts to get annoyingly long, it is probably because the file has been scattered randomly across the disk's "geography." When this happens, the read/write heads of your disk drive must move to different parts of the disk to read and write parts of the file. You can see just how badly a file is broken up by using the CHKDSK FILENAME form of the command. If the file resides in several non-contiguous blocks, you can use the COPY command to copy it to a new disk, which gathers the file into a contiguous block.

TYPICAL OPERATION

In this activity you use the CHKDSK command to check the amount of disk space on an OS/2 diskette. Begin at the OS/2 prompt, [C:\].

1. Type **CHKDSK A:** and press **Return**; notice the following display:

```
[C:\]CHKDSK A:

  Volume SCRATCH created  4-4-1988  1:26 pm

 362496 bytes total disk space.
  22528 bytes in 2 hidden files.
 139264 bytes in 24 user files.
 200704 bytes available on disk.

[C:\]
```

2. Type **CHKDSK A:*.*** and press **Return**; notice a display similar to the following:

```
[C:\]CHKDSK A:*.*

  Volume SCRATCH created  4-4-1988  1:26 pm

 362496 bytes total disk space.
  22528 bytes in 2 hidden files.
 135168 bytes in 23 user files.
 204800 bytes available on disk.

All specified file(s) are contiguous.
```

Note that if your diskette contains files with non-contiguous blocks, your display is similar to the following:

```
&C:\?CHKDSK A:*.*

  Volume SCRATCH created  4-4-1988  1:26 pm

 362496 bytes total disk space.
  22528 bytes in 2 hidden files.
 135168 bytes in 23 user files.
 204800 bytes available on disk.

A:\LETTER1.TXT
   Contains 2 non-contiguous blocks.
A:\LETTER2.TXT
   Contains 3 non-contiguous blocks.
```

3. Turn to Module 63 to continue the learning sequence.

Module 12

CLEAR SCREEN (CLS)

DESCRIPTION

The CLS command clears the display screen and redisplays the OS/2 prompt at the upper left-hand corner of your screen. This command is an internal OS/2 command. The form of the CLS command is

```
CLS
```

APPLICATIONS

The primary application of the CLS command is to remove unwanted clutter from the display screen, or to start commands at the top of the screen. When automatic execution (*batch files*) are used, the last command is often a CLS to remove confusing clutter and to display the cursor at the top of a "clean slate." If you want to dump a directory from your screen to your printer using Shift-PrtSc, you may want to clear your screen, display the directory, and then do the printing. Here again, CLS removes unwanted text from your screen.

TYPICAL OPERATION

In this activity you use the CLS command to clear information from your screen. Begin at the OS/2 prompt, [C:\].

1. Type **DIR** to display a disk directory to the screen.
2. Type **CLS** and press **Return**; notice that your screen is clear:

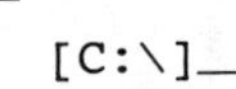

```
[C:\]_
```

3. Turn to Module 61 to continue the learning sequence.

Module 13

CMD

DESCRIPTION

The CMD.EXE command is the OS/2 Mode command processor. By executing this command you can start another command processor in OS/2 mode.

By entering

```
CMD
```

you start another command processor. This command processor inherits its environment from the previous command processor. However, any changes to the environment of this command processor are only known to this command processor. It does not affect the previous command processor environment.

When you start another command processor, you can also give the command processor a command to execute. Enter

```
CMD /K DIR A:
```

or

```
CMD /C DIR A:
```

and the command processor begins and executes the DIR A:. The /C parameter instructs the command processor to terminate when it completes the DIR command. The /K parameter instructs the command processor to remain an active OS/2 session when it completes the DIR command. You can type EXIT and the command prompt to terminate a command processor. Note that if the command passed to the command processor has piping, filters, or grouping commands then the command must be enclosed in quotes. For example, a command like

```
CMD /K "DIR >LPT1"
```

requires quotes so that the redirection is associated with the DIR command and not the CMD command.

For more information about the command processor, see the modules on piping commands (Module 44), filter commands (Module 33), and grouping commands (Module 36).

APPLICATIONS

When you start another command processor you also create a new command environment, with the environment from the previous command processor copied to the new one. Sometimes it is desirable to change the environment variables and then be able to return them to their original values. By starting another command processor, changing the environment, running the desired program, and then exiting back to the previous command processor, the system maintains the original environment values for you.

TYPICAL OPERATION

In this operation you execute another copy of the command processor and then return to the previous command processor. Start at the OS/2 prompt, [C:\].

1. Type **CMD** and press **Return** to begin another command processor.
2. Type **PROMPT = NEW CMD.EXE = = = = = = $g** and press **Return**. Notice the new prompt:

   ```
   NEW CMD.EXE ======>
   ```

3. Type **EXIT** and press **Return**. Notice that the command processor terminated and returned to the previous command processor and that the prompt for this command processor was not modified.
4. Turn to Module 16 to continue the learning sequence.

Module 14

CODE PAGE SWITCHING

DESCRIPTION

If you work with data from a country other than the United States, you may choose to use the national language support features of OS/2, through the use of language-specific code pages. Code page switching lets you select various character sets that are unique to a variety of countries. When loaded, the characters displayed, printed, or entered from the keyboard satisfy the requirements of the national language. These include the letters of the alphabet, numbers, and special symbols (such as accent marks).

The default character set of U.S.-built microcomputers is called the *hardware code page*. To select an alternate code page, you must enter the appropriate command lines into your CONFIG.SYS, STARTUP.CMD and AUTOEXEC.BAT files. These lines change the input/output environment (or the way that keystrokes are interpreted, characters are displayed on the screen, and printed).

Each code page set contains 256 characers. Most of the characters within code pages are common with the exception of a few that are unique to the selected language. If you have the proper hardware, you can examine the effect of each code page by experimenting with the code page switching commands.

OS/2 supports five different code pages. Each code page has a unique number. They are

Language	*Code Page Number*
English	437
Multilingual	850
Portugese	860
French (Canada)	863
Nordic	865

The multilingual (850) code page is used for the following countries and regions:

Australia	Germany	Spain
Belgium	Italy	Sweden
Canada (English and French)	Latin America	Switzerland (French and German)
Denmark	Netherlands	United Kingdom
Finland	Norway	United States (English)
France	Portugal	

OTHER NATIONAL LANGUAGE SUPPORT

OS/2 also provides national language support through the use of the country code and the keyboard code.

- A country code defines the country you live or work in. OS/2 uses this code to determine which default code page to prepare for you to use on your system. OS/2 supports 19 country codes.
- A keyboard code defines which type of keyboard is on your system. OS/2 supports 17 different keyboard codes.

CONFIG.SYS COMMANDS The precise format of command lines within the CONFIG.SYS file is presented in the configuration files module (Module 18).

Your CONFIG.SYS file may include one or more of the following commands:

CODEPAGE Prepares primary and secondary code pages for the system.

COUNTRY Includes a specific country number followed by the appropriate code page number. The following table lists country (nnn) and code page (xxx) numbers; also included are keyboard code numbers (yy). The KEYB command, described in Module 38 and alluded to later in this module, includes the country (nnn) and keyboard (yy) codes.

Country	*nnn*	*xxx*	*yy*	*Country*	*nnn*	*xxx*	*yy*
United States	001	437	US	Arabic	785	850	None
Canada (Eng)	001	850	US	Australia	061	850	US
France	033	863	FR	Belgium	032	850	BE
Spain	034	850	SP	Canada (Fr)	002	863	CF
Italy	039	850	IT	Denmark	045	850	DK
United Kingdom	044	850	UK	Finland	358	850	SU
Germany	049	850	GR	Hebrew	972	850	None
Latin America	003	850	LA	Netherlands	031	850	NL
Norway	047	865	NO	Portugal	351	860	PO
Sweden	046	850	SV	Switzerland (Fr)	041	850	SF
				Switzerland (Gr)	041	850	SG

DEVICE Specifies certain compatible printer or display device drivers.

DEVICEINFO Specifies code pages supported by devices.

Your STARTUP.CMD or AUTOEXEC.BAT file may include the following commands:

KEYB Loads keyboard support for the selected language.

CHCP Changes current code page for the system and all prepared devices.

SYSTEM CODE PAGE COMMANDS

There are three system code page commands used to prepare or change the active code page. These commands are

CHCP — This command is an internal OS/2 command that is entered from the keyboard. Literally, it means "CHange Code Page." When entered, it changes or displays the active code page for all devices, i.e., printers and displays, that have been prepared in the CONFIG.SYS file. The NLSFUNC command is always entered prior to CHCP. An example of the CHCP command that changes the code page to 860 is CHCP 860. Remember, however, that code page 860 must have been prepared using the approriate MODE command and device driver within your CONFIG.SYS file.

COUNTRY — The COUNTRY command is included as a line in the CONFIG.SYS file. It inputs the code page number corresponding to the country of your choice. This changes such things as date and time formats that correspond to the code page number. For example, the command line COUNTRY = 033 selects France.

COMMANDS USING CODE PAGE SWITCHING

The following commands interact with code page switching by using established parameters:

GRAFTABL — The GRAFTABL command is used to display graphics characters above 127. The specific characters are compatible with the selected code page. The characters are displayed when the computer is in the graphics mode. The GRAFTABL command is usually included in your AUTOEXEC.BAT file.

KEYB — The KEYB command, which is often included in your AUTOEXEC.BAT file, loads keyboard support for a specified language. The result is a changed keyboard layout that corresponds to the selected code page.

SORT — The SORT command honors the country-specific sorting hierarchy that corresponds to the selected code page.

Four other OS/2 commands (date, time, backup, restore) use country specific conventions based on the code pages you use.

APPLICATIONS

Code page switching is used when you wish to configure your display, keyboard, and printer for use with one or more languages other than English. The selected code page overlays the default hardware code page (number 437) with the one selected. It is placed in your computer's memory.

If you are using mulitple languages, you can prepare multiple code pages. The printer and display device drivers should be loaded into your CONFIG.SYS file for compatablity with printer and display devices that take advantage of various character sets. These devices include IBM Model 4201 Proprinters, Model 5201 Quietwriters, Enhanced Graphics Adapters, and LCD displays.

TYPICAL OPERATION

If you are not using code page switching, you can go to Step 6 and skip this activity.

In this activity you create a CONFIG.SYS file, a STARTUP.CMD file, and an AUTOEXEC.BAT file. In these files you are entering the appropriate commands to use the Spanish language with a computer equipped with an EGA monitor and an IBM Model 4201 Proprinter. Start at the OS/2 prompt.

1. Insert a scratch diskette into drive A.
2. Use the COPY command to create a CONFIG.SYS file on the disk in drive A. End each line by pressing **Return**. The last line is entered by pressing **Ctrl-Z** and pressing **Return**.

```
COPY CON A:CONFIG.SYS
REM -- COUNTRY = 34 is for Spain ; Codepage of 437 and 850 alt.
COUNTRY=034
REM -- DEVICE = EGA is for an EGA monitor
DEVICE=C:\OS2\EGA.SYS
REM -- DEVINFO = 4201 is for the IBM Model 4201 Proprinter
DEVINFO=PRN,4201,C:\OS2\4201.DCP
FILES=20
BUFFERS=20
^Z
```

3. Create the following STARTUP.CMD file on the disk in drive A by typing the following lines. End each line by pressing **Return**. The last line is entered by pressing **Ctrl-Z** and pressing **Return**.

```
COPY CON A:STARTUP.CMD
ECHO OFF
REM -- KEYB SP is for Spanish keyboard
KEYB SP
CLS
^Z
```

4. Create the following AUTOEXEC.BAT file on the disk in drive A by typing the following lines. End each line by pressing **Return**. The last line is entered by pressing **Ctrl-Z** and pressing **Return**.

```
COPY CON A:AUTOEXEC.BAT
ECHO OFF
REM -- KEYB SP is for Spanish keyboard
KEYB SP
REM -- CHCP 850 is for Multilingual code page
CHCP 850
CLS
^Z
```

If these files were copied to the C:\ directory and you rebooted, your system would be configured for Spanish, EGA, and IBM 4201 printer.

5. Turn to Module 38 to continue the learning sequence.

Module 15
CODEVIEW

DESCRIPTION

The CODEVIEW program is a programmer's diagnostic utility that allows you to debug computer applications written in Basic, C, Fortran, Pascal, and assembler language. In this module you are introduced to the CODEVIEW program and some of its common commands. In fact, just so you know how to use it, you can follow along with the example to see how it works. However, because CODEVIEW is such an extensive assembler language debugger, no attempt is made to provide examples for every CODEVIEW command. Also, if you are not an assembler language programmer and are not familiar with the 80286/80386 microprocessor architecture and its instruction set, many of the commands will have no meaning to you.

The CODEVIEW debugger has numerous features. Among them, it allows the programmer to

- Single step through a program
- Stop execution at breaking points
- Watch values of variables change during execution
- Debug at the source level, with symbols
- Debug at the assembly level, with symbols
- Debug at both source and assembly level, with symbols
- Switch between CODEVIEW output and your program output
- Display memory in different formats
- Edit memory
- Change values of interal registers and flags
- Interface with a mouse
- Create pull-down menus to simplify operator input
- Execute OS/2 commands and other programs during debug session

Other CODEVIEW features include the following:

- Built in assembler
- Built in disassembler, reverse engineer the program
- Expression evaluator with program symbols

PROGRAM PREPERATION

Before programs can be debugged with CODEVIEW they must be compiled with options so that debug information can be included within the .EXE program. After you debug your program, recompile without the CODEVIEW options so that the .EXE is smaller and therefore loads faster.

The following is a list of compile options for each language to indicate that you plan on debugging with CODEVIEW:

ASSEMBLY	MASM	/ZI		program;
BASIC	BASCOM	/Zi		program;
C	CL	/Zi	/Od	program.c
C	MSC	/Zi	/Od	program;
FORTRAN	FL	/Zi	/Od	program.for
LINK	LINK	/CODEVIEW		program;

STARTING CODEVIEW

The form for the CODEVIEW command is

```
CV  cv-options  PROGRAM.EXE  program-arguments
```

where

CV is codeview
cv-options are the arguments for codeview (see below)
PROGRAM.EXE is the program to debug
program-arguments are the arguments to the program being debugged.

The codeview arguments are:

/W	*Codeview to use window mode
/B	*Codeview to output to two color monitor
/S	Codeview to output to non-IBM or a graphics program you wish to see the output screen on
/F	*Use flipping to see both codeview and output screen (F4 key)
/D	Non-IBM interrupt trapping
/I	Enable Control-C on non-IBM
/T	Use sequential mode
/M	Don't use mouse
/43	*Use 43 lines on EGA card
/2	You have two monitors on your computer
/Ccommand	Codeview to execute commands when codeview begins execution

CODEVIEW EXECUTION

CODEVIEW is controlled by use of the keyboard, the function keys, and a mouse. It is controlled by the keyboard when you type commands at the prompt. Commands are also given by pressing the function keys. Clicking the mouse at designated locations give commands and/or display menus that have commands on them, which can be selected via arrow keys or the mouse.

The keyboard and function keys have the following effects on CODEVIEW:

F1	Displays the HELP 1.0 sreen menu
F2	Toggles the display of the registers on the right-hand side of the screen
F3	Switches between source, assembly, or mixed source/assemble mode
F4	Switches to the application output screen
F5	Executes to the next breakpoint or end of program if no breakpoint is encountered

F6	Toggles keyboard between dialog window and program window
F7	Sets a breakpoint on current program line
F8	Executes one statement
F9	Clears breakpoint on current program line
F10	Executes one program step through a function call

CONTROL-U	Moves the display/dialog separator line up one line
CONTROL-D	Moves the display/dialog separator line down one line
Up Arrow	Moves the cursor up one line
Down Arrow	Moves the cursor down one line
PgUp	Scrolls up one page
PgDn	Scrolls down one page
HOME	Scrolls to top of program or command buffer
END	Scrolls to end of program or command buffer

CODEVIEW DIALOG COMMANDS

All CODEVIEW commands can be entered through the keyboard as dialog commands. A list of the most commonly used commands follows. You can use this list for a quick reference.

Command	*Description*
T x	Traces X source lines of code, one at a time, even into another module.
P x	Traces X source lines of code. Function calls execute and count as one line.
G	Starts execution of program.
E	Starts execution of program in slow motion.
L	Moves to beginning of program.
S –	Shows program in assembly code.
S +	Shows program in source code.
S&	Shows program in source and assembly together.
DB x y	Displays memory in bytes, where X is the starting address, and Y is the ending address. X can be a program symbol.
DW x L y	Displays memory in words, where X is the starting address, L means length where Y is the length to display. X can be a symbol.
DA x L y	Displays memory in ASCII, where X is the starting address, L means length where Y is the length to display. X can be a symbol.
? BY x	Displays first byte at X, which is an address or symbol.
? WO x	Displays first word at X, which is an address or symbol.
? x	Displays value of symbol X.
X?m!r.s	Displays symbol S in routine R in module M.
X?m!r.*	Displays all symbols in routine R in Module M.
X?*	Displays all symbols in the current routine.
X*	Displays all module names.
S x L y "zzz"	Searches from address X for length Y for string ZZZ, and displays all addresses of matches.
I x	Inputs from port X and displays input value.
R	Displays registers and values.
7	Displays registers in math co-processor.

BP x	Sets a breakpoint at X.
BC x	Clears breakpoint at X.
BD x	Disables breakpoint at X.
BE x	Enables breakpoint at X.
BL	Lists all breakpoints.
WP? x	Sets a watchpoint X. Break if X becomes non-zero. X is usually a comparison, like COUNT > 12.
TP? x	Sets a tracepoint at X. Break if X changes.
TPB x L y	Sets a byte trace point at X for length Y.
TPA x y	Sets an ASCII trace point at X to Y.
Y	Deletes watchpoint.
W	Lists watchpoints.
WB x L y	Sets Watch in bytes at X for length Y.
WA x L y	Sets Watch in ASCII at X for length Y.
V x	Displays source line where X is a module, label, or address.
A x	Assembles code beginning at address X.
EB x	Enters data in bytes at X.
EA x	Enters data in ASCII at X.
F x L y z	Fills memory starting at address X for length Y with byte Z.
M x L y	Moves memory from X to Z for length Y.
R x y	Changes register X to value Y.
R F x	Changes flag X to value of X (see table below).
Nx	Changes radix to X.
\	Switches to application screen.

In the commands that display and edit data, there are the following table of values available to you for display format:

Code	*Data type*
B	byte
A	ASCII
I	integer
U	unsigned integer
W	word
D	double word
S	short reals
L	long reals
T	10-byte reals

The following are the flag values:

Flag	*Set*	*Clear*
Overflow (yes/no)	OV	NV
Direction (decrement/increment)	DN	UP
Interrupt (enable/disable)	EI	DI
Sign (negative/positive)	NG	PL
Zero (yes/no)	ZR	NZ
Auxiliary carry (yes/no)	AC	NA
Parity (even/odd)	PE	PO
Carry (yes/no)	CY	NC

CODEVIEW PULL-DOWN MENUS

By pressing Alt-F or clicking the mouse on the FILE option on the Menu Bar, the following screen appears:

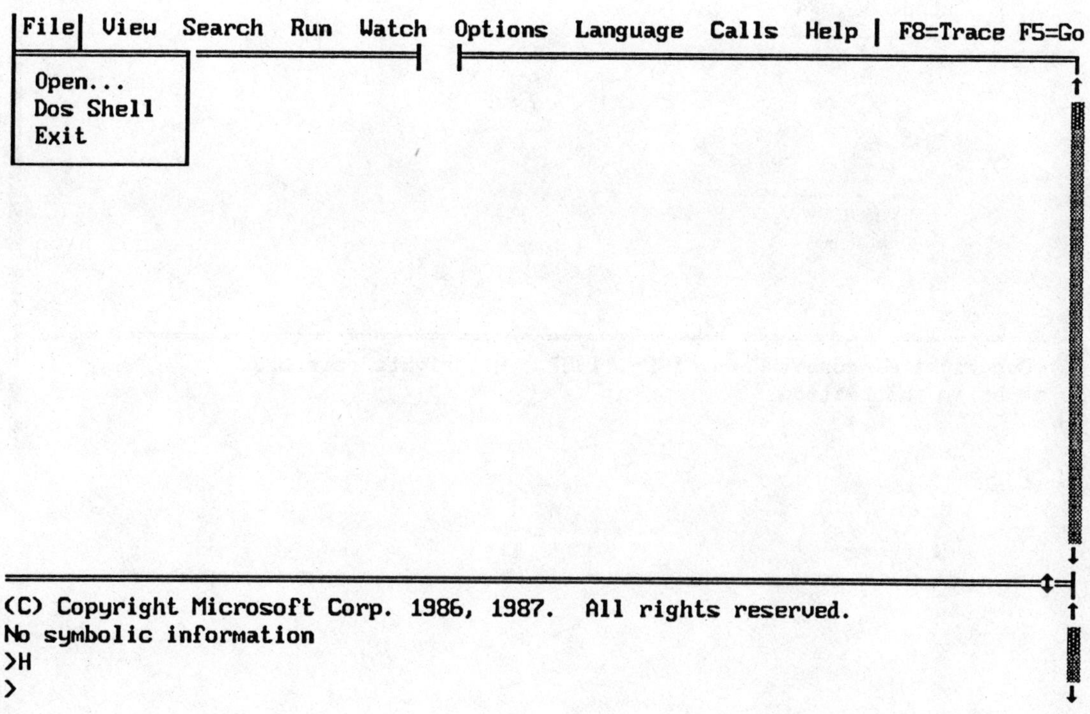

1. If you select Open. . . from this pull-down menu, then CODEVIEW loads a program into memory to debug.
2. If you select DOS Shell, then this debug session is interrupted and the command processor is loaded where you can run OS/2 commands or other programs. Type EXIT and press Return to return to CODEVIEW.
3. If you select Quit, then CODEVIEW terminates and you return to the OS/2 prompt.

By pressing Alt-V or clicking the mouse on the VIEW option on the Menu Bar, the following screen appears:

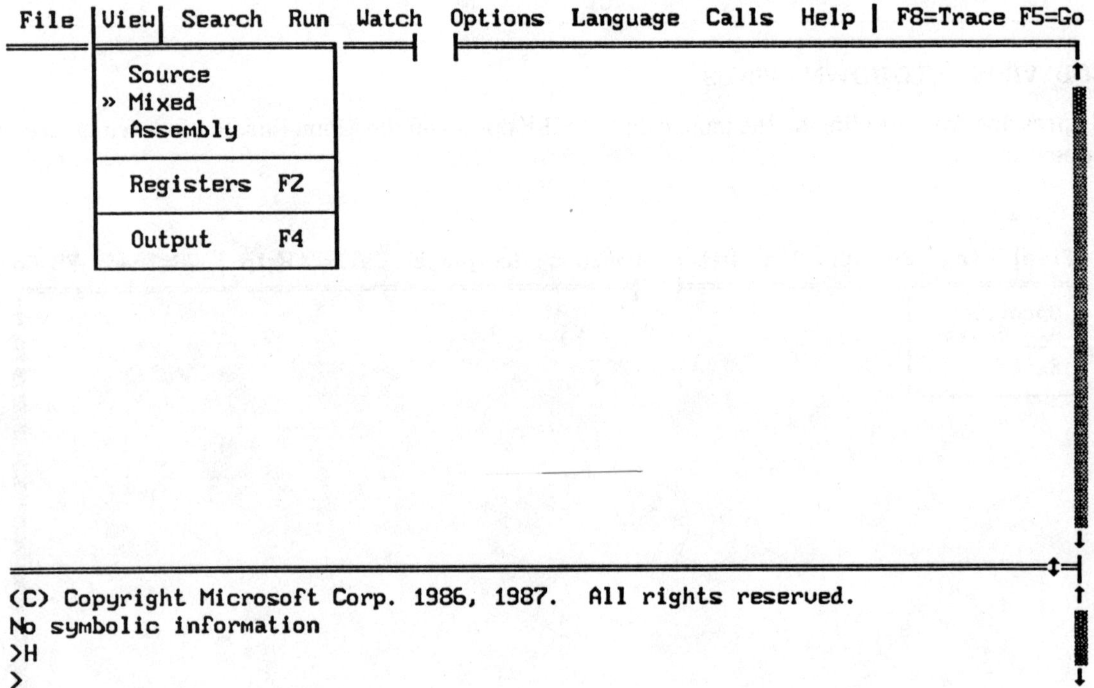

1. If you select Source, then you start debugging the program in the source code mode.
2. If you select Mixed, then you start debugging the program in both the source code and assembly mode.
3. If you select Assembly, then you start debugging the program in the assembly code mode.

By pressing Alt-S or clicking the mouse on the SEARCH option on the Menu Bar, the following screen appears:

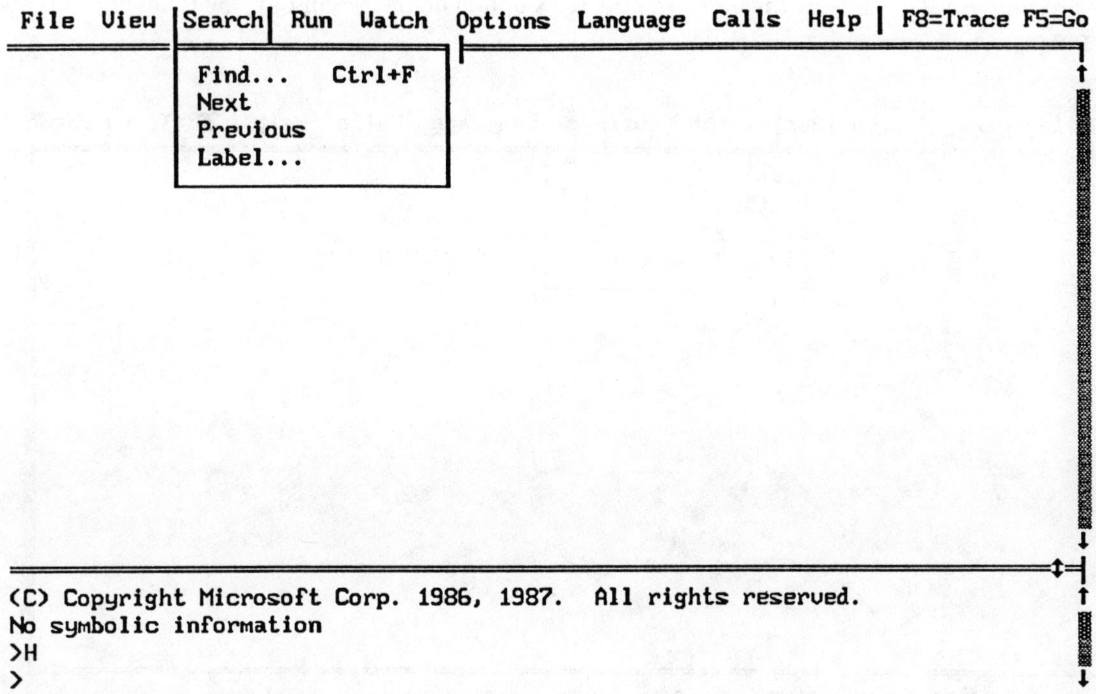

1. If you select Find. . ., you are prompted for a string of text to search for in your program. CODEVIEW finds the string and displays it on the screen for you.
2. If you select Next, then the next occurence of the search string is found and displayed.
3. If you select Previous, then the previous occurrence of the search string is found and displayed.
4. If you select Label, then you are prompted for a label for CODEVIEW to find and display for you.

By pressing Alt-R or clicking the mouse on the RUN option on the Menu Bar, the following screen appears:

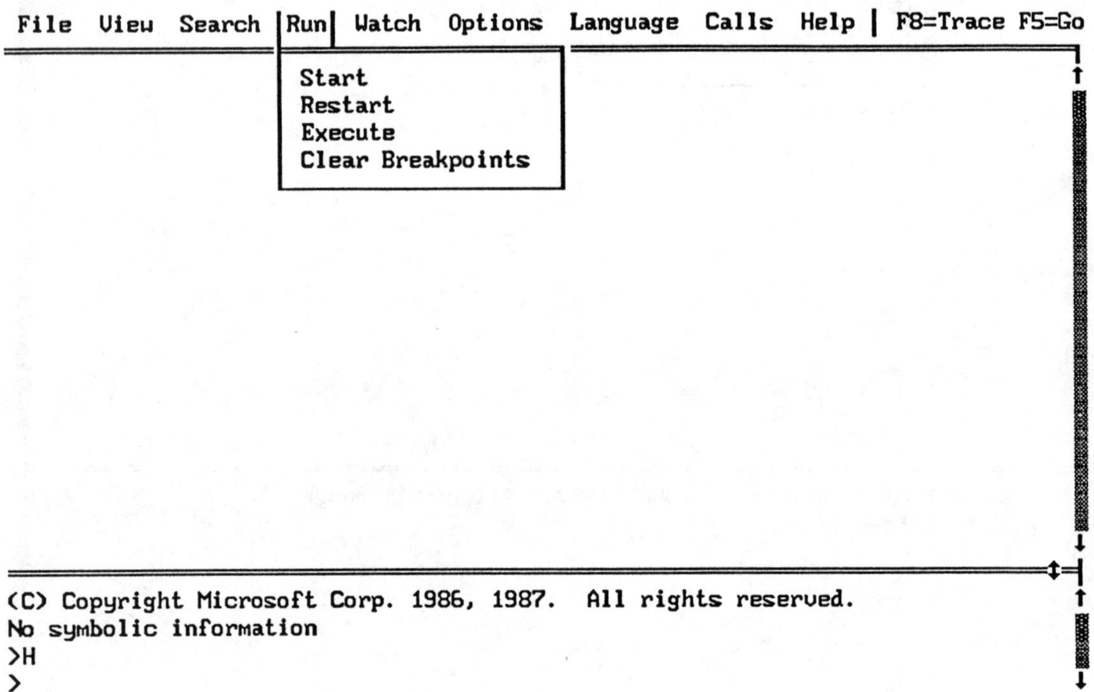

1. If you select Start, then the program being debugged begins execution.
2. If you select Restart, then the location of next instruction to execute is moved to the first statement in your program.
3. If you select Execute, then the program begins execution in slow motion.
4. If you select Clear Breakpoints, then all breakpoints you have set are cleared.

By pressing Alt-W or clicking the mouse on the WATCH option on the Menu Bar, the following screen appears:

```
 File  View  Search  Run |Watch| Options  Language  Calls  Help | F8=Trace F5=Go
                          Add Watch...      Ctrl+W
                          Watchpoint...
                          Tracepoint...
                          Delete Watch...   Ctrl+U
                          Delete All Watch

(C) Copyright Microsoft Corp. 1986, 1987.  All rights reserved.
No symbolic information
>H
>
```

1. If you select Add Watch. . ., you are prompted for a variable or expression you want to watch during program execution, and the variable or expression is displayed on the screen for you.
2. If you select Watchpoint. . ., you are prompted for a watchpoint expression that causes the executing program to break when the watchpoint expression become a non-zero value.
3. If you select Tracepoint. . ., you are prompted for a tracepoint expression that causes the executing program to break when the tracepoint changes value.
4. If you select Delete Watch. . ., you are shown a box with all your currently selected breakpoints. You select the one you want to delete and it is deleted.
5. If you select Delete All Watch, you delete all the watchpoints.

By pressing Alt-O or clicking the mouse on the OPTIONS option on the Menu Bar, the following screen appears:

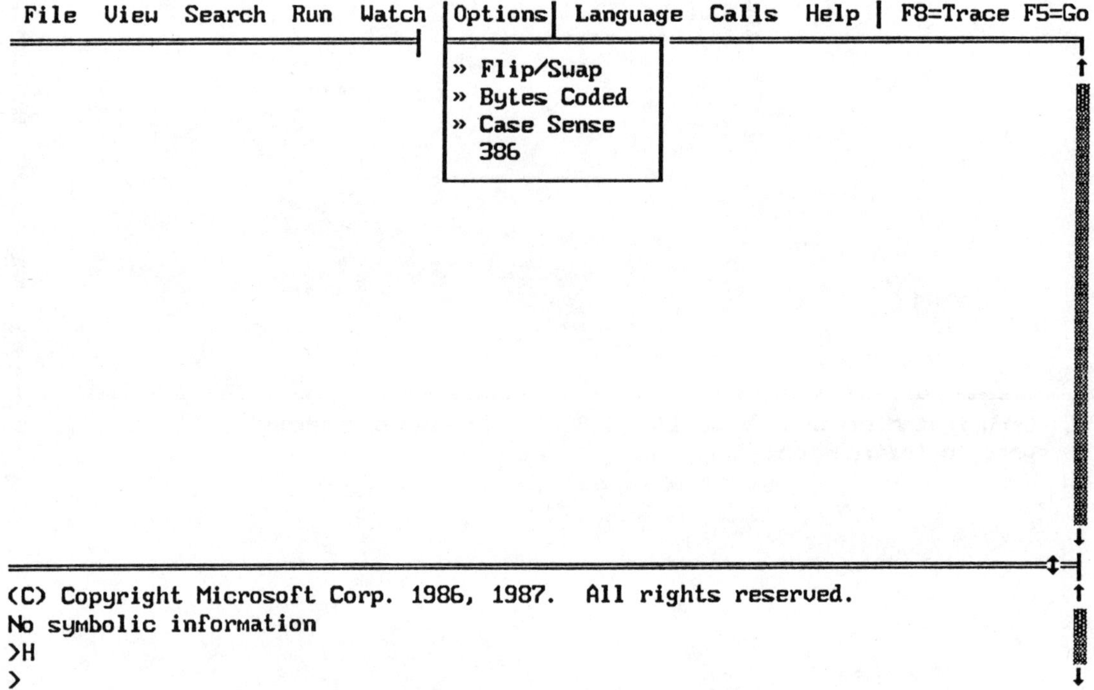

1. If you select Flip/Swap, it toggles the flip/swap screen display mode. When it is off, the screen scrolls smoother, but your application cannot write to the application screen. It is normally on for this reason.
2. If you select Bytes Coded, then the compiler-generated code is displayed with the assembly source.
3. If you select Case Sensitive, it toggles whether CODEVIEW is to take into account upper- and lower-case distinction in input and expressions.
4. If you select 386, you indicate to CODEVIEW that this is a 386 processor.

By pressing Alt-L or clicking the mouse on the LANGUAGE option on the Menu Bar, the following screen appears:

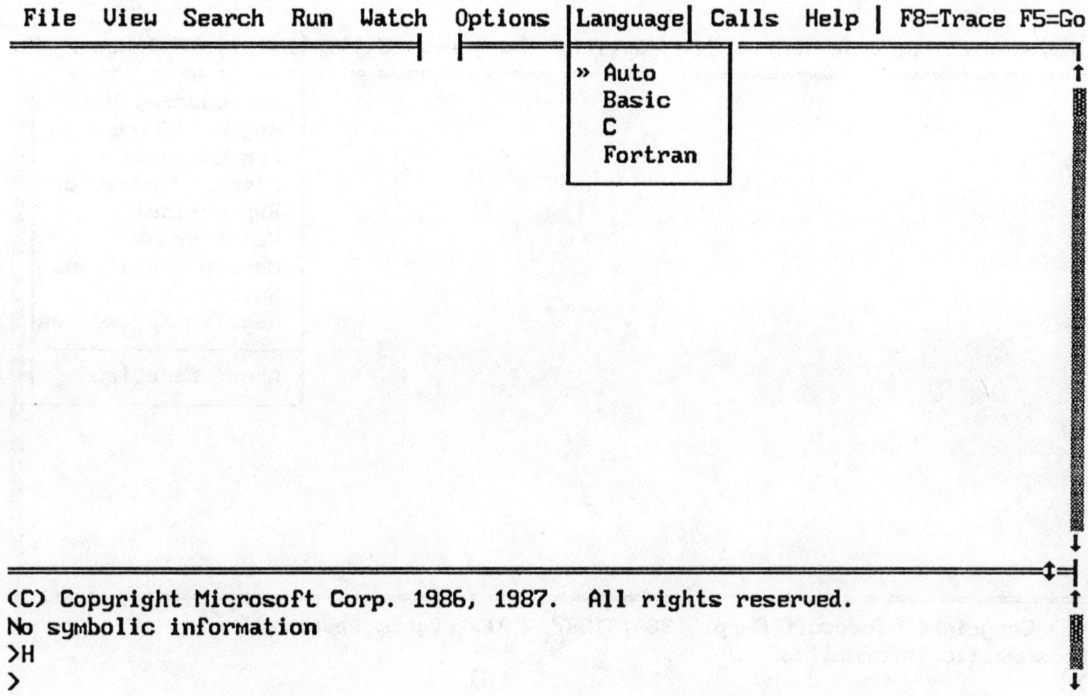

1. If you select Auto, the debugger selects the expression evaluator for you. If the file ends in .BAS, the debugger uses BASIC; if the file ends in .FOR, the debugger uses FORTRAN, and for the rest it uses C.
2. If you select Basic, then the expressions you enter are evaluated in the same way the BASIC programming language does. See HELP screens for more information.
3. If you select C, then the expressions you enter are evaluated in the same way the C programming language does. See HELP screens for more information.
4. If you select Fortran, then the expressions you enter are evaluated in the same way the C programming language does. See HELP screens for more information.

By pressing Alt-H or clicking the mouse on the HELP option on the Menu Bar, the following screen appears:

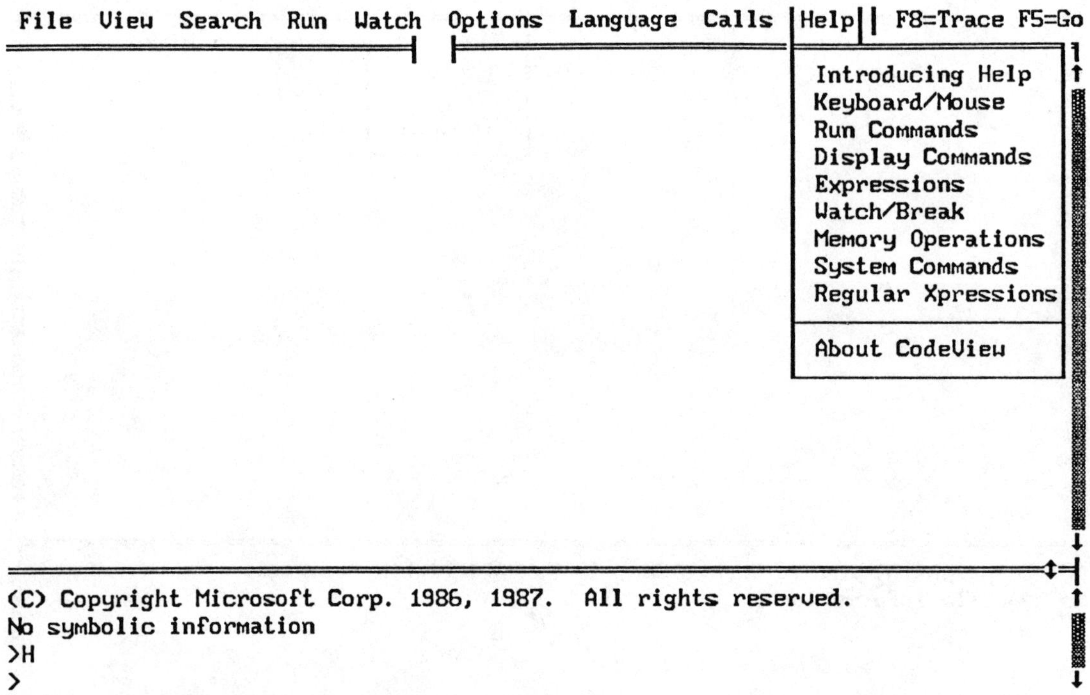

From this menu you can select which specific HELP option you need. It displays the HELP screens, which are in the next section of this module.

By pressing Alt-C or clicking the mouse on the CALLS option on the Menu Bar, the current routine and the trail of program calls that shows how you got to this routine is displayed on the screen.

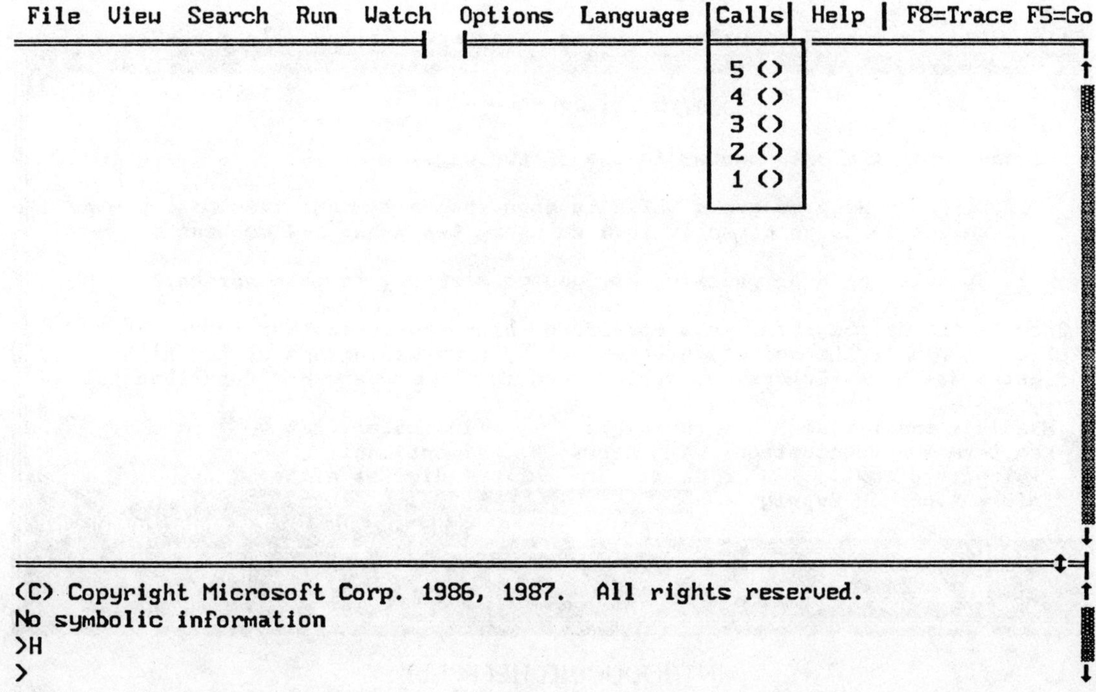

By pressing Alt-T, F8 or clicking the mouse on the TRACE option on the Menu Bar, the next source line is executed in your program.

By pressing Alt-G, F5 or clicking the mouse on the GO option on the Menu Bar, your program begins executing.

CODEVIEW HELP SCREENS

When help is requested, either with a dialog command, the mouse, or through the pull-down menu, a screen similar to one below is displayed:

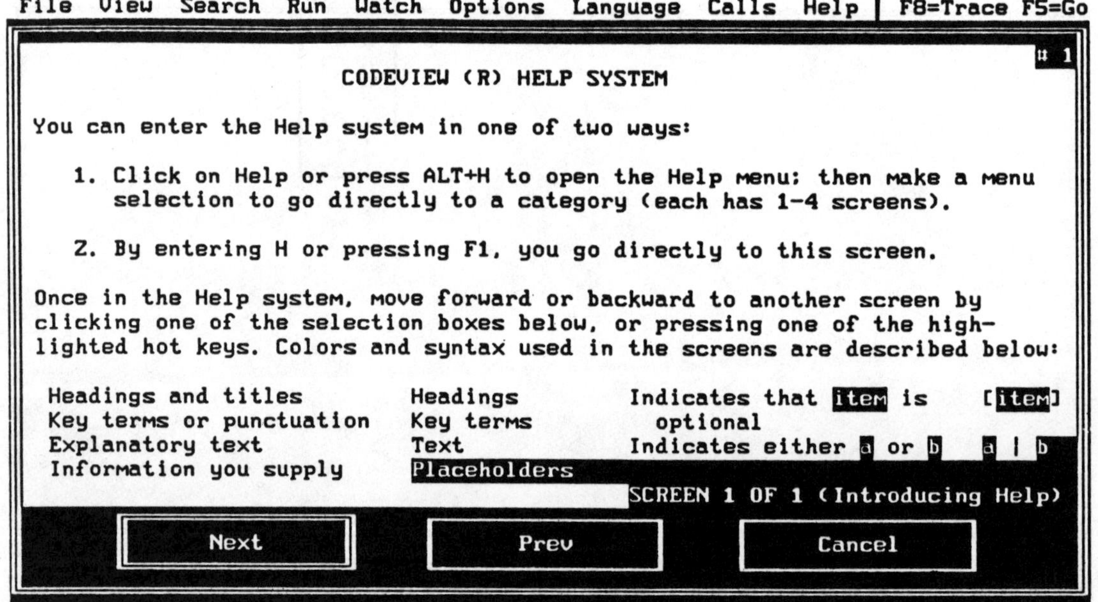

INTRODUCING HELP 1 of 1

From this screen, press N to go to the next screen, P for the previous screen, or C to cancel the HELP operation and return to the prompt.

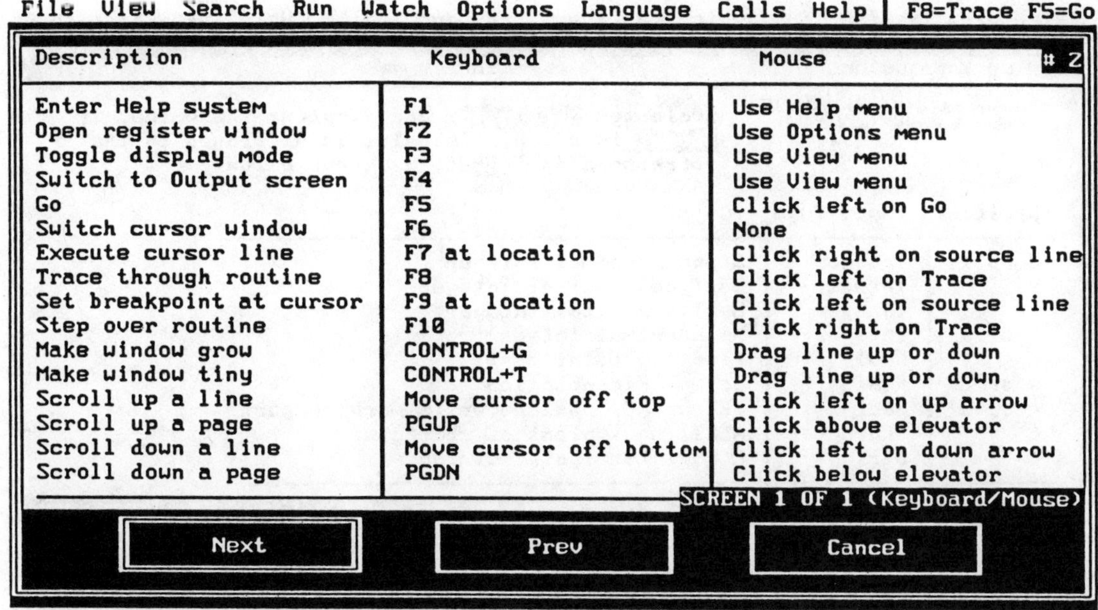

KEYBOARD/MOUSE 1 of 1

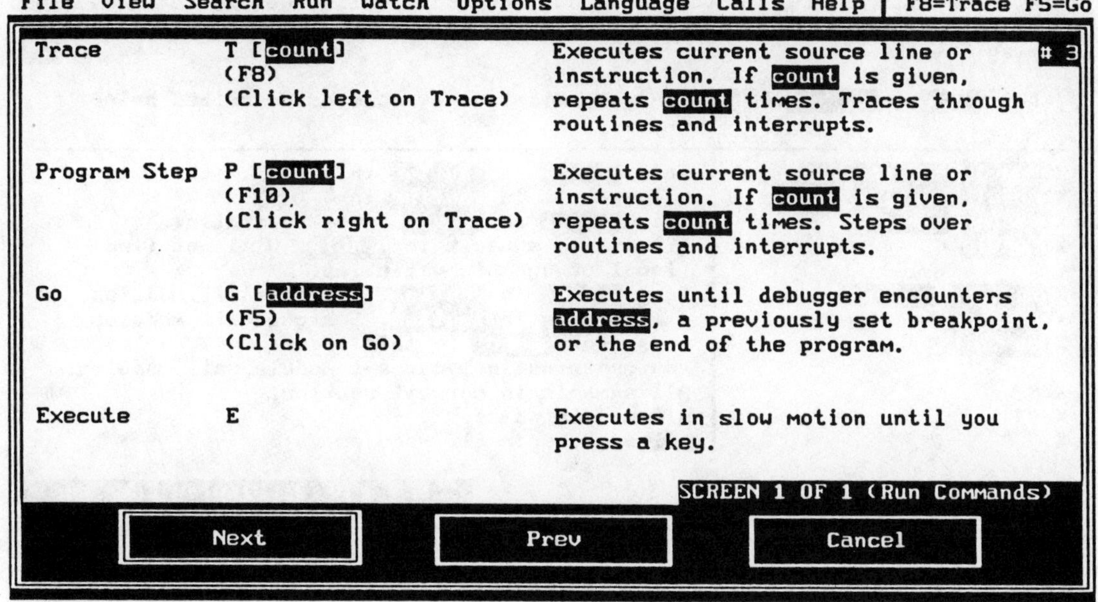

RUN COMMANDS 1 of 1

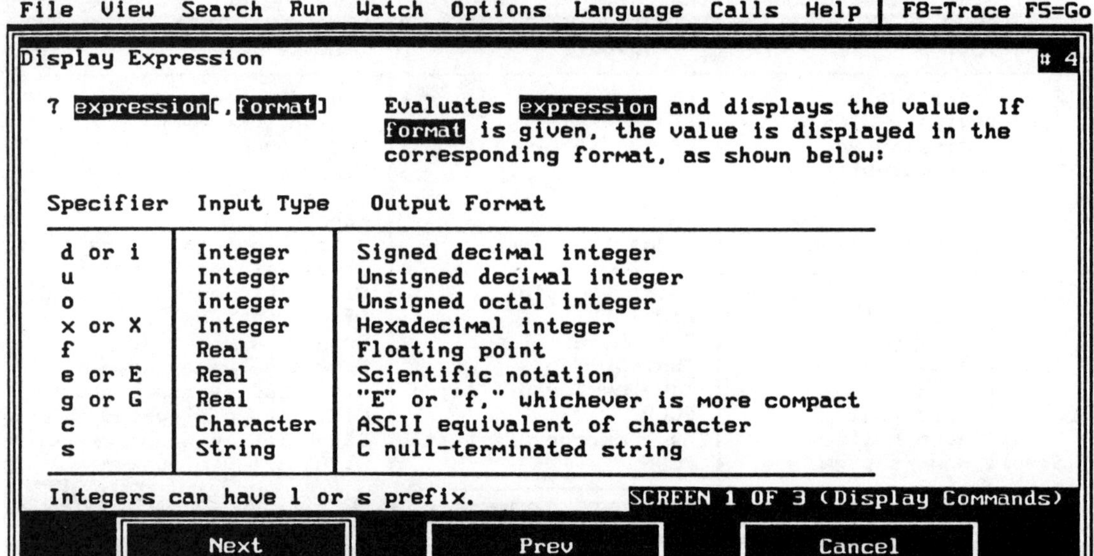

DISPLAY COMMANDS 1 of 3

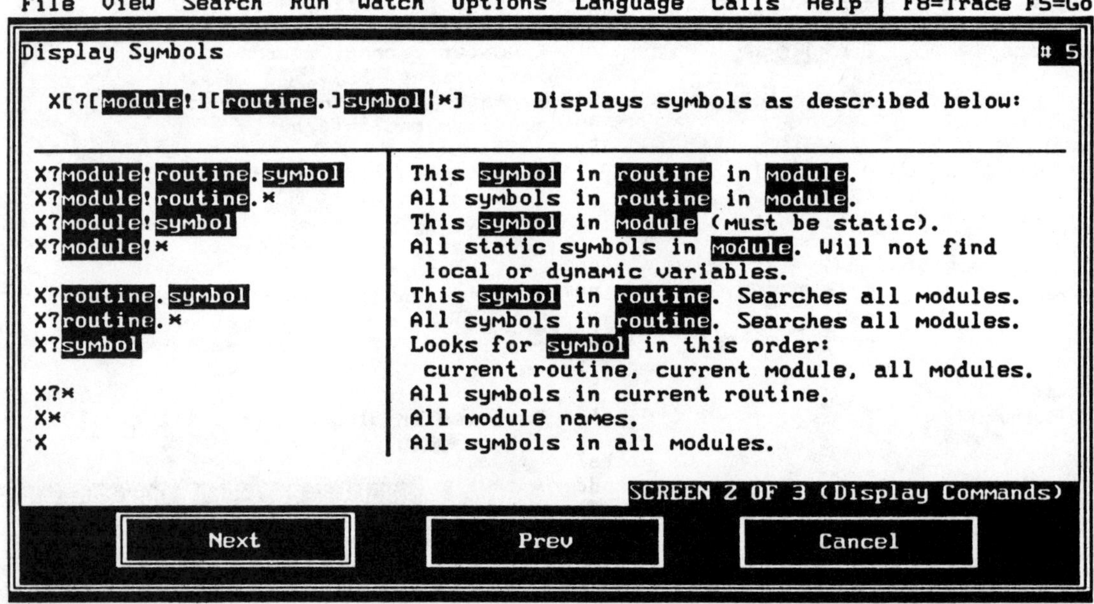

DISPLAY COMMANDS 2 of 3

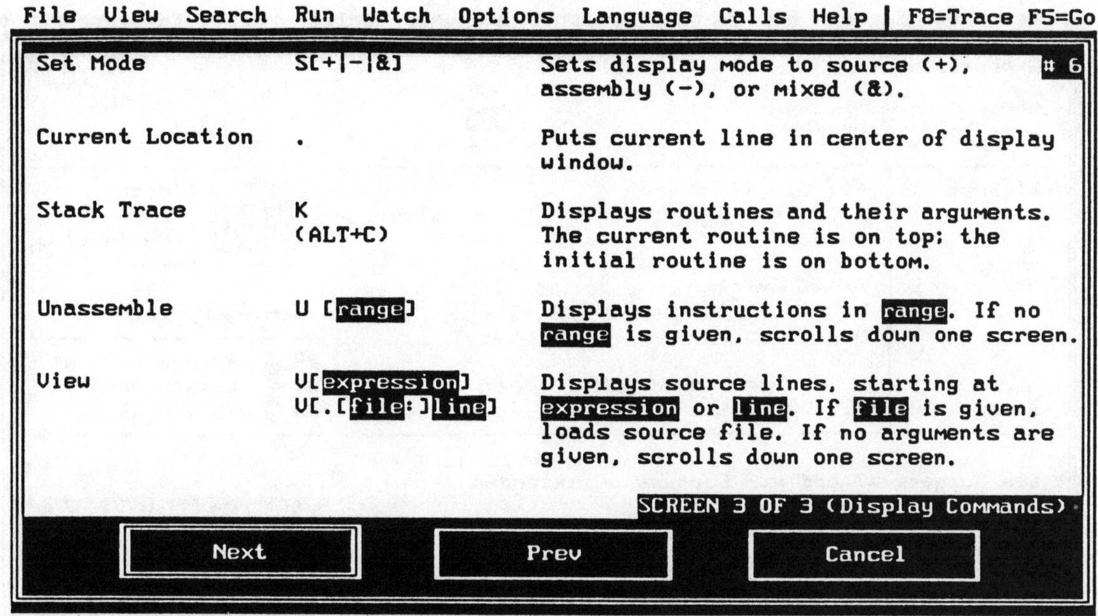

DISPLAY COMMANDS 3 of 3

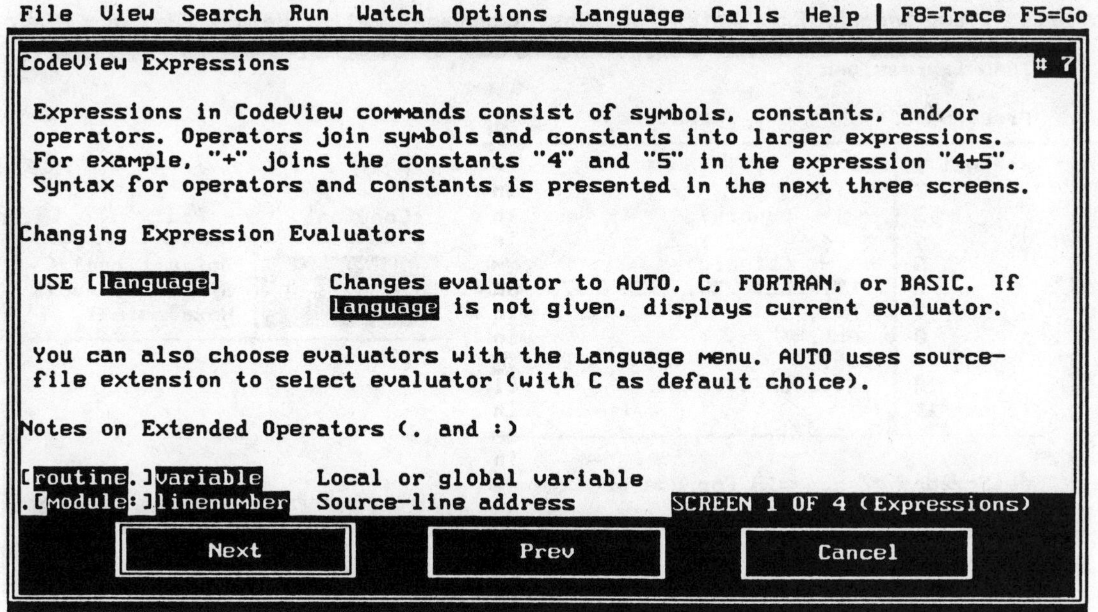

EXPRESSIONS 1 of 4

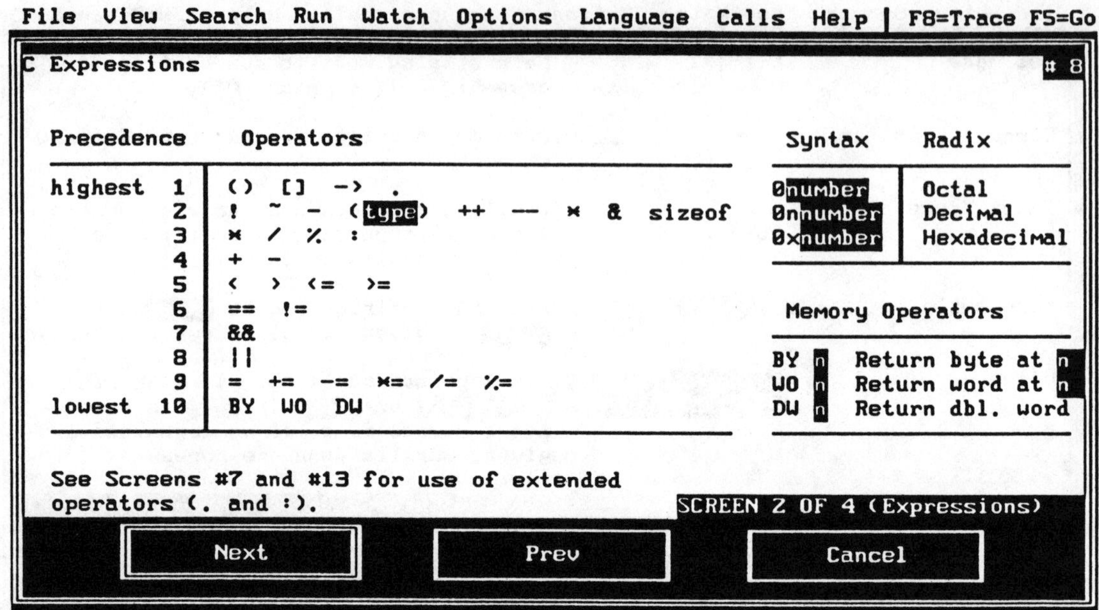

EXPRESSIONS 2 of 4

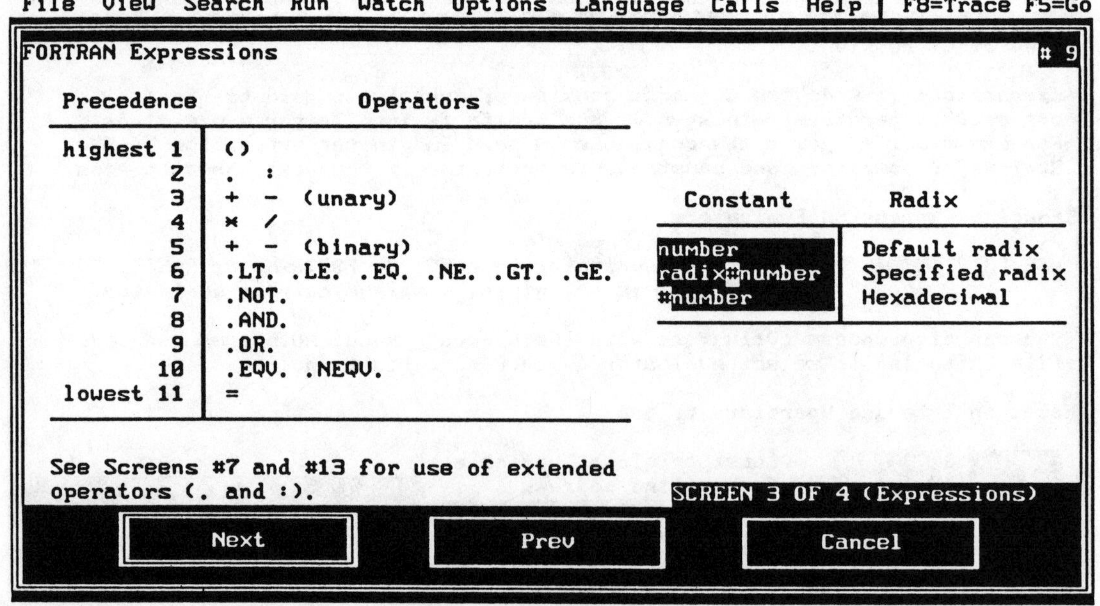

EXPRESSIONS 3 of 4

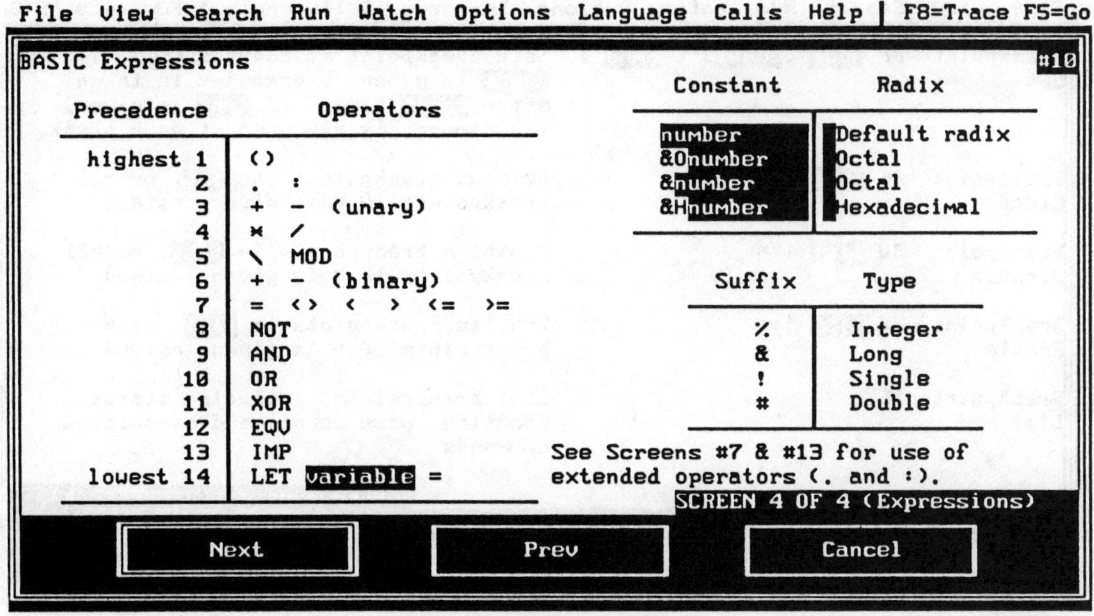

EXPRESSIONS 4 of 4

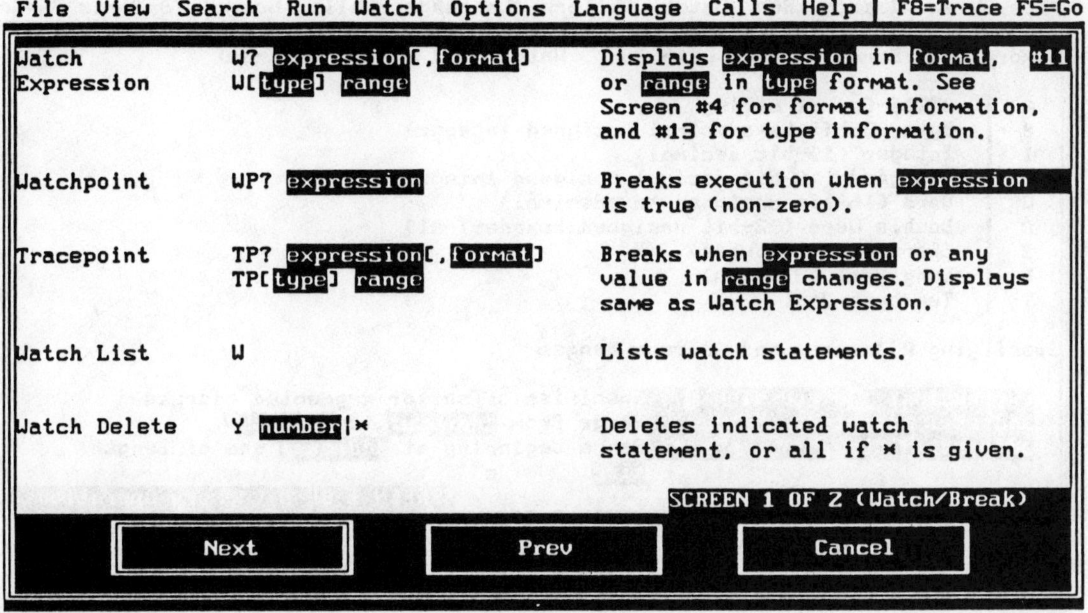

WATCH/BREAK 1 of 2

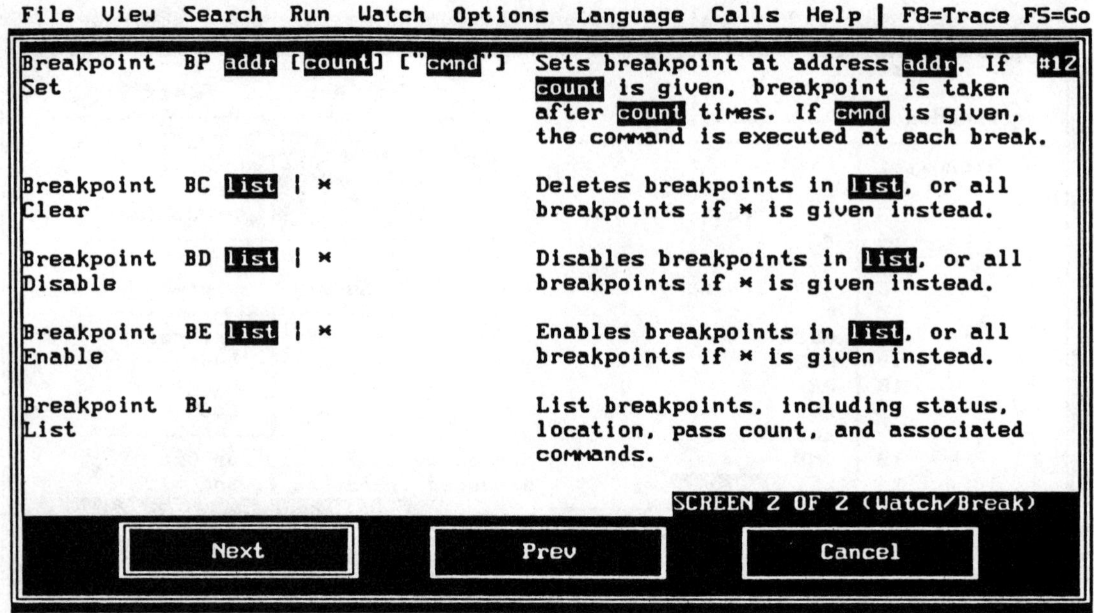

WATCH/BREAK 2 of 2

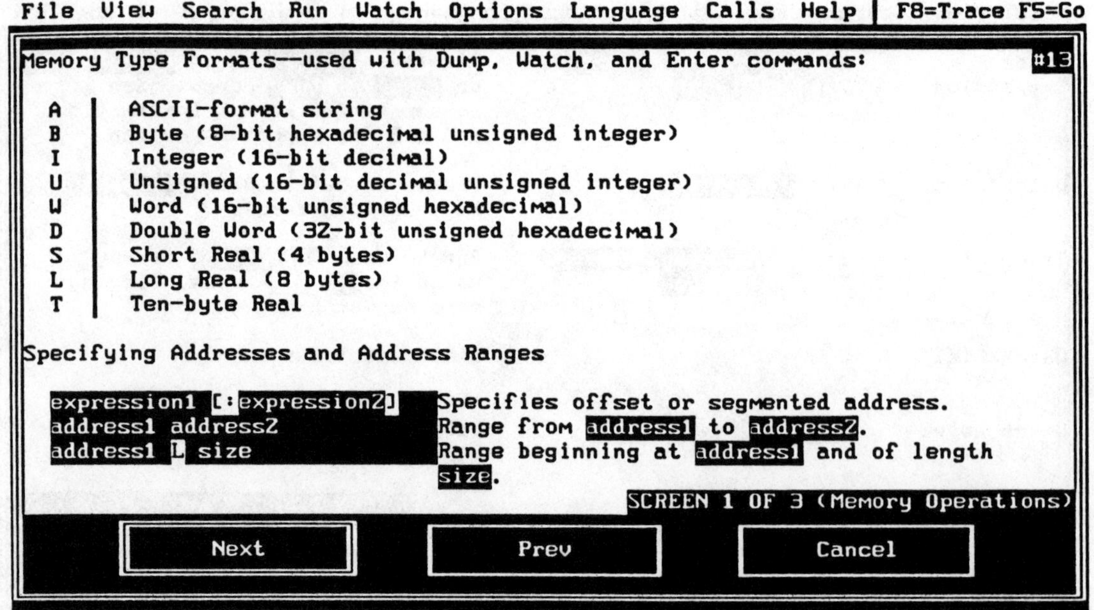

MEMORY OPERATIONS 1 of 3

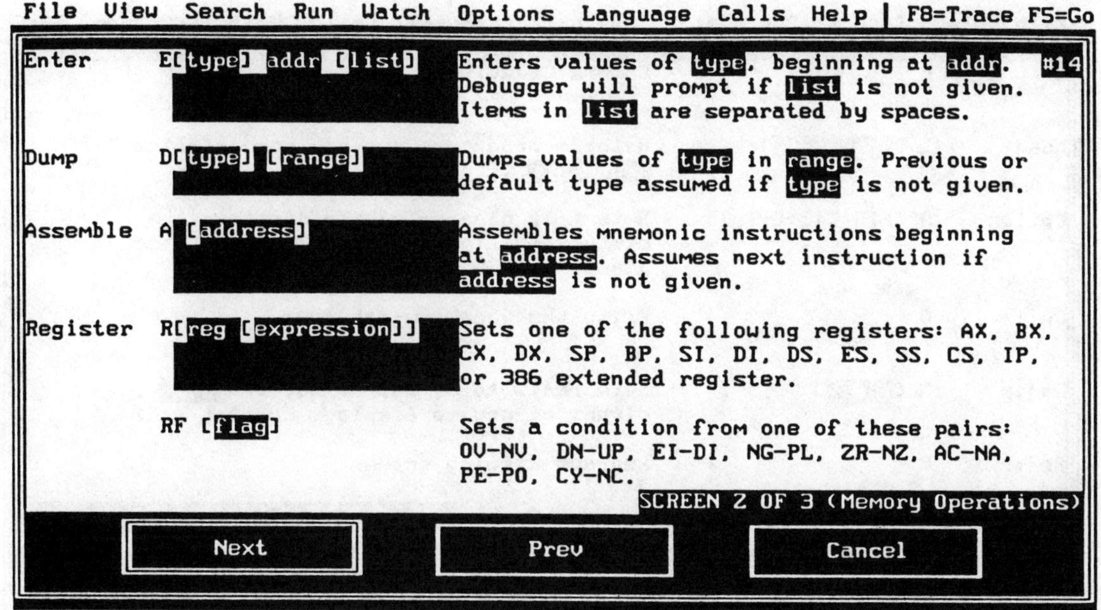

MEMORY OPERATIONS 2 of 3

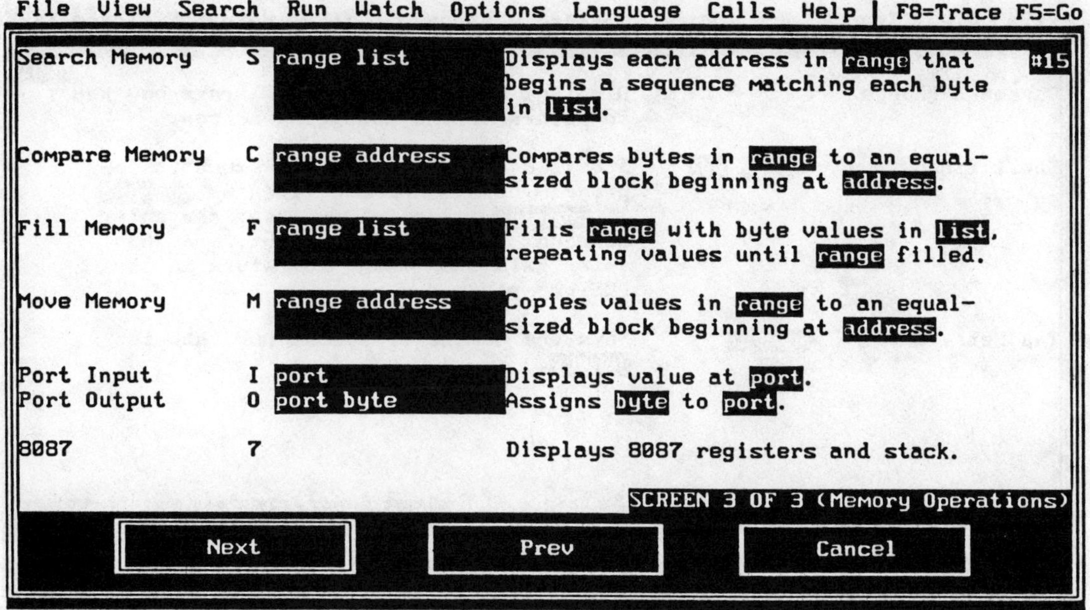

MEMORY OPERATIONS 3 of 3

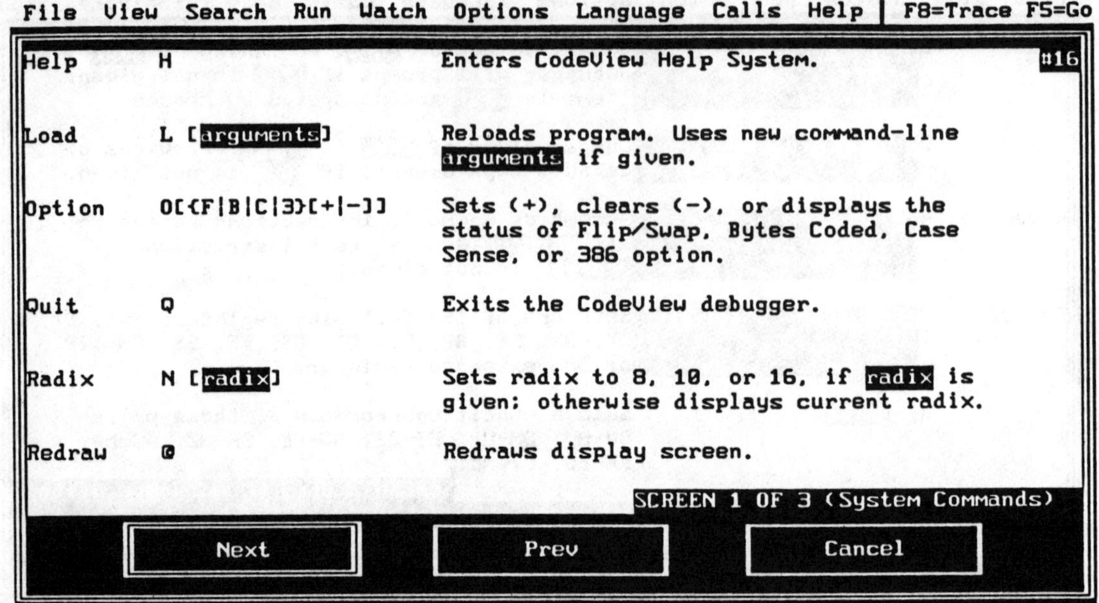

SYSTEM COMMANDS 1 of 3

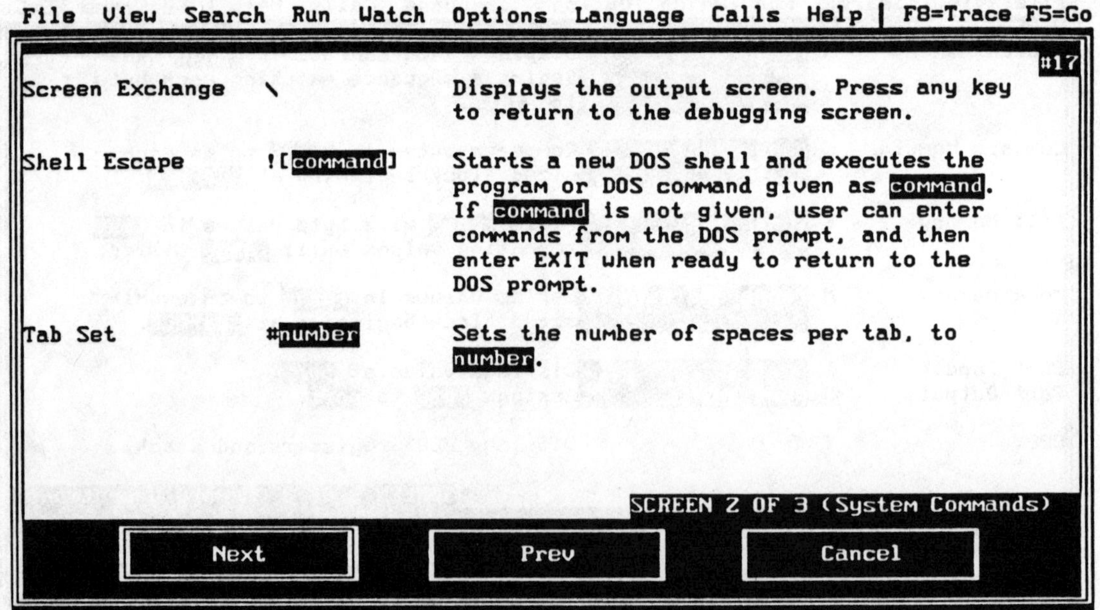

SYSTEM COMMANDS 2 of 3

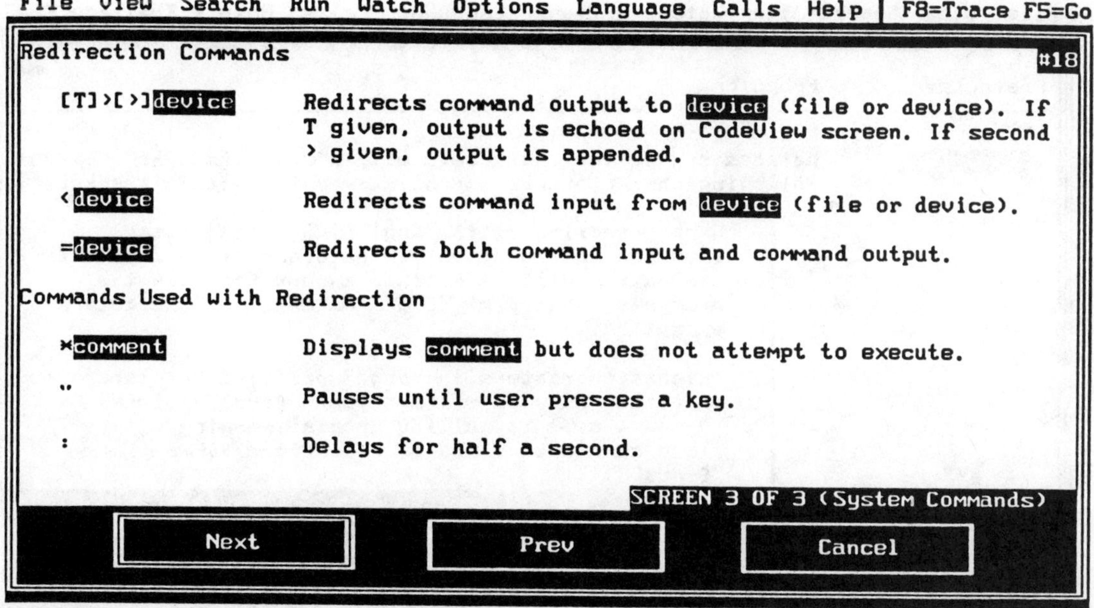

SYSTEM COMMANDS 3 of 3

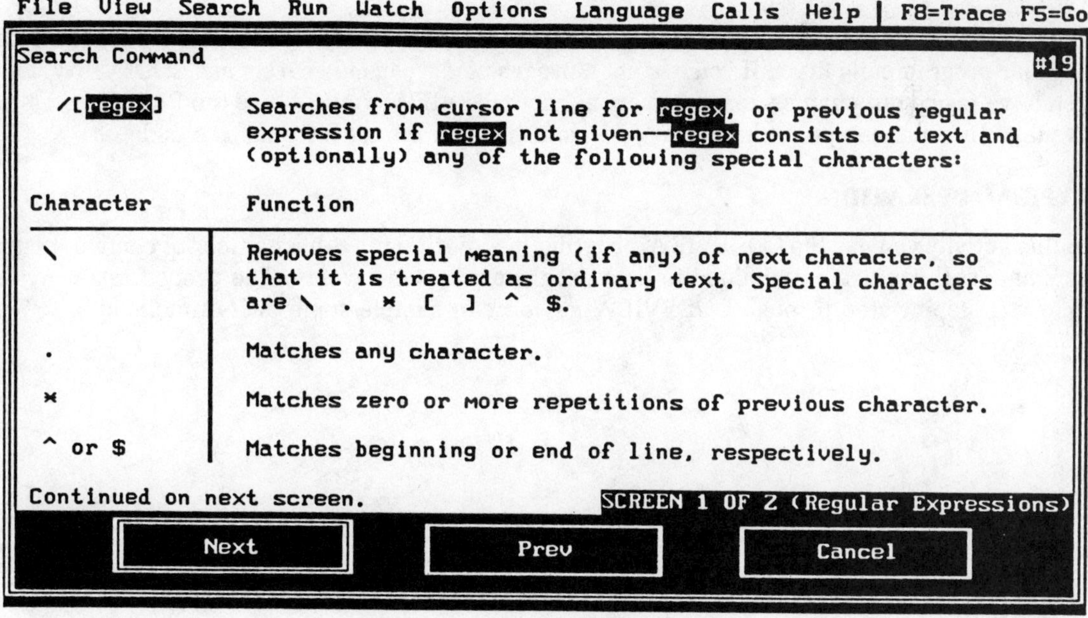

REGULAR EXPRESSIONS 1 of 2

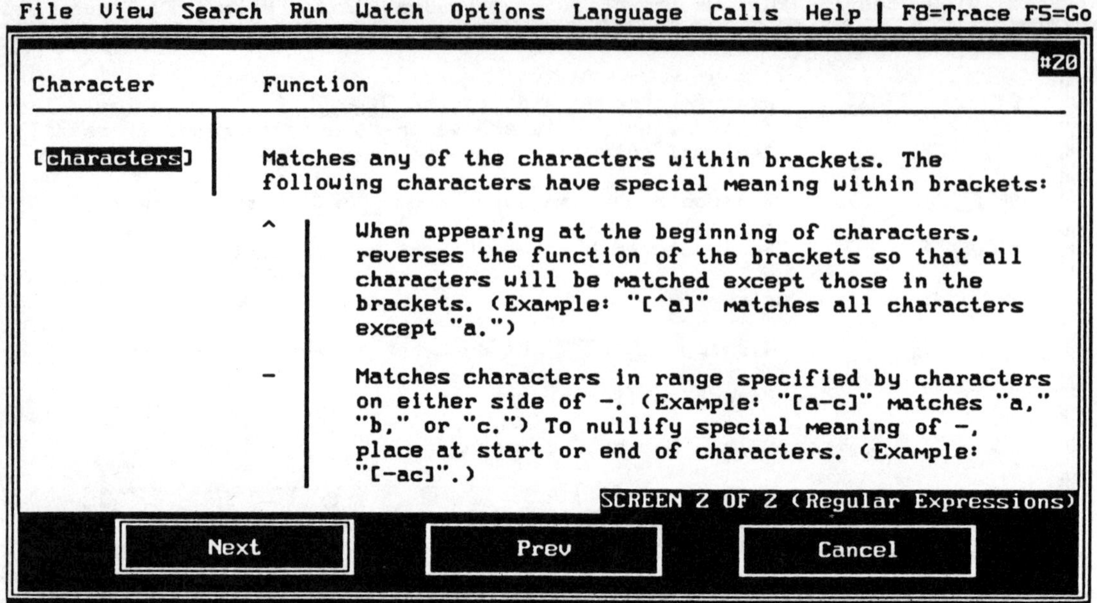

REGULAR EXPRESSIONS 2 of 2

APPLICATIONS

The CODEVIEW program is used by programmers to find program errors and to perform a host of other programming tasks. If you are not a programmer, you may rarely use CODEVIEW. Once you have tested out changes to a program using CODEVIEW, you can use the PATCH command to make the changes permanent to a program that you do not have source code on.

TYPICAL OPERATION

In this activity you use the CODEVIEW program to experiment with a number of commonly used commands. If you are not inclined to be a programmer, don't worry. The procedures provided take you step-by-step through CODEVIEW so you can sample some of its functions.

This activity uses the NAME.ASM program provided in the LINK command module. Start at the OS/2 prompt, [C:\].

1. Type **MASM /ZI NAME;** and press **Return** to assemble the program.
2. Type **LINK /CO NAME;** and press **Return** to link the program.
3. Type **CV name** and press **Return**. (Note, name may be CVP.EXE). The following screen appears:

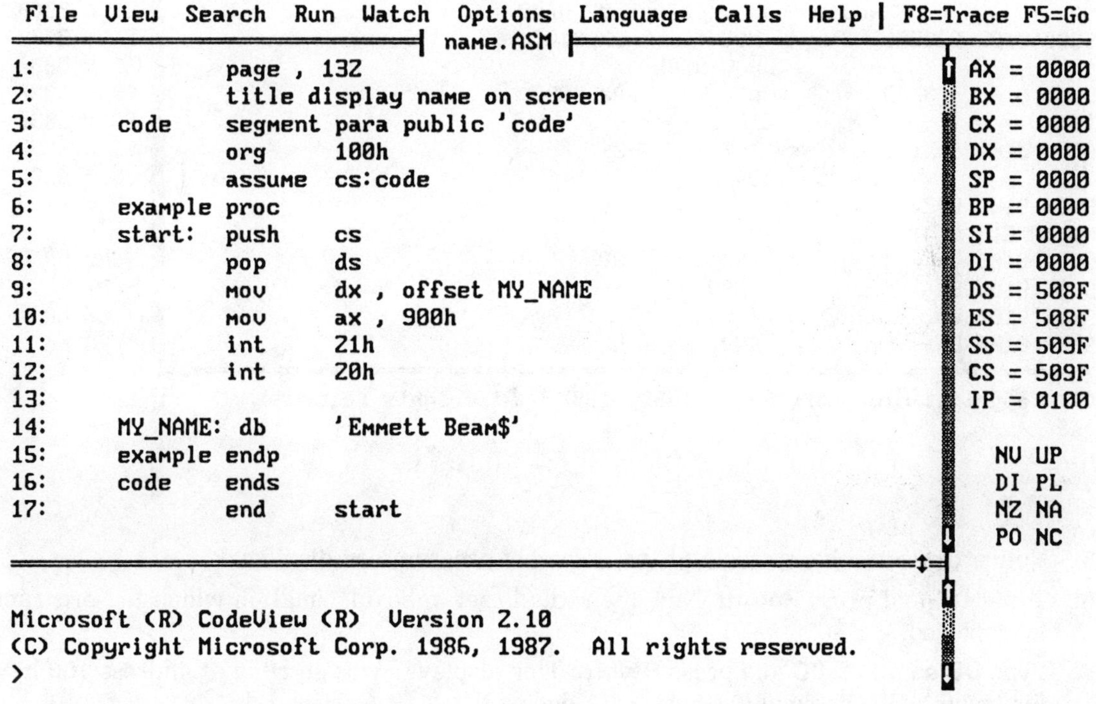

```
 File  View  Search  Run  Watch  Options  Language  Calls  Help | F8=Trace F5=Go
                                   name.ASM
            page , 132                                              AX = 0000
            title display name on screen                            BX = 0000
    code    segment para public 'code'                              CX = 0000
            org     100h                                            DX = 0000
            assume  cs:code                                         SP = 0000
    example proc                                                    BP = 0000
    start:  push    cs                                              SI = 0000
            pop     ds                                              DI = 0000
            mov     dx , offset MY_NAME                             DS = 508F
            mov     ax , 900h                                       ES = 508F
            int     21h                                             SS = 509F
            int     20h                                             CS = 509F
                                                                    IP = 0100
    MY_NAME: db     'Emmett Beam$'
    example endp                                                      NV UP
    code    ends                                                      DI PL
            end     start                                             NZ NA
                                                                      PO NC

Microsoft (R) CodeView (R)  Version 2.10
(C) Copyright Microsoft Corp. 1986, 1987.  All rights reserved.
>
```

The source program is displayed.

4. Type **S&** and press **Return**. The following screen appears:

```
 File  View  Search  Run  Watch  Options  Language  Calls  Help | F8=Trace F5=Go
═══════════════════════════════════════╡ name.ASM ╞══════════════════════════════
START:                                                              AX = 0000
7:         start:  push      cs                                     BX = 0000
509F:0100 0E                  PUSH      CS                          CX = 0000
8:                 pop       ds                                     DX = 0000
509F:0101 1F                  POP       DS                          SP = 0000
9:                 mov       dx , offset MY_NAME                    BP = 0000
509F:0102 BA0C01              MOV       DX,010C                     SI = 0000
10:                mov       ax , 900h                              DI = 0000
509F:0105 B80009              MOV       AX,0900                     DS = 508F
11:                int       21h                                    ES = 508F
509F:0108 CD21                INT       21                          SS = 509F
12:                int       20h                                    CS = 509F
509F:010A CD20                INT       20                          IP = 0100
MY_NAME:
509F:010C 45                  INC       BP                            NV UP
509F:010D 6D                  INSW                                    DI PL
509F:010E 6D                  INSW                                    NZ NA
509F:010F 65                  CWD       65                            PO NC
═══════════════════════════════════════════════════════════════════
(C) Copyright Microsoft Corp. 1986, 1987.  All rights reserved.
>s&
mixed
>
```

5. Notice that now the source and the assembly program are displayed.
6. Type **N16** and press **Return**. Now the radix is set to hexidecimal, in which the program is displayed.
7. Type **DB cs:100 L 0C** and press **Return**. This displays bytes starting at address 100 hex for length of 12 decimal (0C hex = 12 decimal).

The following is displayed: 0E 1F BA 0C 01 B8 00 09 CD 21 CD 20.

8. Type **DA cs:10c L 0B** and press **Return**. This displays ASCII characters starting at 10C for length of 11. This should display your name if you put it in this program, otherwise it displays mine: EMMETT BEAM.
9. Type **DW cs:108 cs:108** and press **Return**. This displays a word from location 108 through 108.
10. Notice that 21CD is displayed. The reason that the bytes are reversed is that the 80286/80386 stores the bytes in a word in "least significant byte first" sequence. As you can tell from Step 7, ASCII strings are stored like you read them.
11. Type **E** and press **Return**. Watch the program run in slow motion.
12. Press **F4** to look at the application screen. Notice that the name in this program is displayed. Press any key to return to the CODEVIEW screen.
13. Type **L** and press **Return**. Now the program is positioned back at the START: statement, ready for the program to run again.
14. Type **S–** and press **Return**. The following screen appears:

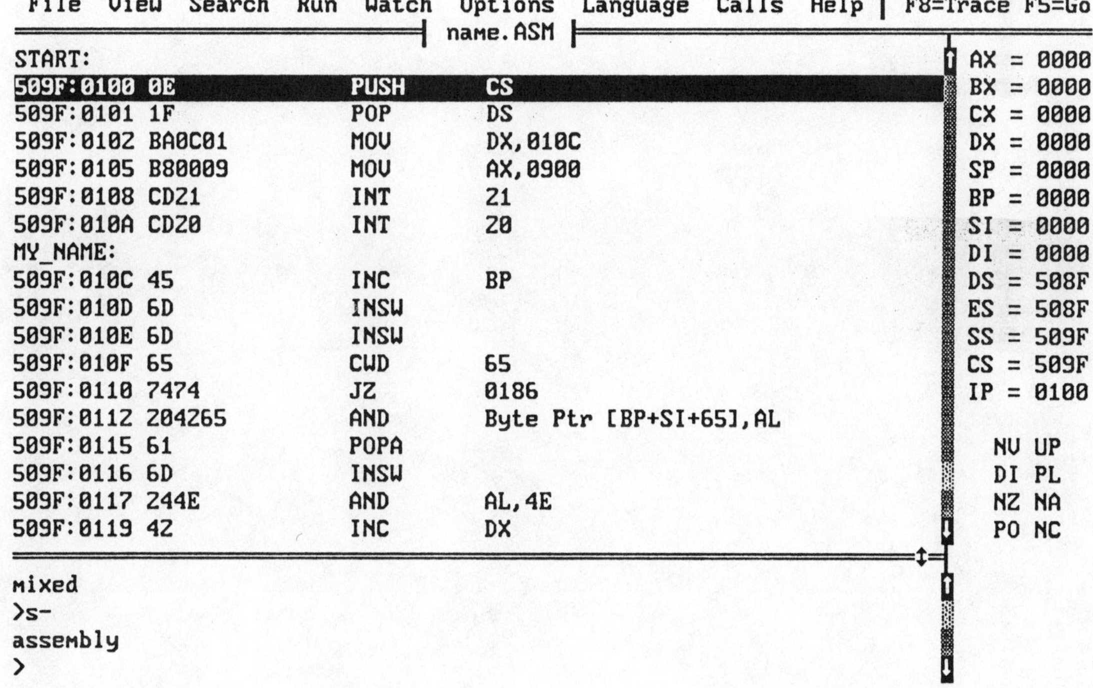

15. Notice that now the assembly program is displayed.

16. Type **EA cs:10C** and press **Return**. Now enter another name in ASCII.
17. Type **Another Name$** and press **Return**. Be sure to end whatever name you type with a $.
18. Press **F5** and notice that the program executes.
19. Press **F4** to flip to the application screen. Notice that another name now appears. You have now modified an assembly language program and successfully executed it. Press any key to return to the CODEVIEW screen.
20. Press **Ctrl-U** six times and notice how the viewing area for dialog command is expanded by six lines.
21. Type **BP cs:108** and press **Return**. You just set a breakpoint.
22. Type **L** and press **Return**.
23. Press **F5** and notice that the program begins executing and stops on the instruction INT 21, which is your break point.
24. Press **F5** and notice that the program finishes executing.
25. Type **Q** to quit and press **Return**; the OS/2 prompt is displayed. You have completed the CODEVIEW activity and the learning sequence.

Module 16
COMMAND

DESCRIPTION

The COMMAND.COM command is the DOS Mode command processor. By executing this command, you can start another command processor in DOS Mode.

By entering

```
COMMAND
```

you start another command processor. This command processor inherits its environment from the previous command processor. However, any changes to the environment of this command processor are only known to this command processor. It does not affect the previous command processor environment.

When you start another command processor, you can also give the command processor a command to execute. Enter

```
COMMAND /C DIR A:
```

and the command processor begins and executes the DIR A:. The /C parameter instructs the command processor to terminate when it completes the DIR command. You can type EXIT and the command prompt to terminate a command processor. Note that if the command passed to the command processor has piping, filters, or grouping commands, then the command must be enclosed in quotes. For example, a command like

```
COMMAND /C "DIR >LPT1"
```

requires quotes so that the redirection is associated with the DIR command and not the COMMAND command.

For more information about the command processor, see the modules on piping commands (Module 44), filter commands (Module 33), and grouping commands (Module 36).

By executing the following command,

```
COMMAND /E:1024 /P
```

you start another command processor with an environment size of 1024 bytes, specified by the /E parameter. The environment size range is from 160 to 32768 bytes long. The /P parameter specifies to make this command processor permanent and not be able to return to the previous command processor with the EXIT command. The only way to remove this command processor is to re-start OS/2.

APPLICATIONS

When you start another command processor, you also create a new command environment, with the environment from the previous command processor copied to the new one. Sometimes it is desirable to change the environment variables and then be able to return them to their original values. By starting another command processor, changing the environment, running the desired program, and then exiting back to the previous command processor, the system maintains the original environment values for you. Also, it is desirable to increase the size of the environment area. The best way to do it is to start another command processor with the desired environment length.

TYPICAL OPERATION

In this operation you execute another copy of the command processor and then return to the previous command processor. Start at the DOS prompt, [REAL C:\]. To start at the DOS prompt means to go to the DOS Mode. You go to the DOS Mode through the Session Manager.

1. If you are not in the Session Manager Program Selector menu, press **Ctrl-Esc** to return to Session Manager. Select DOS Command Prompt in the SWITCH TO A RUNNING PROGRAM window and press **Return** to go to DOS Mode.
2. Type **COMMAND** and press **Return** to begin another command processor.
3. Type **PROMPT=NEW COMMAND.COM ======$G** and press **Return**. Notice the new prompt:

   ```
   NEW COMMAND.COM ======>
   ```

4. Type **EXIT** and press **Return**. Notice that the command processor terminated and returned to the previous command processor and that the prompt for this command processor was not modified.
5. Press **Ctrl-Esc** to return to Session Manager. Select OS/2 Command Prompt in the SWITCH TO A RUNNING PROGRAM window to return to OS/2 Mode.
6. Turn to Module 30 to continue the learning sequence.

Module 17
COMP

DESCRIPTION

The COMP command is an external OS/2 command that compares the contents of two files to ensure that they are identical.

The general form of the COMP command is

```
COMP THISFILE THATFILE
```

where *THISFILE* and *THATFILE* are both on the active disk drive. In this example, *THISFILE* is read first and then compared to *THATFILE*. You can control which file is read first by typing that name first.

If you are comparing a copy of *THISFILE*, located on the disk in drive B:, with the original copy of *THISFILE* on the disk in drive A:, the command form

```
COMP A:THISFILE B:THISFILE
```

is used. If they are identical, the following information is displayed:

```
[C:\OS2]COMP A:THISFILE B:THISFILE

Compare file A:THISFILE and file B:THISFILE

The files compare OK.

Do you want to compare more files (Y/N)?_
```

If you wish to compare additional files, typing Y displays the following prompts:

```
Do you want to compare more files (Y/N)? y
Enter the first filename.
THISFILE
Enter the second filename.
THATFILE

The files are different sizes.

Do you want to continue (Y/N)? n

Do you want to compare more files (Y/N)? n
[C:\OS2]
```

When files are different sizes, there are obviously differences within the files. If you want to see the differences, answer Y to the "Do you want to continue (Y/N)?" question.

When a compare error occurs, the following message is displayed:

```
A COMPARE error occurred at OFFSET 2
Mismatching byte of file 1 = 40
Mismatching byte of file 2 = 41
```

When ten mismatches occur, the following message is displayed:

```
There were 10 or more mismatches in comparing
the files. The system is ending the COMPARE command.

Do you want to compare more files (Y/N)?
```

You can also run the COMP command by typing COMP and pressing Return. The following series of prompts and messages is displayed:

```
[C:\OS2]COMP

Enter the first filename.
CHKDSK.COM
Enter the second filename.
B:

The files compare OK.

Do you want to compare more files (Y/N)? n
[C:\OS2]
```

Wildcards are allowed in COMP commands. For example, you can enter the following command:

```
COMP  C:\SOURCE\*.ASM  A:*.ASM
```

then each .ASM file in the C:\SOURCE subdirectory is compared to the corresponding file on drive A:.

APPLICATIONS

The most notable use of the COMP command is to compare one or more copies of a file to the original file to verify exact reproduction. This is the quickest way to ensure a good quality file copy. If you suspect copy problems, you may wish to use COMP each time you make a copy of a file just to be safe.

TYPICAL OPERATION

In this activity you use the COMP command to verify that a copy is accurate. Begin at the OS/2 prompt, [C:\].

1. Type **COPY C:\OS2\COMP.COM COMPARE.COM** and press **Return**.
2. Type **COMP C:\OS2\COMP.COM COMPARE.COM** and press **Return**. If the copy is good, the following messages and prompt are displayed:

```
[C:\]COMP C:\OS2\COMP.COM COMPARE.COM

Compare file COMP.COM and file COMPARE.COM

The files compare OK.

Do you want to compare more files (Y/N)?_
```

3. Type **N** and press **Return** to return to the system prompt.
4. Type **DEL COMPARE.COM** and press **Return** to erase COMPARE.COM from your disk.
5. Turn to Module 31 to continue the learning sequence.

Module 18

CONFIGURATION COMMANDS

DESCRIPTION

The configuration file, CONFIG.SYS, allows you to customize how OS/2 runs on your computer. The configuration capabilities and corresponding configuration commands give you the ability to control the devices available and the performance of your computer.

The configuration file must have the name CONFIG.SYS. A configuration file is created using the COPY command, an ASCII word processor, or EDLIN in DOS MODE. Configuration files contain one or more lines of commands like the OS/2 command lines in batch files (Module 8). When your computer is turned on, OS/2 checks for the CONFIG.SYS file and adjusts the system configuration accordingly. Configuration commands that are commonly available with OS/2 are included in the following list. Each command is explained in the balance of this section.

There are four categories of configuration commands:

1) Common OS/2 commands you are most likely to use
2) DOS MODE commands
3) OS/2 commands you are not likely to use
4) Country/language specific commands

COMMON OS/2 COMMANDS

BUFFERS = n
— where n is a number from 1 to 99 (the default is 3).

DEVICE = *filename*
— where the *filename* is that of a device driver, such as

```
DEVICE=ANSI.SYS
DEVICE=DRIVER.SYS
DEVICE=VDISK.SYS
```

DISKCACHE = n
— where n is the amount of memory (in kilobytes) to allocate for the cache memory, from 64 to 7200.

LIBPATH = *pathname*
— where the *pathname* specifies the directories that are to be searched for the dynamic link libraries.

PAUSEONERROR = YES or PAUSEONERROR = NO
— determines whether OS/2 pauses during the boot process if it finds an error in the CONFIG.SYS file.

PROTECTSHELL = *filename argument*
— where the *filename* is that of a special command processor for the OS/2 MODE.

PROTECTONLY = *x*
— where *x* = NO will allow PC/MS-DOS programs in DOS MODE.
x = YES will not allow PC/MS-DOS programs.

REM TEXT
— allows you to place comments into the CONFIG.SYS file.

RUN = *filename*
— where filename is a program to begin running during system initalization.

SWAPPATH = *pathname*
— where the *pathname* specifies the directory that is to be used to write/read the swap file.

Each of the commonly used commands and corresponding examples are presented to familiarize you with their use and syntax.

DOS MODE COMMANDS

BREAK = on or BREAK = off
— BREAK specifies the Control-C check. The default is off.

FCBS = *m,n*
— where *m* is the number of files that can be opened at any given time, ranging in value from 1 to 255 (The default is 4). The value *n* is the maximum number of files that may remain open at any given time, ranging in value from 0 to 255. (The default is 0.)

RMSIZE = *x*
— where *x* is amount of memory reserved ofr DOS MODE. The default is 640/512KB (physical below 1Meg.). This option is valid when the configuration command PROTECTONLY = NO is also in the CONFIG.SYS file.

SHELL = *filename*
— where the *filename* is that of a special command processor for the DOS MODE.

SELDOM USED CONFIGURATION COMMANDS

IOPL = *x*
— where *x* is YES or NO to allow data input/output privilege to a process that requests it. Default is NO.

MAXWAIT = *x*
— where *x* is the maximum time a process has to wait before it runs.

MEMMAX = *x,y*
— OS/2 memory option where *x* sets memory swapping on or off, and *y* sets relocating data segments on or off.

PRIORITY = *x*
— where *x* specifies process priority, either ABSOLUTE or DYNAMIC.

TIMESLICE = *min,max*
— where *min* and *max* specify the mininum and the maximum for a program timeslice. This is almost never changed by a user.

THREADS = x
— where x specifies how many program threads to allow for.

COUNTRY/LANGUAGE SPECIFIC COMMANDS

CODEPAGE = *xxx,yyy*
— where *xxx* and *yyy* are three digit codes representing country/language specific character sets to be displayed on your monitor and printer.

COUNTRY = *nnn*
— where *nnn* is a three-digit country code (the default is 001, United States).

DEVINFO = d,s,*f*
— where d is the device name, s is the device type, and *f* is the filename that contains the code page tables.

CONFIGURATION COMMANDS

BREAK The BREAK ON command causes PC/MS-DOS DOS MODE to check for the Ctrl-Break (or Ctrl-C) sequence before performing any program operation. When BREAK OFF is active (which is the default value), operation is interrupted only when an input operation from, or output operation to, a standard device (LPTn, COMn, CON, AUX, etc.) occurs. If your CONFIG.SYS file includes the command line BREAK = ON, then you can press Ctrl-Break to interrupt program operation and return to the DOS prompt. To check the status of BREAK, you can type BREAK and press Return.

BUFFERS A *buffer* is a 528-character (or byte) block of computer memory temporarily used to store data that is either read from or written to your disk. A buffer is used only when the data is less than a "block" of disk space (528 bytes). By temporarily storing small segments of data in memory, disk read/write activity, and therefore data access time, is reduced. The default buffer value is three.

When buffers are used, the program searches them instead of a disk for stored data. However, if too many buffers exist, the search time may exceed the time saved by avoiding disk operations. In addition, buffers reduce the amount of memory available to your program. With each buffer, you lose 528 bytes of memory; 50 buffers occupy 26,400 bytes of memory. A loss of memory may increase disk input/output activity by your program, again increasing time instead of reducing it.

Because the most efficient number of buffers corresponds to the kind and size of program in use, there is no pat answer for how many buffers are best. You can try numbers between ten and 20. If you want a configuration file that establishes 16 buffers, it must contain the line BUFFERS = 16.

CODEPAGE The codepage command lets you select the system code-pages that OS/2 will have available to use. These codes represent country/language specific character sets that are displayed on your monitor and printer. The form of the codepage command is

```
CODEPAGE=xxx,yyy
```

where *xxx* and *yyy* are three digit codes equal to one of the following:

Code Page	*Country*
437	United States
850	Multilingual
860	Portuguese
863	Canada (french)
865	Nordic

For example,

```
CODEPAGE=437,850
```

This parameter sets the primary code-page to the United States and the secondary code-page to Multilingual. Applications that require one of the two code-pages can run. See Code Page Switching (Module 14) for more information.

COUNTRY The COUNTRY command allows you to define international country/language characteristics. The form of the COUNTRY command is

```
COUNTRY=nnn
```

where *nnn* is a country code equal to one of the following:

Country	*nnn*	*Code pages*	*KeybYY*	*Date Format*	*Currency*
United States	001	437,850	US	mm-dd-yy	$
Netherlands	031	437,850	NL	dd-mm-yy	–
Belgium	032	437,850	BE	dd/mm/yy	F
France	033	437,850	FR	dd/mm/yy	F
Spain	034	437,850	SP	dd/mm/yy	
Italy	038	437,850	IT	dd/mm/yy	Lit.
Switzerland	041	437,850	SF,SG	dd.mm.yy	Fr.
United Kingdom	044	437,850	UK	dd-mm-yy	
Denmark	045	865,850	DK	dd/mm/yy	DKR
Sweden	046	437,850	SV	yy-mm-dd	SEK
Norway	047	865,850	NO	dd/mm/yy	KR
Germany	049	437,850	GR	dd.mm.yy	DM
Australia	061	437,850		dd-mm-yy	$
Finland	358	437,850	SU	dd-mm-yy	MK
Israel	972	437		dd/mm/yy	–

COUNTRY sets the DATE and TIME format, the currency symbol, and the decimal character. However, it does not translate the language used in DOS prompts. See Code Page Switching (Module 14) for more information.

DEVICE The DEVICE command lets you specify the name of a file that contains what is called a *device driver*. A device driver is a program that does such things as structuring the data used during communications or printing. At system startup, DOS loads the device driver file into memory, where it resides as an active part of DOS. The form for the DEVICE command is

DEVICE=*filename*

where the *filename* is that of a device driver.

Some versions of DOS are supplied with ready-made device driver files. These files often have the extension .DEV or .SYS. For example, if you see the filename RAMDISK.DEV, you probably have a device driver that creates a logical disk drive in memory. See Module 22 on device drivers for further information.

DEVINFO This command prepares a device for code-page switching. See Code Page Switching (Module 14) for more information. The form for the DEVINFO command is

DEVINFO=*devicename,devicetype,filename,ROM=xxx,yyy*

where Valid device names are KBD$, SCREEN$, PRN, LPT1, LPT2, and LPT3.

A Devicetype for SCREEN$ is EGA.

Valid devicetypes for KBD$ are described in Module 38 on KEYB.

Filename names the file that contains the code-page tables for an output device or keyboard translation tables.

The optional ROM parameter specifies a primary code-page and an optional secondary code-page in a ROM or Cartridge device.

DISKCACHE This command allows you to allocate some of your RAM memory to be used as a disk cache buffer. The form of the command is

DISKCACHE=*n*

where *n* specifies in kilobytes how much memory to allocate to the disk cache buffer. *N* can range in value from 64 to 7200 kilobytes. Disk caching is a technique of allowing OS/2 to keep portions of your commonly used disk data in memory. The system runs faster when the desired data can be found in memory and the system does not have to physically read your disk for the data.

FCBS The FCBS command lets you specify the number of file control blocks (FCBs) that can be open at the same time. It also prevents a program from closing files automatically when it attempts to have more than a specified number of files opened. The form of the FCBS command is

FCBS=*m,n*

where *m* is the total number of files that can be opened at the same time; m can be a number from 1 to 255. The default is 4.

n is the number of files that can remain open; this value is used to prevent a program from closing files automatically during operation. The value of *n* is a number from 0 to 255. The default is 0.

FILES This command lets you change the number of files that can be opened at the same time. The default value is commonly FILES = 8, providing five predetermined DOS "handles" for standard device drivers (input, output, error, auxiliary, and standard printer). This leaves three for program use.

IOPL This command lowers the input/output privilege level such that application programs that request it can input/output privilege. Only set this parameter to YES if you have an application program that requires it. The form for the IOPL command is

```
IOPL=x
```

where *x* is YES or NO. The default is NO.

LIBPATH This command specifies the location of the dynamic link libraries. The default location is the root directory of the disk you booted from. The form for the LIBPATH command is

```
LIBPATH=pathname
```

where *x* is the maximum time a process has to wait before it runs. If *x* has the value two, then all waiting proceses would receive a temporary boost in priority every two seconds.

```
LIBPATH=c:\;c:\myDLL
```

will first search the C:\ directory and then search the C:\MYDLL directory for dynamic link libraries.

MAXWAIT This command specifies the amount of time an active process that has not run must wait before it receives a temporary boost in priority. This allows a low priority task to receive some processor time. The form for the maxwait command is

```
MAXWAIT=x
```

where *x* is the maximum time a process has to wait before it runs.If *x* has the value two, then all waiting processes would receive a temporary boost in priority every two seconds.

MEMMAN This command determines how OS/2 is to do memory management. The form for the MEMMAN command is

```
MEMMAN=x,y
```

where *x* sets memory swapping on or off (SWAP or NOSWAP), and *y* sets relocating data segments on or off (MOVE or NOMOVE). There are two defaults, one when you boot off floppy, and another when you boot off a fixed disk. The default when you boot off a fixed disk is: MEMMAN = SWAP,MOVE. The floppy boot default is: MEMMAN = NOSWAP,MOVE. When swapping is off, system performance and efficiency decreases since there is no sharing of memory resources. If you are running off a hard disk but are booting off a floppy in an office environment, consider placing the following MEMMAN command in your CONFIG.SYS file: MEMMAN = SWAP,MOVE.

PAUSEONERROR This command determines whether OS/2 pauses during the boot process if it encounters an error. If OS/2 finds and error in the config.sys file and PAUSEONERROR equals YES, then OS/2 displays an error message, pauses, and displays this message:

```
Press ENTER to continue
```

The default is YES. If you do not wish for OS/2 to pause if it encounters an error in the CONFIG.SYS file during the boot process, place the following command in the CONFIG.SYS file:

```
PAUSEONERROR=NO
```

PRIORITY This command determines how OS/2 will schedule processes (programs) to run. When this option is set to dynamic (the default), then OS/2 has flexibility in making sure all processes receive some processor time, not just the highest priority ones. The typical user will never set this option to absolute. The form for the PRIORITY command is

```
PRIORITY=x
```

where x specifies process priority, either ABSOLUTE or DYNAMIC.

PROTECTONLY This command informs OS/2 whether to reserve memory for DOS MODE PC/MS-DOS programs to run. The default is NO. The form for this command is

```
PROTECTONLY=x
```

where x = NO, reserve memory for PC/MS-DOS programs to run.
x = YES, do not reserve memory for PC/MS-DOS programs, make all of memory available to OS/2.

PROTECTSHELL The PROTECTSHELL command lets you use a special command processor in place of OS/2's standard command processor program CMD.EXE The PROTECTSHELL command should not be needed unless you are a system programmer or have been supplied with an alternate command processor. Sometimes this command is included to specify the location of the command processor.

REM The REM command allows you to place comments in the CONFIG.SYS file. An example of this command is:

```
REM  The next statement must be done before the spooler begins!!!
```

The text in the REM statement is not executed and does not appear on the screen during the boot process, it is for documentation and informational purpose only within the CONFIG.SYS file.

RUN The RUN command starts a program running in the background during the initialization process. The form for this command is

```
RUN=filename
```

where *filename* is a program to begin running. For example, if you have an alarm clock program that you want started at initialization time, you will enter the command in your CONFIG.SYS file like this: run = alarm /4. Note that parameters are allowed just like you have available from the command processor.

SHELL The SHELL command lets you use a special command processor in place of DOS's standard command processor program COMMAND.COM. The SHELL command should not be needed unless you are a system programmer or have been supplied with an alternate command processor. Sometimes this command is included to specify the location of the command processor.

SWAPPATH This command instructs OS/2 where to place the swap file. This is the file that OS/2 uses when it is performing memory management and is only valid if the MEMMAN command allows swapping. The form for this command is

```
SWAPPATH=pathname
```

where the *pathname* specifies the directory that is to be used to store the temporary swap file.

TIMESLICE The TIMESLICE command controls how much processor time a process receives before OS/2 checks for other processes. This command should almost never be changed by the user. Only change it if an application directs you to change it. The form for this command is

```
TIMESLICE=min,max
```

where *min* and *max* specify the mininum and the maximum for a program timeslice.

THREADS This command informs OS/2 how many threads (paths of execution) to allow for. The default is 48, which is sufficient for most users. An application is composed of one and often many threads. If you have lots of programs running at once, you may have to increase the number of threads that are available to OS/2. Note, however, that this consumes more memory also. The form for the THREADS command is

```
THREADS=x
```

where x specifies how many program threads to allow for.

APPLICATIONS

The system configuration is determined by the commands within the CONFIG.SYS file. Each time your computer is turned on or re-booted OS/2 configures itself according to the command in your CONFIG.SYS file. Some configuration commands have defaults when not included in the COONFIG.SYS file. The CONFIG.SYS file is created for you initially when OS/2 is installed on the computer system. After that, it can be customized for your particular needs.

TYPICAL OPERATION

In this activity you list your config.sys file and compare it to my CONFIG.SYS file. Start at the OS/2 prompt, [C:\].

Here is my CONFIG.SYS file:

```
rem                          CONFIG.SYS
buffers=30
shell=c:\os2\command.com /P /e:1024 c:\os2
protshell=c:\shell.exe c:\cmd.exe /k c:\os2init.cmd
rmsize=640
protectonly=NO
break=OFF
threads=64
iopl=YES
libpath=c:\;c:\os2;
memman=SWAP,MOVE
diskcache=64
maxwait=3
swappath=C:\
device=c:\os2\mousea02.sys,serial=com1
device=c:\os2\pointdd.sys
device=c:\os2\ansi.sys
run=c:\os2\spool.exe c:\spool /o:lpt1 /d:lpt1
```

1. Type **COPY C:\CONFIG.SYS LPT1:** and press **Return**.
2. Study your CONFIG.SYS file listing to know how your computer system is configured. Compare it to my copy of CONFIG.SYS.
3. Turn to Module 22 to continue the learning sequence.

Module 19
COPY

DESCRIPTION

The COPY command is an internal OS/2 command. It is used to:

1. Copy one or more specified files to another disk with the same filename, date, and time information.
2. Copy one or more specified files to the same or to another disk with a different filename.
3. Copy one or more specified files to the same or to another disk with the current system date and time.
4. *Concatenate* (or combine) two or more files into a single file.
5. Create a new file by copying what is typed on the screen (CON:) to a designated file.

The general form of the COPY command is

```
COPY SOURCEFILE TARGETFILE
```

Notice that a space separates the two filenames. The *SOURCEFILE* is the filename of the file being copied. The *TARGETFILE* is the filename of the file created by the COPY command. If no target filename is given, the source filename is used automatically. You can also use disk drive designators (like A: or B:) and pathnames. Here is an example of the COPY command with disk and pathnames:

```
COPY C:\FORMS\FORM.LTR A:\MAIL\JOHNBOY.LTR
```

This command copies a file named FORM.LTR from directory pathname FORMS on disk C to a new file named JOHNBOY.LTR in directory pathname MAIL on disk A.

It is only necessary to specify a target filename if you want to change the filename. Otherwise, the existing filename is used. There are a number of variations to the COPY command. The following list presents most of the useful forms:

COPY OLDNAME NEWNAME—Makes a copy of the file OLDNAME on the active disk drive. The copied file is given the new filename NEWNAME.

COPY OLDNAME B:—Makes a copy of the file OLDNAME on the active disk drive and places it on the disk in drive B. The copy retains the original name, date, and time information.

COPY OLDNAME B: /V—Makes a copy of the file OLDNAME on the active disk drive and places it on the disk in drive B as in the previous example. The /V parameter verifies the integrity of the data as it is copied. Although verification is rarely needed, you can use /V when you suspect copy problems, or in cases where you want to avoid the risk of data errors.

COPY B:MYWORDS.TXT A:—Makes a copy of the file MYWORDS.TXT, which is located on the disk in drive B, and copies it to the disk in drive A with the original filename, date, and time. The A: is optional, as the default (or active) disk drive is assumed by OS/2.

COPY OLDNAME B:NEWNAME—Makes a copy of the file OLDNAME, which is located in the active disk drive, and places it on the disk in drive B with the filename NEWNAME.

COPY STUFF.TXT + THINGS.TXT COMBO.TXT—Combines the files STUFF.TXT plus THINGS.TXT into a new file named COMBO.TXT. The new file COMBO.TXT is given the current date and time. You can concatenate several files this way.

COPY FIRST + SECOND + THIRD + FOURTH—Adds (sometimes called *appends*) the named files to the end of the first file. The result is copied to the FIRST file.

COPY OLDNAME + ,,—Updates the date and time to the file OLDNAME, which is located in the active disk drive.

COPY *.TXT ALL.TXT—Copies all files having the .TXT extension into one file named ALL.TXT.

COPY *.TXT + *.LTR LTR&TXT.ALL—Copies all files having the .TXT and .LTR extensions into one file named LTR&TXT.ALL.

COPY HANDY.TXT + *.TXT—Adds all files (except HANDY.TXT itself) having the .TXT extension to the end of the file HANDY.TXT.

COPY TEXT.ONE + B:PROG.COM/B + B:TEXT.TWO /A COMBO.A&B—Combines ASCII (standard text) and binary (program) files into a single file named COMBO.A&B. Notice that three files are combined: TEXT.ONE, which is an ASCII file located on the default disk; PROG.COM, which is a binary file located on the disk in drive B; and TEXT.TWO, which is another ASCII file located on the disk in drive B. The "/B" and "/A" parameters let you combine binary and ASCII file types. When either /B or /A are used, they apply to the previous file and all following files until another /B or /A is encountered. Dissimilar file types (ASCII and binary) cannot be combined without using the /A or /B parameter.

COPY CON: NEWNAME—(typed text) Ctrl-Z—This combination of two or more lines copies what is typed on the screen (or *console*) to the named file. The last character must be a Ctrl-Z (or F6), which is recognized by OS/2 as an end-of-file marker. Each line in the typed file is completed by pressing the Return key.

COPY CON: LPT1:—Copies the contents of the screen to your parallel printer.

COPY FILE1 CON:—Copies (or displays) FILE1 to the screen.

COPY LETTER.ONE NUL:—Used for testing. NUL is a dummy device name.

COPY \PATH1\LETTER.ONE \PATH2—Makes a copy of the file LETTER.ONE in directory PATH1 on the active disk drive and places it in directory PATH2. The copy retains the original name, date, and time information.

COPY *.* \TEXT—Copies all files in the active directory to the directory having the pathname TEXT. You can substitute a period for the *.*. The period represents all filenames in the current path. If you use a double period, all files in the parent directory are copied.

COPY *.* \—Copies all files in the active directory to the parent directory.

Parameter Summary

/A When used with a source filename, it causes the file to be treated as an ASCII file so that the copy ends when the end-of-file (Ctrl-Z) character is reached.

/A When used with a target filename, it causes an end-of-file character to be appended to the end of the target file.

/B When used with a source filename, it causes the file to be treated as a binary file so that the copy does not end when a Ctrl-Z character is reached.

/B When used with a target filename, no end-of-file character is appended to the target file.

/V Verifies that each sector is written correctly.

APPLICATIONS

The many forms of the COPY command allow a substantial amount of flexibility in copying and combining files on the same disk or from one disk to another. In addition to copying, using reserved device names with the COPY command lets you create, display, and print files. The NUL device name lets you test COPY command operations. Finally, the /A and /B (ASCII and binary) parameters let you combine dissimilar files. All of these functions offer you an extensive repertoire of file-handling utilities.

TYPICAL OPERATION

In this activity you use the COPY command to create, copy, and combine files. Begin at the OS/2 prompt, [C:\].

1. Place a formatted scratch disk in drive A and close the load lever.
2. Type **COPY CON: A:FILE1** and press **Return.**
3. Type the following text, ending each line with **Return.** (Press **Ctrl-Z** and then press **Return** on the last line to obtain the ^Z character.)

```
This is file number one.
It contains three lines.
This is the last line.
^Z
```

4. Type **COPY A:FILE1 CON:** and press **Return**; notice that your new file is displayed on the console (screen) similar to the following:

```
[C:\]COPY A:FILE1 CON:

This is file number one.
It contains three lines.
This is the last line.
    1 file(s) copied.
[C:\]
```

5. Type **COPY A:FILE1 A:FILE2** and press **Return**.
6. Type **DIR A:FILE*** and press **Return** to display a directory of your newly created files. Your display should resemble the following:

```
  [C:\]DIR A:FILE*

 Volume in drive A has no label
 Directory of A:\

FILE2               128   6-16-88    1:03p
FILE1               128   6-16-88    1:03p
        2 File(s)      21440 bytes free
```

7. Type **COPY A:FILE1 + A:FILE2 A:FILE3** and press **Return**.
8. Type **COPY A:FILE3 CON:** and press **Return**; notice that your new combined file is displayed on the console (screen).

```
[C:\]COPY A:FILE3 CON:

This is file number one.
It contains three lines.
This is the last line.
This is file number one.
It contains three lines.
This is the last line.

[C:\]
```

9. Type **DIR A:FILE*** and press **Return** to display a directory of your newly created files. Your display should resemble the following:

```
[C:\]DIR A:FILE*

 Volume in drive A has no label
 Directory of  A:\

FILE2               128   6-16-88   1:03p
FILE1               128   6-16-88   1:03p
FILE3               153   6-16-88   1:06p
        3 File(s)      21287 bytes free

  [C:\]
```

10. To preserve disk space, you can delete your experimental files by typing **DEL A:FILE*** and pressing **Return**.
11. Turn to Module 25 to continue the learning sequence.

Module 20
DATE

DESCRIPTION

The DATE command is an internal OS/2 command which means that you do not see the DATE command file when a directory of your OS/2 files is displayed. The DATE command is run automatically when you insert the OS/2 disk and turn on your computer. You can also run the DATE command by typing DATE and pressing Return from the OS/2 prompt. The following screen is displayed:

```
[C:\OS2]DATE
The Current date is: Tue  1-01-1980
Enter the new date: (mm-dd-yy)
```

Respond by typing the date notation for the national language in use. For example, if you are configured for the U.S., type the current month, day, and year in the form 09-01-88 and press Return. The date is recorded by OS/2. If the date is not important to you, you can respond to the DATE prompt simply by pressing Return.

You can also enter the date by typing DATE followed by the proper date. This inputs the date on a single line without displaying the date prompt.

APPLICATIONS

Why enter the date when it is so much easier simply to press the Return key? There is a valid reason. When you enter the current date, files that are saved to disk are tagged with that date. This lets you examine a directory to determine which files are most current.

There are a number of programs that use the system date to tag files and display calendar information. Although it may seem like a lot of trouble to enter the date, it is recommended for these reasons.

Most microcomputer now come with a clock-calender option included. If your computer does not now have one, you can buy a clock-calendar option board to eliminate the need to type the date and time every time you turn on your computer. These boards use a battery to maintain clock and calendar operation, even when the computer is turned off or disconnected from a power source.

TYPICAL OPERATION

In this "hands-on" activity you use the DATE command to enter the current date. Start at the OS/2 prompt, [C:\].

1. Type **DATE** and press **Return**; notice the DATE prompt.

```
[C:\]DATE
The Current date is: Tue  1-01-1980
Enter the new date: (mm-dd-yy)
```

2. Type the current date in the indicated form (separate month, day, year with hyphens) and press **Return**.
3. The current date is now recorded. To verify the current date, you can repeat Step 1 above. If you do not want to change the date, press **Return** to redisplay the OS/2 prompt. Pressing Return leaves the system date unchanged.
4. Turn to Module 59 to continue the learning sequence.

Module 21
DETACH

DESCRIPTION

The DETACH command is an internal OS/2 command. The DETACH command lets you execute some programs and OS/2 commands in the background while you continue to execute other programs. The one restriction that applies to programs that are detached is that they are not allowed console input/output. The background programs must execute independently, without operator intervention.

The form for the DETACH command is

```
DETACH PROGRAM
```

where *PROGRAM* is your application program, batch (.cmd) file, or an OS/2 commmand you want to execute in the background. The detached program, batch file, or command is called a "process" in OS/2 terms. They are also called non-interactive since they do not have keyboard input nor output to a display.

When you detach a process, OS/2 assigns the process a *Process Identification Number* (Pid), displays the Pid to you, begins the execution of the process, and returns a prompt to you. You can now continue with other commands or programs while the detached process runs simultaneously in the background.

When you detach a program you can add parameters, input/output redirection, and piping functions. To detach a process to sort your OS/2 commands directory and place the output into a file on drive A named OS2-SORT.DIR, enter the following command:

```
DETACH DIR C:\OS2 ¦ C:\OS2\SORT >A:OS2-SORT.DIR
```

Let's look at how this command follows the restriction placed on detached processes. First, the DIR command is executed with the parameter of *C:\OS2*. The input to this command is from the directory on disk of *C:\OS2*. The output from DIR is into a pipe. Next the SORT command receives its input from the pipe. Finally SORT redirects its output to a disk file.

NOTE

- The background process does not have access to the keyboard for operator input, nor a screen to output an informational or error message to the operator.
- OS/2 will execute any program you command it to with the DETACH command.
- If you detach a process that you should not, you could lock a file, ruin a file, or lose valuable information.

- Since a background process does not have access to the keyboard, you cannot CTRL-C to abort a detached process — it continues to run until it comes to an end on its own.

APPLICATIONS

A normal purpose and application for the DETACH command is to execute an application print program in the background while you edit a document or update a spreadsheet in the foreground. Another good time to run DETACH commands is during end-of-day processing. You can be spooling several reports or lists and reorganizing your database, all while you are backing up your data files onto floppy disks.

This capability of concurrent processing at end-of-day will save you time. Since the detached background processes can be batch files, it will simpify many tasks that you normally do.

TYPICAL OPERATION

In this activity you use the DETACH command to produce an alphabetical listing of your OS2 directory and place the output on a floppy disk in drive A:. Begin at the OS/2 prompt, [C:\].

1. Insert a scratch floppy disk into drive A:.
2. Type **DETACH DIR C:\OS2 | C:\OS2\SORT >A:OS2-SORT.DIR**. Notice the screen display (however, the number is different):

```
The Process Identification Number is 999.

[C:\]
```

3. Type **DIR** and press **Return**. Notice that while the directory of drive C: is listing, the light on drive A: is blinking as the output of the SORT command is being written to the diskette in drive A:, demonstrating that both commands are working at the same time.
4. Type **TYPE A:OS2-SORT.DIR**. Notice that the output is an alphabetical list of the directory C:\OS2.
5. Type **DEL A:OS2-SORT.DIR** and press **Return** to delete the file OS2-SORT.DIR from drive A:.
6. Turn to Module 57 to continue the learning sequence.

Module 22
DEVICE DRIVERS

DESCRIPTION

Each piece of hardware on you computer computer (keyboard, disk, printer) has a device driver associated with it and built into OS/2. There are drivers for the keyboard, the disk drives, the communications port, the printer, and the clock. When an application program accesses one of the devices on your computer, the device driver is the piece of software that communicates with the hardware. Because most device drivers utilize software in the computers' system ROM (read only memory) to actually communicate with the device, device drivers are usually portable between computer manufacturers.

One commonly used device driver is for a virtual disk, often called a RAM disk. This device driver simulates a disk drive through the use of another hardware device on your computer, RAM memory. To your programs the RAM disk acts just like a hardware fixed disk or floppy disk drive.

When you purchase additional hardware for your computer (mouse, tape backup), the manufacturer provides with it an associated device driver, usually on floppy disk. When you install the hardware in you computer, you must also make OS/2 aware of the new hardware. The way you make OS/2 aware of the new device and how to use the device is by installing the software device driver. First copy the device driver onto your boot disk. Next make an entry into the CONFIG.SYS file for the new hardware with the DEVICE command. Lastly reboot your computer as the only time OS/2 reads the config.sys file is at system startup. The form for the DEVICE command is

```
DEVICE=drivername
```

where *drivername* is the path/filename of the device driver.

COMMON DEVICE DRIVERS

The ANSI.SYS Driver This device driver affects only the DOS Mode operation. With this device driver loaded application programs can use the ANSI escape sequence for video and keyboard control. The counterpart to this device driver in Protected Mode is the OS/2 command ANSI, described in Module 4.

The ANSI.SYS device driver provides DOS Mode applications extended screen and keyboard control features. Documentation supplied with programs requiring the ANSI.SYS driver usually tells you to load the ANSI.SYS driver in your CONFIG.SYS file. Some programs do not operate properly without it or require the ANSI.SYS driver on non-IBM branded microcomputers. For example, programs compiled with Nantucket's Clipper Compiler require the ANSI.SYS driver to operate properly on some AT&T microcomputer models. See Module 4 for a description of the ANSI.SYS device driver functions.

The COM.SYS Driver The COM.SYS device driver supports asynchronous communications to other computers via COM1 or COM2 serial port. The form for the COM.SYS device driver is

```
DEVICE=COM.SYS /COMn:baud,parity,data,stop,recv,xmit ,P
```

where *n* is either 1 or 2, specifing COM1: or COM2:

data defines number of data bits: 5, 6, 7, or 8

stop defines stop bits: 1, 2, or 5 (for one-and-half)

recv defines receive buffer size in bytes

xmit defines the transmit buffer size in bytes

P defines the timeouts for RLS, DSR, and CTS to infinite

NOTE

- The MOUSEA02.SYS device driver must be installed before the COM.SYS device driver if you have a serial mouse.
- The COM.SYS device driver is named COM01.SYS for IBM's OS/2 for the IBM PC-AT, and named COM02.SYS for the PS/2.

The EGA.SYS Driver This device driver supports a mouse device on EGA systems. To install the EGA.SYS driver, enter the following line in the CONFIG.SYS file:

```
DEVICE=EGA.SYS
```

The EXTDSKDD.SYS Driver This driver is used to establish floppy disk drive parameters. The form of the command is

```
DEVICE=EXTDSKDD.SYS /D:n [/T:n] [/S:n] [/H:n] [/C] [/N] [/F:n]
```

where: /D:*n* specifies a drive designator between 0 and 255.

The numbers 0, 1, and 2 are the first, second, and third physical diskette drives. The numbers 128 and 129 are the first and second physical fixed (or hard) disks.

The following EXTDSKDD.SYS options are discretionary:

/T:n Tracks per side, from 1 to 999; default = 80
/S:n Sectors per track, from 1 to 99; default = 9
/H:n Heads per drive, from 1 to 99; default = 2
/C Requires changeline support
/N Specifies a non-removable device, such as a fixed disk
/F:n Designates drive type and form factor; default = 2
Values for n are:
0 = 160, 180, 320, and 360KB
1 = 1.2MB
2 = 720KB
7 = 1.44MB

To setup a 720KB external disk drive on a PC-XT having drives A and C, use

```
DEVICE=EXTDSKDD.SYS /D:2/F:2
```

Note that the /F:2 is the default value and not required.

To copy files from one 1.2MB diskette to another in a PC AT equipped with one hard drive, one 1.2MB drive, and one 360KB drive, use the following EXTDSKDD.SYS command:

```
DEVICE=EXTDSKDD.SYS /D:0 /T:80 /S:15 /H:2 /F:1
```

The new logical drive (/D:0) is D, with 80 tracks per side (/T:80), 15 sectors per track (/s:15), two heads (/H:2), and a drive form factor of one (/F:1) for the 1.2MB drive. Note that /T:80 and /H:2 could have been omitted as these are default values.

The MOUSEAxx.SYS Driver The MOUSEAxx.SYS device drivers support mouse devices. The three mouse drivers supplied are MOUSEA02.SYS for Microsoft serial mouse, MOUSEA03.SYS for Microsoft parallel bus mouse, and MOUSEA04.SYS for Microsoft parallel InPort mouse. The form for this driver is

```
DEVICE=MOUSEAxx.SYS ,SERIAL=device ,MODE=m ,QSIZE=q
```

where xx is 02,03, or 04

device is COM1: or COM2:; use on serial mouse only.

m is R for Real Mode, P for Protected Mode, and B for both.

q is the queue size in bytes for each protected-mode screen group, for values 1 to 100, with a default of 10.

The POINTDD.SYS Driver This driver works in conjuction with the MOUSEAxx.SYS device driver. The POINTDD.SYS driver displays the pointer image on the screen for the mouse driver. The form for this driver is

```
DEVICE=POINTDD.SYS
```

The VDISK.SYS Driver The VDISK.SYS file lets you establish a *virtual disk*. This is a memory disk. The line in the CONFIG.SYS file that establishes your virtual disk is

```
DEVICE=VDISK.SYS nnn sss ddd
```

where nnn is the virtual disk size (64K default)

sss is the sector size (128, 256, or 512) in bytes (128 default)

ddd is the number of directory entries (2 to 512), (64 default)

The line

```
DEVICE=VDISK.SYS 64 128 64
```

establishes a 64KB virtual disk with 128-byte sectors and 64 possible directory entries.

```
DEVICE=VDISK.SYS 256 512 128
```

establishes a 256KB virtual disk with 512-byte sectors and 128 possible directory entries.

You can have multiple virtual disks by placing multiple VDISK command lines in your CONFIG.SYS file. The first virtual disk drive letter assumes the next letter following the highest one in use. For example, a system with physical drives A: and B: uses C: as the first virtual drive, D: as the second, and so on.

Turn to Module 4 to continue the learning sequence.

Module 23
DIRECTORY COMMANDS (DIR, MKDIR, RMDIR, CHDIR)

DESCRIPTION

A directory is a list of filenames that is automatically displayed on the screen when you type DIR and press Return from the system prompt. The DIR command is an internal OS/2 command. Multiple disk directories allow directory subdivisions. This feature lets you group common files into separate directories. This is similar to subdividing information into file cabinet drawers and file folders. This is particularly convenient when you use a fixed disk containing hundreds of files. Instead of listing all files in one directory, you can list files in smaller, more manageable subdirectories. The following DIR commands are explained later in this section:

Command	*Purpose*
MKDIR or MD	Make a new directory
CHDIR or CD	Change to another directory
RMDIR or RD	Remove (or delete) a directory from the disk

Each subdirectory is assigned a unique *pathname*. Therefore, you might create a word processing pathname, a database manager pathname, a spreadsheet pathname, and so on. More about pathnames later in this section.

FORMS OF THE DIRECTORY COMMAND There are many forms of the DIR command. Each form is described in the following list:

DIR	Lists a directory of the disk located in the active (or logged) disk drive. (Disk A: if the [A:\] prompt is displayed, B: if the [B:\] prompt is displayed, and so on.)
DIR D:	Lists a directory of the specified disk D:.
DIR /P or DIR D:/P	Pauses the directory listing when the screen is full. Press any key to see the next screen load of filenames. Typing DIR ¦MORE achieves a similar result.
DIR /W or DIR D:/W	Displays a wide directory. This listing, however, omits file size, date, and time information.
DIR *filename.ext*	Displays the specified filename; used to verify the presence of a file on the logged or specified disk.
DIR *filename.** or DIR *filename.???*	Displays a directory of all files having the same filename with different extensions.

DIR *.ext or DIR ????????.ext	Displays a directory of all filenames having the specified extension.
DIR *pathname* or DIR *D:pathname*	Displays a directory of all filenames within the specified subdirectory (pathname).
DIR *pathname**filename*	Displays a directory of the specified filename within the specified pathname.
DIR *pathname**pathname*	Displays a directory of the second-tier subdirectory. (Subdirectories can have subordinate directories of their own. This is called *branching*.)
DIR .. or DIR \\	Displays a parent directory from a subdirectory.

PAUSING AND RESTARTING A DIRECTORY In addition to the /P parameter with the DIR command, there are two other ways to pause the directory display. First, you can press Ctrl-S, which stops the directory display in its tracks. Press any key to resume the display. You can pause the display with the MORE filter. This is done by typing DIR ¦MORE. Pausing the display is often necessary when the directory listing exceeds the number of lines on your screen.

SORTING YOUR DIRECTORY ALPHABETICALLY Another handy tool on OS/2 is the SORT filter. Using SORT with the directory command arranges the directory listing in alphabetical order, making it easier to locate specific filenames. The command for sorting your directory is

```
DIR ¦ SORT
```

If you wish to sort the directory into a file, use DIR ¦SORT >*filename*. You direct the sorted directory to your printer with DIR ¦SORT >PRN (or LPT1, as appropriate).

SUBDIRECTORIES Imagine your directory structure in the shape of an inverted tree. There is a top directory (the root) and subdirectories (the branches). This relationship is often referred to as parent and children directories. The following diagram shows a typical directory structure:

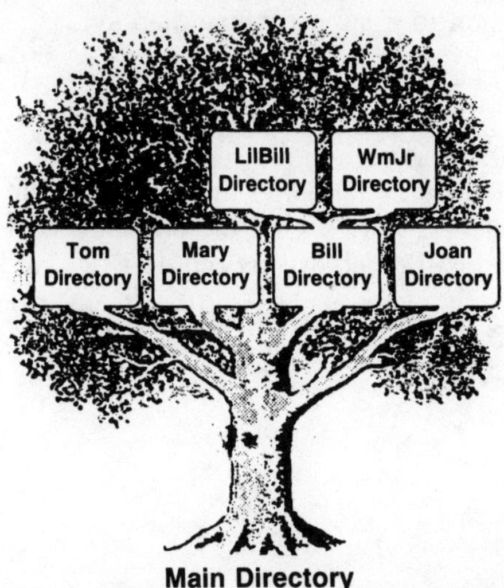

Notice that the Bill directory has two subdirectories. Therefore, Bill is a parent to LilBill and WmJr. Both LilBill and WmJr can have subdirectories, or children, if desired. Once directories are created with the MKDIR (or MD) command, you can move in and out of the directories with the CHDIR (or CD) command. You can remove directories with the RMDIR (or RD) command. These three commands are described in the following paragraphs.

The MKDIR Command The MKDIR (or MD) command is used to make (or create) a new subdirectory that is subordinate to the currently logged directory. To make a subdirectory having the pathname WP (for word processing), log your root directory, type MKDIR WP, and press Return. You may prefer the short form of this command, which is MD.

If you list a directory of the disk containing your new WP subdirectory, the subdirectory listing is displayed:

```
WP     <DIR>     6-07-88    11:25p
```

The CHDIR Command The CHDIR (or CD) command is used to change from one directory to another. If you are in the main directory and wish to move down to the BILL directory, type CD BILL and press Return.

To move to WMJR (one level down), use CD WMJR or CD \BILL \WMJR. To move back up to the parent (one directory level up), type CD .. and press Return. To move to the root directory from any logged subdirectory, use CD \. You can move directly to any directory (or filepath) from another by including the complete pathname in your CD command. For example, the command CD \BILL \WMJR takes you directly to the \BILL \WMJR filepath from any logged location.

The RMDIR Command The RMDIR (or RD) command is used to remove a subdirectory. First you must delete all files within a subdirectory before it can be deleted. If necessary, you can copy the files you want to keep to another directory with the COPY command, and then delete them from the subdirectory to be deleted. To remove an empty subdirectory having the pathname WP, go to the directory level immediately above the one to be removed and type RD WP.

The following two lines are common to a subdirectory display.

```
.              <DIR>      6-08-88    5:10p
..             <DIR>      6-08-88    5:10p
         2 File(s)     28560 bytes free
```

The single dot represents the directory being listed, while the double dot indicates the parent directory. With some versions of OS/2, you can list the parent directory by typing DIR .. and pressing Return. You can list the local directory by typing DIR . and pressing Return.

Regardless of the currently logged directory, you can view the files in another subdirectory by using a command like DIR \BILL \WMJR.

APPLICATIONS

The directory command is essential in knowing what files exist on a specified disk. In addition to listing filenames, the command tells you how many files are present and how much disk space remains. The ability to create subdirectories lets you organize your files into logical groups. The subdirectory capability is especially helpful for large fixed disks capable of containing hundreds of files.

TYPICAL OPERATION

In this activity you use the DIR command to view a disk directory in the conventional and wide form. Begin at the OS/2, [C:\].

1. Place a floppy disk with some files on it in drive A:.
2. Type **A:** and press **Return** to log to drive A:. Notice the prompt on drive A:, [A:\].
3. Type **DIR** and press **Return**; notice a similiar display:

```
[A:\]DIR

Volume in drive A has no label
Directory of A:\

COMMAND   COM   17792   3-17-87   12:00p
ANSI      SYS    1664   3-17-87   12:00p
FORMAT    COM    6912   3-17-87   12:00p
   :       :       :       :        :
MORE      COM     384   3-17-87   12:00p
BASIC     COM   16256   3-17-87   12:00p
BASICA    COM   26112   3-17-87   12:00p
       23 File(s)    28672 bytes free
```

4. Type **DIR /W** and press **Return**; notice the display:

```
[A:\]DIR /W

 The volume in drive A has no label
 Directory of A:\

COMMAND  COM   ANSI      SYS   FORMAT    COM   CHKDSK   COM   SYS       COM
DISKCOPY COM   DISKCOMP  COM   COMP      COM   EDLIN    COM   MODE      COM
FDISK    COM   BACKUP    COM   RESTORE   COM   PRINT    COM   RECOVER   COM
ASSIGN   COM   TREE      COM   GRAPHICS  COM   SORT     EXE   FIND      EXE
MORE     COM   BASIC     COM   BASICA    COM
       23 File(s)   28672 bytes free
```

5. Type **MKDIR FORFUN** and press **Return.**
6. Type **DIR** and notice that the FORFUN subdirectory is displayed:

```
[A:\]DIR

Volume in drive A has no label
Directory of A:\

COMMAND  COM    17792   3-17-87  12:00p
ANSI     SYS     1664   3-17-87  12:00p
FORMAT   COM     6912   3-17-87  12:00p
   :       :       :       :        :
BASIC    COM    16256   3-17-87  12:00p
BASICA   COM    26112   3-17-87  12:00p
FORFUN       <DIR>      6-08-88   6:12p
       23 File(s)    28672 bytes free
```

7. Type **CD FORFUN** and press **Return** to change directories; notice the display:

```
[A:\FOREFUN]
```

8. Type **DIR** and press **Return**; notice the display:

```
[A:\FOREFUN]DIR

 Volume in drive A has no label
 Directory of  A:\FORFUN

.          <DIR>      6-08-88    6:12p
..         <DIR>      6-08-88    6:12p
     2 File(s)        28560 bytes free
```

9. Type **CD . .** and press **Return**; you are now back in the original directory.

10. List a directory of the FORFUN subdirectory by typing **DIR FORFUN** and pressing **Return**. Notice the display:

```
[A:\FOREFUN]DIR

 Volume in drive A has no label
 Directory of   A:\FORFUN

.            <DIR>     6-08-88    6:12p
..           <DIR>     6-08-88    6:12p
     2 File(s)    28560 bytes free
```

11. Type **RD FORFUN** and press **Return**; you have just removed the FORFUN directory from your disk.
12. Verify that the FORFUN subdirectory is gone by listing the directory one last time. Type **DIR** and press **Return**; notice the display:

```
[A:\]DIR

Volume in drive A has no label
Directory of A:\

COMMAND   COM     17792    3-17-87   12:00p
ANSI      SYS      1664    3-17-87   12:00p
FORMAT    COM      6912    3-17-87   12:00p
  :        :        :         :        :
MORE      COM       384    3-17-87   12:00p
BASIC     COM     16256    3-17-87   12:00p
BASICA    COM     26112    3-17-87   12:00p
       23 File(s)     28672 bytes free
```

13. Type **C:** and press **Return** to return to drive C:.
14. Turn to Module 60 to continue the learning sequence.

Module 24
DISKCOMP

DESCRIPTION

The DISKCOMP command is an external OS/2 command that compares the contents of two floppy disks to ensure that they are identical.

The general form of the DISKCOMP command is

```
DISKCOMP A: B:
```

where the disk in drive A: is read first and then compared to the disk in drive B. You can control which disk is read first by using the appropriate disk drive designator A:, B:, C:, etc.

After two disks are compared, the prompt "Compare another diskette (Y/N)?" is displayed. Typing Y (for "yes") lets you compare another disk; typing N (for "no") redisplays the OS/2 prompt.

Diskettes of compatable size, type, and density must be compared:

- 5¼ to 5¼ inch diskette
- 3.5 to 3.5 inch diskette
- single sided to single sided
- double sided to double sided
- low density to low density
- high density to high density

If you compare identical disks, the display resembles the following screen illustration:

```
[C:\]DISKCOMP A: B:

Insert source diskette in drive A:

Insert target diskette in drive B:

Press Enter to continue.


Comparing 40 tracks
9 sectors per track, 2 side(s).

Compare has ended.

Compare another diskette (Y/N)? _
```

If you have used the COPY *.* command instead of DISKCOPY, the disks will not compare "ok." This is because the location of each file changes when files are copied individually.

If you compare two dissimilar disks, DISKCOMP displays a screen with a message similar to this:

```
[C:\]DISKCOMP A: B:

Insert source diskette in drive A:

Insert target diskette in drive B:

Press Enter to continue.


Comparing 40 tracks
9 sectors per track, 2 side(s).

Comparison error(s) on side 0 track 0

Comparison error(s) on side 1 track 0

Comparison error(s) on side 0 track 1
      :

Compare has ended.

Compare another diskette (Y/N)? _
```

APPLICATIONS

The most common use of DISKCOMP is to compare one or more copies of a master disk to the master to verify exact replication. This is the quickest way to ensure a good quality copy. If you suspect copy problems, you may wish to use DISKCOMP each time you make a disk copy just to be on the safe side.

TYPICAL OPERATION

In this activity you use the DISKCOPY command to make a copy of OS/2, and then the DISKCOMP command to verify that the copy is accurate. Begin at the OS/2 prompt, [C:\].

1. Insert an OS/2 diskette in drive A. Then type **DISKCOPY A: A:** and press **Return**. Exchange diskettes as prompted.
2. Type **DISKCOMP A: A:** and press **Return**. Exchange diskettes as prompted. Notice the following display:

```
[C:\]DISKCOMP A: A:

Insert source diskette in drive A:

Press Enter to continue.
```

3. Press **Return**; and notice the following display:

```
Comparing 40 tracks
9 sectors per track, 2 side(s).

Insert target diskette in drive B:

Press Enter to continue.
```

4. Press **Return**; and, if your copy is good, notice the following display:

```
Compare has ended.

Compare another diskette (Y/N)? _
```

5. Type **N** and press **Return** to return to the system prompt.
6. Turn to Module 17 to continue the learning sequence.

Module 25
DISKCOPY

DESCRIPTION

The DISKCOPY command is an external command that is available with all versions of OS/2. It makes a verbatim copy of one removable disk (the *source* disk) on another (the *target* disk). Never specify a fixed disk with the DISKCOPY command. If the target disk is unformatted, DISKCOPY formats it for you during the copy operation.

The form of the DISKCOPY command is

```
DISKCOPY A: B:
```

where A: is the disk drive that contains the source disk (the disk being copied) and B: is the disk drive containing the target disk (the disk to which the copy is transferred).

The DISKCOPY command makes an exact replica of the source disk. If the target diskette is not formatted, DISKCOPY formats the target diskette with the same number of tracks and sectors per track as the source diskette.

When copying is complete, the prompt "Copy another diskette (Y/N)?" is displayed. Typing N discontinues the DISKCOPY process and returns you to the system prompt. Typing Y lets you repeat the DISKCOPY command, allowing you to make multiple copies of the source disk.

If you copy two similar disks, the display resembles the following screen illustration:

```
[A:\]DISKCOPY A: B:

Insert source diskette in drive A:

Insert target diskette in drive B:

Press Enter to continue.


Copying 40 tracks,
9 sectors per track, 2 side(s).


Copy has ended.
Copy another diskette (Y/N)? _
```

NOTE

- DISKCOPY destroys the contents of the target diskette.
- Diskette types must be compatable. (1.2MB cannot fit on a 360KB floppy.)
    - 5¼ to 5¼ inch diskette
    - 3.5 to 3.5 inch diskette
    - single sided to single sided
    - double sided to double sided
    - low density to low density
    - high density to high density
- DISKCOPY cannot work on drives used in the SUBST or JOIN commands under DOS Mode.
- The source and target diskettes cannot be virtual disks.

If you try to copy incompatible disk types, DISKCOPY displays the following message:

```
Drive types (double-sided, high capacity)
or diskette types not compatible.
```

If you only have one disk drive, DISKCOPY prompts you to insert the source and target disks at the appropriate times and waits for you to press any key before continuing.

If DISKCOPY finds errors on either diskette, it displays the drive, track, and side of the error, and continues the copy.

You should know that as files are created and modified, they begin to occupy available disk space in a random fashion. For example, when a file is first created and saved on a new disk, it occupies contiguous (or end-to-end) sectors. As other files are created and edited, they begin to occupy the disk's geography in a random, helter-skelter fashion.

After several reading, editing, and writing sessions, you may detect some degradation in file access time. If it reaches an annoying level, you may wish to copy the files to a new disk. You should use the COPY and XCOPY commands to do this, rather than the DISKCOPY command. Why? Because these commands collect files one at a time and writes them in contiguous sectors to the target disk. DISKCOPY, on the other hand, simply copies everything in its original configuration, without regard to poor file organization.

Here is the recommended way to recollect your scattered files into contiguous disk geography. First, format your target disk and place it in a target drive, such as B:. Place your source disk in the source drive, such as A:, and type COPY *.* B: and press Return.

APPLICATIONS

The DISKCOPY command is most often used to make working copies of new program disks or backup copies of disks containing important data files, programs, or both. The format feature of DISKCOPY saves valuable time. If you wish to make several copies of a disk, using DISKCOPY eliminates the need to use a two-step format/copy procedure.

TYPICAL OPERATION

In this activity you use the DISKCOPY command to make a copy of an OS/2 disk. Begin at the OS/2 prompt, [C:\].

1. Place an OS/2 disk in drive A: and close the load lever.
2. If you have a second drive, place a new or used disk in drive B: and close the load lever.

CAUTION

In the following step, the disk in drive B: is formatted. This destroys any files that may reside on the disk in drive B:. If the disk to be formatted contains files, be sure that they are expendable. The DISKCOPY command erases these files.

3. Type **DISKCOPY A: B:** and press **Return**.

```
[C:\]DISKCOPY A: B:

Insert source diskette in drive A:

Insert target diskette in drive B:

Press Enter to continue.
```

4. Insert the diskettes and press **Return**. Notice the display:

```
Copying 40 tracks,
9 sectors per track, 2 side(s).
```

5. Notice that the red disk drive lights indicate read-write activity. Also, if you are formatting a high-capacity diskette, it has 80 tracks and 15 sectors per track.
6. If you only have one drive, DISKCOPY prompts you to insert the source and target disks at the appropriate times and waits for you to press any key before continuing. Change the diskettes at the appropriate times and press any key to continue.
7. Type **N** in response to the "Copy another diskette (Y/N)?" prompt. Notice that the system prompt is redisplayed.

```
Copy has ended.
Copy another diskette (Y/N)? _

[C:\]_
```

8. Turn to Module 28 to continue the learning sequence.

Module 26

DPATH

DESCRIPTION

The DPATH command is an internal OS/2 command. It is used to provide access to data files located in other directory paths or other disks. The DPATH command is usually entered as a line in STARTUP.CMD, OS2INIT.CMD or another *batch* file, which most often contains one or more OS/2 commands. The STARTUP.CMD file is automatically executed upon system turn on to establish desired parameters. The OS2INIT.CMD batch file, when present, is executed each time a session is begun. Other batch files are executed upon command. When used, each command in the batch file executes as it is encountered in the file. The creation and use of batch files is described in Module 8.

To illustrate the DPATH command, assume you have a file named GATOR.DAT that is located in a subdirectory. You are not sure if it is on disk C or disk A, so you want to search both disks and TYPE the file when found. To complicate matters, you are not sure if the program is in the SWAMP subdirectory or the MUD subdirectory.

Here is where the DPATH command comes to your rescue. To set up a search for GATOR.DAT, you can specify the disk and directories using the DPATH command. While logged on disk C, assuming that you have a fixed disk system, type

```
DPATH \SWAMP;\MUD;B:\SWAMP;B:\MUD
```

When you enter TYPE GATOR.DAT, OS/2 first searches the C:\SWAMP subdirectory, then the C:\MUD subdirectory. Next, it searches the B:\SWAMP subdirectory. Finally, it searches the B:\MUD subdirectory where GATOR.DAT is found and typed on your monitor.

You also can use the DPATH command to display the data path setup. To do this, type DPATH and press Return. A display similar to the following is displayed:

```
[C:\OS2]DPATH

DPATH=\SWAMP;\MUD;B:\SWAMP;B:\MUD
```

To cancel the data path settings, type DPATH; and press Return. The semicolon is the critical agent in this DPATH command. Now when you check your paths with the DPATH command, the message "DPATH = " is displayed.

APPLICATIONS

As you may suspect, a primary use of the DPATH command is to provide access to data files located in multiple subdirectories. This provides you with the flexiblity to organize your data files in meaningful ways without having to recompile your application programs.

TYPICAL OPERATION

In this activity you use the DPATH command to establish a directory search and then use it to display the established routing. Finally, the data paths are restored. Begin at the OS/2 prompt, [C:\].

1. Type **DPATH** and press **Return**. Write down the current dpath setting. (If there is one).
2. Type **DPATH \SWAMP;\SWAMP\MUD** and press **Return**.
3. Type **DPATH**, press **Return**, and notice the following display:

```
[C:\]DPATH

DPATH=\SWAMP;\SWAMP\MUD
```

4. Cancel the path by typing **DPATH;** and pressing **Return**.
5. Type **DPATH** and check for the following display:

```
[C:\]DPATH
DPATH=
```

6. Restore the dpath value saved from Step 1 by performing Step 2 with the saved dpath value.
7. Turn to Module 5 to continue the learning sequence.

Module 27

EDLIN

DESCRIPTION

EDLIN is a *line editor* program that is available on OS/2 only in Dos Mode. A line editor is used to create and save text and program files. It also lets you modify file contents through insertion and deletion commands.

A line editor uses line numbers to display and edit text. This is different from what are called *full-screen* editors. Full-screen editors, which describes most word processing programs, let you move the cursor anywhere on a displayed screen of text. Although line editing may sound crude in comparison to full-screen editing, you will find EDLIN quite fast for creating files and performing minor touch-up work. Just a few keystrokes lets you create and modify text files.

When an existing text file is edited and saved, EDLIN automatically converts the original file to a backup file (with a .BAK extension) for safekeeping. Then, when you view your directory, you see that the edited file exists with its original filename and extension, as well as with the filename and a .BAK extension.

Now that you know what EDLIN does, you can learn how to use EDLIN by experimenting with the commands described in the following pages of this module. Although EDLIN commands may seem awkward at first, you should begin to appreciate the way EDLIN behaves with just a few minutes of practice.

In this module, the term DOS refers to the OS/2 compatiblility box or Real Mode (DOS Mode), that runs PC/MS-DOS 3.x and earlier programs. This module is modernized with my Real Mode prompt of [REAL A:\], which I use so that I am always reminded that I am in the Real Mode (DOS Mode).

To create a new text file (or "document") with EDLIN, just type EDLIN *filename* and press Return. A screen similar to the following is displayed:

```
[REAL A:\]EDLIN MYTEXT
New file
*
```

The asterisk (*) is EDLIN's prompt, similar to DOS' [REAL A:\] prompt. You can quit EDLIN by typing Q (for "quit") and pressing Return; the DOS prompt is redisplayed.

EDLIN COMMANDS

Because the EDLIN prompt does not tell you any more than the DOS prompt, it is necessary to know EDLIN commands before using it. A list of EDLIN commands follows. With use, they should become just as familiar as DOS commands. Either upper or lower case is acceptable.

NOTE

All EDLIN commands are followed by pressing the Return key. EDLIN's *pointer* is a conceptual place within a document. For example, if you want to edit text in line 5, you can "move the pointer" to line 5 by typing 5 and pressing Return. If you want to check the position of the pointer, you can type . (a period) and press Return.

Table 27-1 EDLIN Commands and Examples

Command	*Meaning*

NOTE

The asterisk (*) is shown in the examples within this table to designate EDLIN's prompt; it is not typed as part of the commands.

Return — Executes the typed EDLIN command, or moves the pointer to the next line in the document. If you edit a line and change your mind, press Ctrl-C to cancel the changes and return to the EDLIN prompt. Table 20-2 is a list of EDLIN editing keys.

— Moves the pointer one line below the last line of the document.

Example:

```
*#i          Inserts a new line at the bottom of the file.
```

. (period) — Displays the current line (the last line edited).

Example:

```
*.
     1: This is text for line number 1.
     1: _
```

number 1 to 65529 — Typing a line number moves the pointer to that line. The cursor is at the beginning of the line ready for you to make changes. The change process is described later.

Examples:

```
*3
     3: This is the text on line number 3.
     3: _

*+2       Moves pointer two lines down.
*-10      Moves pointer 10 lines up.
```

A — Append (or add) a specified number of lines to the bottom of the current file (which is loaded in your computer's memory). This command is used with the W (write) command. When memory becomes full, you can write the first portion of your file to disk with the Write command. Then use Append to add more lines from disk to the end of that part of the file in memory. The message "End of input file" is displayed if the last line of the input file is read into memory.

Table 27-1 EDLIN Commands and Examples (Continued)

Command	Meaning
	Example:
	`•100A` Adds 100 lines to the end of your file.
C	Copies specified lines to another location in the file, beginning at the designated line. An optional count can be used to make multiple copies. Following lines are automatically renumbered. If you want 3 copies, the count is 3. Copied lines cannot overlap, i.e., you cannot copy lines 4 through 6 to lines 4, 5, or 6.
	Format: (beginning line),(ending line),(target line),(no. of copies)c
	Examples:
	`•3,10,15C` Copy lines 3 through 10 to line 15.
	`•3,5,9,2C` Copy lines 2 through 5 to line 9 twice (2 copies).
D	Deletes specified lines from the file.
	Format: (beginning line),(ending line)d
	Examples:
	`•4,6D` Deletes lines 4 through 6 from the file.
	`•,10D` Deletes lines beginning with the current line number through line 10.
	`•6D or 6,D` Deletes line 6 from the file.
	`•D` Deletes the current line from the file.
E	End editing and save the file to disk.
	Example:
	`•E` Ends editing session and saves the file to disk. If the file already existed, the previous version is converted to a backup file with the .BAK extension.
I	Inserts a line in the document beginning at the current pointer location. Pressing Return inserts another new line. Following lines are automatically renumbered. Pressing Ctrl-C or Ctrl-Break ends the insert operation and redisplays the EDLIN prompt.
	Examples:
	`•6I` Inserts a line in front of line 6.
	`•#I` Inserts a line at the bottom of the file.
	`•I` Inserts a line in front of the current line.
L	Lists lines on the screen; the current line is marked by * following the displayed line number. You can list ranges of lines by specifying one or more line numbers.
	Format: (beginning line),(ending line)l

Table 27-1 EDLIN Commands and Examples (Continued)

Command	Meaning
	Examples:
	`•3,12L` Lists lines 3 through 12.
	`•,12L` Lists 11 lines beginning with line 12.
	`•8,L or •8L` Lists 23 lines beginning with line 8.
	`•L` Lists 23 lines of text including 11 lines before the current line, the current line, and 11 lines following the current line.
M	Moves specified lines from one location in the file to another.
	Format: (beginning line),(ending line),(target line)m
	Examples:
	`•3,5,9M` Moves lines 3 through 5 to line 9; lines are automatically renumbered.
	`•,+5,25M` Moves the current line plus five more lines to line 25.
	`•,-3,9M` Moves the three lines preceding the current line and the current line to line 9.
	`•5M` Moves the current line ahead of line 5.
P	Lists specified lines of text (or a "page") on the screen. You can use this command to move through a document. Unlike the List command, the Page command changes the current line number.
	Format: (beginning line),(ending line)p
	Examples:
	`•5,25P` Displays lines 5 through 25.
	`•P` Displays 23 lines; the last line displayed becomes the current line.
Q	Quit EDLIN without saving the file.
	Example:
	`•Q` EDLIN asks, "Abort edit (Y/N)?" Typing **Y** abandons the file and displays the DOS prompt.
R	Replaces the first text string (or *find string*) with the second (or *replace string*) within a designated range of lines.
	NOTE You can use Ctrl-Z in place of F6 in the Replace command line. The question mark is optional and is used when you want EDLIN to give you a Yes or No replacement option each time the search string is found. Omitting the Replace string deletes the search string. Upper- and lower-case characters must be matched.

Table 27-1 EDLIN Commands and Examples (Continued)

Command	*Meaning*
	Format: (beginning line),(ending line)?r(find string)(F6)(replace string)
	Examples:
	•1,25?RSmith**F6**Jones — Replaces Smith with Jones within lines 1 through 25. Displays O.K.? prompt before each replacement.
	•1,25RDobbs**Ctrl-Z**Evans — Replaces every occurrence of Dobbs with Evans within lines 1 through 25.
	•RDobbs**F6**Jones — Replaces every Dobbs with Jones throughout the entire file.
	•1,25Rvery**F6** — Deletes every occurrence of the word "very." This is the same as replacing it with nothing.
S	Searches for a specified text string within a designated range of lines.
	Format: (beginning line),(ending line)?s(search string)
	Examples:
	•10,30?STotal — Finds "Total." The ? causes the text line containing the search string to be displayed. The search is made within lines 10 through 30.
	•10,30S — Finds the last search string used; searches within lines 10 though 30.
	•STotal — Finds "Total" beginning with the line following the current line and ending with the last line in the file.
	•S — Finds the last search string used following the current line.
T	Reads (or transfers) a named file into the current file ahead of a designated line.
	Format: line T D:*filename.ext*
	Examples:
	•6T B:LOVE.LTR — Reads (transfers) the file named LOVE.LTR on the disk in drive B: to the current file beginning at line 6.
	•T MYFILE — Reads (transfers) MYFILE from the default disk beginning at the current line.
W	Writes a specified number of lines from the current file to disk, beginning with line number 1. Used when memory becomes full. After writing lines to disk, you can resume editing. You may wish to append additional lines to the bottom of the file using the Append command.
	Format: number of lines w
	Example:
	•500W — Writes 500 lines to disk, beginning with the first line in memory.

Table 27-2 EDLIN Editing Keys

Command	Use
Ctrl-C	Returns to the EDLIN prompt without changing the current line.
F1	Displays the next character on the current line each time F1 is pressed.
F3	Displays all text on the current line.
F5<cr>	Cancels changes to the current line without changing the original text.
F6	Used with the replace command to identify the replace string.
Ins	Inserts a blank space to the right of the cursor.
Del	Deletes the character at the cursor.

EDLIN PRACTICE SESSION The only way to see whether you like EDLIN is to try it out. The Typical Operation Section of this module lets you experiment with some of EDLIN's commands.

APPLICATIONS

Because EDLIN occupies a minimum amount of disk space, is fast, and is easy to use, many people use EDLIN to write and edit program source files and documents. The disk space issue is particularly important if you are creating large files on a microcomputer with floppy disks. Many word processors occupy nearly all the available space on early technology removable disks. EDLIN uses less than 5,000 bytes (or characters) of disk space, making it one of the smallest editors available.

TYPICAL OPERATION

In this activity you use the EDLIN program to create and edit a practice file. Begin at the DOS prompt, [REAL C:\].

1. Type **EDLIN MYFILE** and press **Return**. Notice the following display:

```
[REAL C:\]EDLIN MYFILE
EDLIN has created a new file.
*
```

2. Type **i** (for insert) and press **Return** to begin entering text. Notice that the cursor moves to line 1.

```
[REAL C:\]EDLIN MYFILE
EDLIN has created a new file.
*i
      1:*
```

The asterisk following 1 designates that line 1 is the current line.

3. Type the following file, pressing **Return** at the end of each line until you reach line 6.

```
1: This is a new document named myfile.
2: Edlin is being used to create it.
3: Notice how a new line number is displayed each time I press
4: the RETURN key.
5: Now that I've created this document, I can save it.
6: _
```

4. Press **Ctrl-C** to redisplay the EDLIN prompt.
5. Type **e** and press **Return** to exit EDLIN and save the file.
6. Start EDLIN again by typing **EDLIN MYFILE** and pressing **Return**. Notice the following screen:

```
[REAL C:\]EDLIN MYFILE
The entire input file has been read.
*
```

7. Type **L** and press **Return** to list the file.

```
[REAL C:\]EDLIN MYFILE
The entire input file has been read.
*L
     1:*This is a new document named myfile.
     2: Edlin is being used to create it.
     3: Notice how a new line number is displayed each time I press
     4: the RETURN key.
     5: Now that I've created this document, I can save it.
*
```

8. Change the word "RETURN" on line 4 to "Enter" as follows:
   a. Type **4** and press **Return**; notice the following display:

```
*4
     4:*the RETURN key.
     4:*_
```

9. Press **F1** four times to move the cursor to the space following "the."
10. Type **Enter**.
11. Press the **Del** key once.
12. Press **F3** to display the rest of the line; then press **Return**. Your document should now resemble the following:

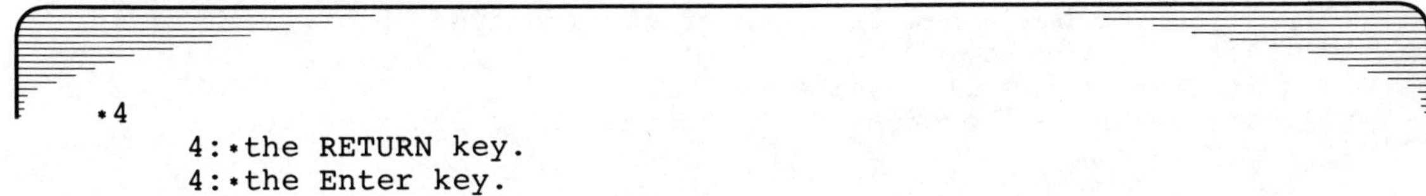

```
*4
      4:*the RETURN key.
      4:*the Enter key.
*
```

13. Type **L** and press **Return** to list the document; notice the display. The asterisk indicates that line 4 is the active line.

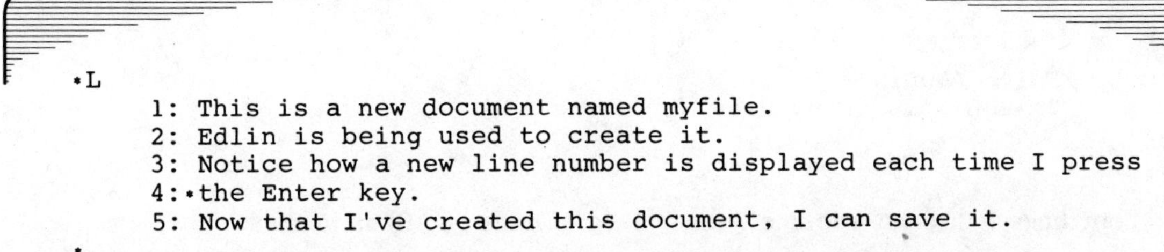

```
*L
      1: This is a new document named myfile.
      2: Edlin is being used to create it.
      3: Notice how a new line number is displayed each time I press
      4:*the Enter key.
      5: Now that I've created this document, I can save it.
*
```

14. Insert a line ahead of line 5 as follows:
    a. Type **5i** and press **Return**.
    b. Type **This is new line number 5.**.
    c. Press **Return** at the end of the line.
    d. Press **Ctrl-C** to return to the EDLIN prompt.
    e. Check to see if your screen resembles the following:

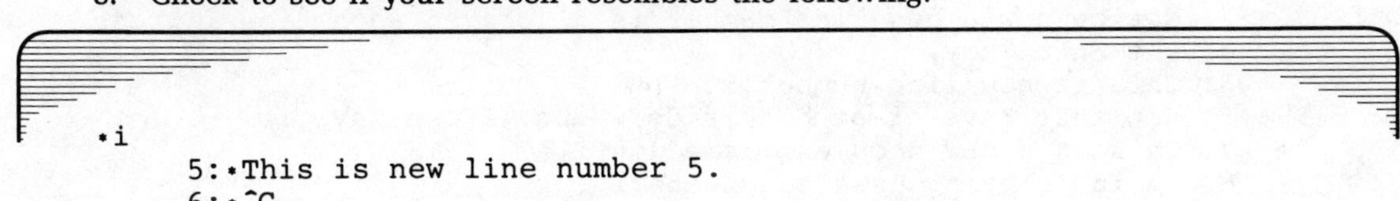

```
*i
      5:*This is new line number 5.
      6:*^C
*
```

15. Type **L** and press **Return** to list the file; notice that it resembles the following screen:

```
•L
        1: This is a new document named myfile.
        2: Edlin is being used to create it.
        3: Notice how a new line number is displayed each time I press
        4: the Enter key.
        5: This is new line number 5.
        6:•Now that I've created this document, I can save it.
•
```

16. Replace the word "Edlin" with "EDLIN" as follows:

    a. Type **2,5rEdlin**, press **Ctrl-Z** (or **F6**), type **EDLIN**, and press **Return**.
    b. Notice the display:

```
•2,5rEdlin^ZEDLIN
        2:•EDLIN is being used to create it.
•
```

17. Copy lines 1 through 4 to line 7 (lines 1 - 4 to lines 7 - 10) as follows:

    a. Type **1,4,7c** and press **Return**.
    b. Type **L** and press **Return** to list the file; notice the following screen:

```
•1,4,7c
•l
        1: This is a new document named myfile.
        2: Edlin is being used to create it.
        3: Notice how a new line number is displayed each time I press
        4: the Enter key.
        5: This is new line number 5.
        6: Now that I've created this document, I can save it.
        7:•This is a new document named myfile.
        8: Edlin is being used to create it.
        9: Notice how a new line number is displayed each time I press
       10: the Enter key.
•
```

18. Move lines 1 through 4 to line 6 as follows:
    a. Type **1,4,6m** and press **Return**.
    b. Type **L** and press **Return** to list the change. Notice the results of the move:

```
*1,4,6m
*l
        1: This is new line number 5.
        2:*This is a new document named myfile.
        3: Edlin is being used to create it.
        4: Notice how a new line number is displayed each time I press
        5: the Enter key.
        6: Now that I've created this document, I can save it.
        7: This is a new document named myfile.
        8: Edlin is being used to create it.
        9: Notice how a new line number is displayed each time I press
       10:  the Enter key.
*
```

19. Type **e** and press **Return** to end editing and save the file.
20. This concludes the practice EDLIN session. To conserve disk space, delete the files MYFILE and MYFILE.BAK by typing **DEL MYFILE.*** and pressing **Return**.
21. Press **Ctrl-Esc** to return to Session Manager. Select OS/2 Command Prompt in the SWITCH TO A RUNNING PROGRAM window to return to OS/2 Mode.
22. Turn to Module 44 to continue the learning sequence.

Module 28

ERASE (OR DELETE)

DESCRIPTION

The DELETE (or ERASE) command removes files from a diskette and reallocates the disk space that the file previously occupied. DELETE is an internal command. The shortest form of the command is DEL; therefore, DEL is used as the command form in this module. However, there are some OS/2 users who have adopted the alternatiave form, ERASE.

The general form of the command is

DEL *filename*

The form for DOS Mode is

    DEL*filename*

with NO space before the filename. Under OS/2 the space is optional.

Another form of the command for OS/2 Mode is

    DEL *filename filename filename*

where you can delete multiple files with one DEL command.

Regardless of the logged drive or filepath, you can delete a file from any disk by placing the disk directory pathname in the command, such as

```
DEL C:\DATA\TEMP.DTA
```

Be cautious when deleting a file. Once deleted, a file is gone forever, unless you have a file recovery utility. Even then, if additional disk operations occur, the recovery utility may be rendered useless.

You can delete multiple files by using the wild card in your DEL command line. For example, if you want to delete all .OBJ files on the disk in drive B, you can use DEL B:*.OBJ. This command deletes every filename that has the extension .OBJ. You can also delete every file on a disk with DEL *.*. However, OS/2 alerts you to the fact that you are on the brink of possible disaster by displaying "Are you sure (Y/N)?" Typing Y (for "Yes") followed by Return does the deed. Typing N cancels the deletion and redisplays the OS/2 prompt without deleting any files. For instance, the command

```
DEL C:\TEMP\*.*
```

deletes all files in the C:\TEMP subdirectory. The command

```
DEL C:\TEMP
```

also deletes all files in the C:\TEMP subdirectory.

APPLICATIONS

The DEL command is used normally to delete individual, unwanted files from a disk. Many programs automatically create backup files that occupy valuable disk space. The EDLIN program, MicroPro's WordStar word processing program, and Ashton-Tate's dBASE series are examples of such programs. The backup files have the extension .BAK. This makes it easy to delete your old backup files with the command DEL *.BAK.

TYPICAL OPERATION

In this activity you use the DEL command to erase an unneeded file. Begin at the OS/2 prompt, [C:\].

1. Create a temporary file using the COPY command as follows:

   a. Type **COPY CON: TESTFILE** and press **Return**.
   b. Type **This is a test file.** and press **Return**.
   c. Press **Ctrl-Z** and then press **Return** to write the file to disk.

2. Type **DIR TESTFILE** and notice the following display:

```
[C:\]DIR TESTFILE

 Volume in drive C has no label
 Directory of   C:\

TESTFILE            20   7-13-88    8:04a
         1 File(s)   5197824 bytes free
```

3. Type **DEL TESTFILE** and press **Return** to delete the file from your disk.
4. Verify that the file is gone by typing **DIR TESTFILE**; notice the following display:

```
[C:\]DIR TESTFILE

 Volume in drive C has no label
 Directory of   C:\

SYS0002: The system cannot find the file specified.
```

5. Turn to Module 50 to continue the learning sequence.

Module 29

EXE2BIN

DESCRIPTION

The EXE2BIN command converts compiled program files, usually having the extension .EXE, to binary command files, which use the the extension .COM. This is where the name EXE2BIN was derived. The utility is used to convert an executable .EXE file to a BINary file.

The form of the EXE2BIN command is

EXE2BIN *file1.exe file1.com*

If the .EXE extension is not used with the source filename, the extension .EXE is assumed. If the .COM extension is not used with the target filename, the extension .BIN is assigned to the target filename, where BIN stands for "binary." You may then rename the file with the REN command to change the .BIN extension to .COM. The Typical Operation section of the LINK command module uses EXE2BIN to convert a file.

The EXE2BIN command converts program files with the extension .EXE to a "memory image." Once converted, the program is smaller and loads faster. The resulting program must be smaller than 64KB.

NOTE

This command may not be supported by OS/2. You may have to use your PC/MS-DOS version to create your .COM programs in DOS Mode.

APPLICATIONS

If you are a programmer and have compiled and linked a program, you can convert that program to a "COM file" using EXE2BIN. Otherwise, you will not have an application for the EXE2BIN utility.

TYPICAL OPERATION

Because this is an advanced OS/2 command requiring you first to write a program source file and then compile and link it to an object file, the Typical Operation activity is not appropriate for the general audience of this book. However, if you are a programmer, you can use EXE2BIN to convert your compiled program files into COM files using the form of the EXE2BIN command shown in the Description section of this module. You can also review the LINK command module to see how EXE2BIN interacts with other commands.

Turn to Module 42 to continue the learning sequence.

Module 30

EXIT

DESCRIPTION

The EXIT command is an internal OS/2 command. The EXIT command allows you to terminate the execution of the CMD.EXE or COMMAND.COM program and return to the program that started the command processor, usually another command processor.

The form for the EXIT command is

```
EXIT
```

With the Session Manager in OS/2 you can execute several copies of the command processor (CMD.EXE) at one time. This is one way you can multitask with OS/2 because from each command processor executing you can run all OS/2 programs and commands. To terminate a copy of the command processor, type EXIT. When you do this, CMD.EXE terminates and returns its memory resources to OS/2.

Also, from either command processor (COMMAND.COM or CMD.EXE), you can execute the command processor. To terminate the executing version, type EXIT and press Return, and the command processor terminates and returns its memory resources to OS/2 or DOS.

If type EXIT on the first copy of COMMAND.COM, it ignores the EXIT command because one copy of the DOS command processor must be running at all times. However, you can EXIT from all copies of the OS/2 command processors because you can start another copy via the Session Manager.

APPLICATIONS

To do multitasking on OS/2 you can run multiple copies of the command processor (CMD.EXE). Each copy of CMD.EXE requires a certain amount of resources and overhead. During processing, you may want to free many of the resources you have allocated to run a program that runs considerably faster the more memory it can allocate. To do this, you will terminate all command processors, except one, to return to single tasking. To terminate a command processor, simply type EXIT at the command prompt.

TYPICAL OPERATION

In this activity you use the EXIT command to terminate a copy of the command processor. Start at the OS/2 prompt, [C:\].

1. Press **Ctrl-Esc** to return to the Session Manager.
2. Move to the START A PROGRAM section and position on OS/2 Command Prompt and press **Return**. Notice that the following message appears on the screen:

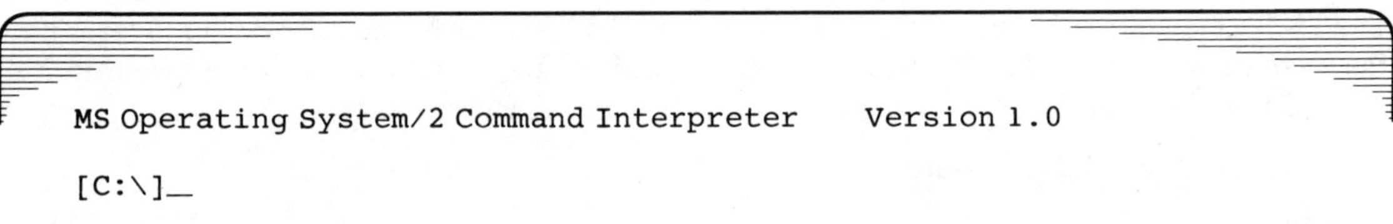

This new command processor is ready to execute a command.

3. Press **Ctrl-Esc** to return to the Session Manager. Notice that in the SWITCH TO A RUNNING PROGRAM window there are two copies of the CMD.EXE program (OS/2 Command Prompt). Move to the last copy of the OS/2 Command Prompt and press **Return**.
4. Type **EXIT** and press **Return** to terminate this copy. Notice that when the CMD.EXE program terminates, it returns to the Session Manager which started it. Now notice in the SWITCH TO A RUNNING PROGRAM window that there is only one copy of the OS/2 Command Prompt (CMD.EXE).
5. Select OS/2 Command Prompt in the SWITCH TO A RUNNING PROGRAM window to return to OS/2 Mode.
6. Turn to Module 20 to continue the learning sequence.

Module 31
FDISK

DESCRIPTION

The FDISK command is an external OS/2 command that prepares a fixed (or hard) disk for use. It is used to organize your fixed disk into *partitions*, which allocates disk space to separate usable areas.

The FDISK command is used after your fixed disk has received a low-level format. The low-level format process is described briefly in Module 34. You may have to perform a low-level format yourself if you purchase a new fixed disk and controller card directly from the manufacturer or a distributor. If you purchase your computer from a reputable dealer, the fixed disk should be formatted for you. Most dealers also install the OS/2 Operating System on the hard disk for their customers.

You may not have to run FDISK, but if you do, it is easy because it has menus to lead you through each procedure. To see if you need to run FDISK, turn the power on to your computer. If OS/2 starts, then you do not have to run FDISK.

FIXED DISK GEOGRAPHY AND PARTITIONING

Fixed disks are divided into what are called *cylinders*. If you have a 10-, 20-, or even 40-megabyte fixed disk (where a megabyte is a million characters), your disk probably contains 305 cylinders beginning with cylinder number 000 and ending with cylinder number 304. A typical cylinder has a 34,816-character capacity. The cylinder number varies with capacity and number of heads used by your fixed disk.

The maximum size of a fixed disk partition is 32 megabytes. Each partition has its own operating system. If DOS is the only operating system you wish to use, then you can assign the entire fixed disk to OS/2, up to 32 megabytes. However, if your disk is larger than 32 megabytes, you can use primary and extended OS/2 partitions to utilize the whole hard disk.

OS/2 and PC/MS-DOS can share the same hard disk since their hard disk partitioning and disk and file layouts are the same. If you want to install OS/2 on a computer that is currently using PC/MS-DOS, then read the instructions that come with OS/2, because it can be done.

PREPARING A NEW HARD DISK

The steps in setting up a hard disk are as follows:

1. Perform a low-level format on the disk. You most likely do not have to do this because it is usually done by the manufacturer of the hard disk. If you need to perform another low-level format, then see FORMAT (Module 34) for further instructions.

2. Run FDISK to partition the disk. Each OS/2 partition can be up to 32 megabytes. You can partition (section) your hard disk according to your particular needs. Most people allocate the whole hard disk to OS/2. Note that it can be shared with PC/MS-DOS.
3. Run FORMAT on each OS/2 partition. You can select one of the partitions on the hard disk to be the active partition. This means that when your computer starts, it looks in the active partition for the operating system to start from. When you format the active partition, you must use the /S option on FORMAT so that the operating system is moved into that partition.
4. Run the install program furnished on the installation diskette that comes with the OS/2 Operating System.

You may have to run some or all of the above steps.

WARNING

Be sure you know the state of your computer system hard disk before doing anything as you do not want to destroy any valuable data. Look before you leap!

A procedure for formatting, transferring OS/2, and copying external files to a fixed disk is described. In addition, a description of partitioning also is provided.

PREPARING YOUR FIXED DISK FOR OS/2

To prepare a fixed disk for use with OS/2, perform the following procedure.

CAUTION

If your fixed disk is already formatted, performing this procedure erases all stored data. Therefore, you may wish to read the procedure instead of actually using it. Your disk must also have received a low-level format.

1. Place your OS/2 system diskette in drive A: and turn on your computer.
2. Type FDISK and press Return; notice a screen similar to the following:

```
Personal Computer
Fixed Disk Setup Program Version 1.00

FDISK options

Current Fixed Disk Drive: 1

Choose one of the following:

     1.  Create a Microsoft Operating System/2 partition
         or a logical drive
     2.  Change the active partition
     3.  Delete a Microsoft Operating System/2 partition
         or a logical drive
     4.  Display the partition data
     5.  Select the other fixed disk drive


Enter choice: [1]


Press Enter to continue or
Esc to return to Microsoft Operating System/2
```

3. Type 1 and press Return; you should see

```
Create Microsoft Operating System/2 Partition

Current Fixed Disk Drive: 1


     1.Create primary Microsoft Operating System/2 partition
     2.Create extended Microsoft Operating System/2 partition


Enter choice: [1]

Press ESC to return to FDISK options
```

4. Press Return to accept 1. Check the following display.

```
Create Primary Microsoft Operating System/2 Partition

Current Fixed Disk Drive:  1

Do you want to use the maximum
size for a Microsoft Operating System/2 partition (Y/N) .....?


Press ESC to return to FDISK Options
```

5. Type Y to allocate the maximum for OS/2. This also makes OS/2 the default operating system when you turn on your computer or reset with Ctrl-Alt-Del. The cylinder numbers are displayed on your screen as they are allocated.
6. When the process is finished, check to see that your OS/2 diskette is in drive A: and press any key in response to the "Press any key. . ." prompt.
7. Press any key, such as Spacebar, and the OS/2 prompt is redisplayed.

NOTE

In the following steps, the fixed disk is formatted, and it is assumed that the fixed disk is drive C:.

8. Type FORMAT C: /S/V and press Return; the following prompt is displayed:

```
[A:\]FORMAT C: /V
Press any key to begin formatting drive C:
```

9. Press a key to begin the formatting process. Notice that the head and cylinder numbers are displayed.
10. Wait until the following message is displayed:

```
Formatting has been completed.
System file transfer is in progress...
The System files have been transfered.

Enter up to 11 characters for the volume label,
or Press ENTER for no volume label.
```

11. Type a volume name and press Return, or just press Return if you do not want a volume name. Your fixed disk is now formatted and the system prompt is redisplayed.

12. Your hard disk is now ready to receive OS/2. Follow the instructions furnished with OS/2 to complete the installation process.

CREATING EXTENDED DOS PARTITION

You can use FDISK to create an extended partition if (1) your hard disk is larger than 32 megabytes (the maximum OS/2 partition size), or (2) you wish to designate several logical partitions on one hard disk.

If you wish to create an extended partition, you select option 2 in response to the prompt on the following screen:

```
Create Microsoft Operating System/2 Partition

Current Fixed Disk Drive: 1


     1.Create primary Microsoft Operating System/2 partition
     2.Create extended Microsoft Operating System/2 partition

Enter choice: [1]

Press ESC to return to FDISK options
```

Type 2 and FDISK displays a menu like this one:

```
Create Extended Micorsoft Operating System/2 Partition

Current Fixed Disk Drive: 1

Partition Status   Type  Start  End Size
 C: 1          A   PRI DOS     0  612  613


Total disk space is 1263 cylinders.
Maximum space available for partition
is 650 cylinders.

Enter partition size........... [ 650]

Press ESC to return to FDISK options
```

This screen shows you the total number of cylinders available for an extended partiton. The default is either the maximum size allowed or the remaining portion. Press the Return key if you want the default; otherwise, enter the number of cylinders you want for the partition and press Return. You can create several logical drives on extended partitions. This allows you to segregate an application and its data files to its own drive letter.

However, if you have already allocated the entire disk to OS/2, you see a screen similar to the following one. Notice the message "No space to create an Operating System/2 partition.":

```
Create Extended Micorsoft Operating System/2 Partition

Current Fixed Disk Drive: 1

Partition Status   Type  Start  End Size
 C: 1         A    PRI DOS     0  612  613


No space to create an Microsoft Operating System/2
partition.

Press ESC to return to FDISK options
```

CHANGE PRIMARY PARTITION (Option 2)

You can change the primary partition by using Option 2 of the first FDISK menu. Typing 2 and pressing Return displays a screen similar to the following one. Notice that this screen indicates a primary and an extended partition:

```
Change primary partition

Current Fixed Disk Drive: 1

Partition Status   Type  Start  End Size
 C: 1         A    PRI DOS     0  612  613
    2              EXT DOS   613 1225  613


Total disk space is 1226  cylinders

Enter the number of the partition you
want to make active...............: [ ]


Press ESC to return to FDISK options
```

The A status indicates the active disk partition. To change the active partition to 2, type 2 and press Return. Use Esc to back your way out of the FDISK utility.

DELETING A PARTITION (OPTION 3)

You can delete either the primary or extended partition using Option 3 of the first FDISK menu. Typing 3 and pressing Return displays the following information:

```
Delete Microsoft Operating System/2 Partition

Current Fixed Disk Drive: 1

Choose one of the following

     1.Delete primary Microsoft Operating System/2 partition
     2.Delete extended Microsoft Operating System/2 partition


Enter choice: [ ]

Press ESC to return to FDISK options
```

Typing 1 and pressing Return displays the following screen:

```
Delete Microsoft Operating System/2 Partition

Current Fixed Disk Drive: 1

Partition Status   Type  Start  End Size
 C: 1       A    PRI DOS     0  149  150
    2            EXT DOS   150  306  156


Warning! Data in the Primary Microsoft Operating
System/2 partition will be lost. Do you want
to continue.....................? [N]


Press ESC to return to FDISK Options
```

Pressing ESC or return redisplays the first FDISK menu, canceling the delete operation. Typing Y and pressing Return deletes the partition.

DISPLAY PARTITION INFORMATION (Option 4)

This option displays information similar to the following:

```
Display Partition InformationCurrent Fixed Disk Drive: 1

Partition Status   Type  Start  End Size
 C: 1        A   PRI DOS     0  612  613


Total disk space is 613  cylinders

Press ESC to return to FDISK options
```

The preceding display represents what you see with a single partition. The Delete and Change Partition examples contain screens that are typical of a fixed disk that contains two partitions.

APPLICATIONS

The FDISK command is vital if you have a system with a fixed disk. The ability to share the fixed disk with different operating systems or to have multiple partitions is often convenient, if not necessary. If you have a 40-, 70-, or 120-megabyte disk, you must use partitions to take advantage of the entire disk.

If you own programs that operate on non-OS/2 or PC/MS-DOS operating systems, such as Xenix, UNIX, or CP/M-86, you must install that operating system on a partition other than the one allocated for OS/2. This is accomplished by using format utilities supplied with the other operating systems. When multiple partitions are used, you will use FDISK to switch between them, to change their size, and possibly to delete partitions used for programs that you no longer want to use.

TYPICAL OPERATION

In this activity you use the FDISK command to display the status of your fixed disk. Begin at the OS/2 prompt, [C:\].

1. Type **FDISK** and press **Return**. Notice a display similar to the following:

```
Personal Computer
Fixed Disk Setup Program Version 1.00


FDISK options

The Current Fixed Disk Drive is: 1

Choose one of the following:

     1.  Create a Microsoft Operating System/2 partition
         or a logical drive
     2.  Change the active partition
     3.  Delete a Microsoft Operating System/2 partition
         or a logical drive
     4.  Display the partition data
     5.  Select the other fixed disk drive


Enter choice: [1]

Press Enter to continue or
Esc to return to Microsoft Operating System/2
```

2. Type **4** and press **Return**; notice a display similar to the following:

```
Display Partition Information

The Current Fixed Disk Drive is: 1

Partition Status      Type   Start   End  Size
 1  C:        A      PRI DOS      0   731   732

Maximum capacity of the fixed disk is 732 cylinders.

Press Esc to return to FDISK Options [_]
```

3. Press **Esc** twice to redisplay the OS/2 prompt.
4. Turn to Module 9 to continue the learning sequence.

Module 32
FILENAMES

DESCRIPTION

It is important to understand OS/2 file naming conventions and their use. This module describes filenames and some special filename "tools" called *wild cards* and *literals*.

WHAT IS A FILENAME?

Every program and data file is given a name to differentiate it from other programs and data files. A program is one or more computer instructions collected into a file. A data file is normally a collection of characters (or *data*) that make up a document, like a letter, or a database, like a collection of accounting transactions or customer records.

You should use descriptive filenames. For example, if you create and save a letter to Mom, you might give it the filename MOM.LTR. A letter to Dad could be called DAD.LTR. A word processing program file might have the filename WP.COM. Examine these filenames a little closer.

First, notice that each filename is meaningful. This is important if you want to know what is in a file by looking at its name. Obscure filenames are of little use when viewing a disk directory (or filename list).

Also notice that the filenames have two parts separated by a period. In our filename examples, the first part was used to differentiate Mom's letter from Dad's. The second part of the filename, called an *extension*, specifies the file type. These files are letters, so (for convenience) we assigned the extension .LTR. When we look at a list of filenames, we can tell which ones are letters by looking at extensions; we can tell who the letters are to by reading the first part of the filenames. The extension COM designates a command file type. Command files and files having the extension EXE are *executable* program files. You can run files having the extension COM or EXE by typing the first part of the filename. For example, in the WP.COM example, typing WP and pressing Return causes the WP program to run. It is not necessary to type the filename extension. If you have program files having extensions like OVR, WKS, DBF, or HLP, use some other extension to avoid possible confusion.

FILENAME RULES

There are a few simple rules associated with filenames. These are:

1. Filenames are one to eight characters in length with an optional one- to three-character filename extension.

2. Filenames can includc any of the following characters:
   A - Z (or a - z)
   0 - 9
   $ & # @ ! % ' ' ( ) – { } _
   Other characters are not allowed, such as : , ; ¦ +, since they have special meanings.
3. The following symbols and device names cannot be used as filenames or file extentions:
   . " \ / [ ] : ? * ¦ < > + = ; , & ^
   CLOCK$ COM1 COM2 CON KBD$ LPT1 LPT2 LPT3
   MOUSE$ NUL POINTER$ PRN SCREEN$
4. A period is used to separate the first part of a filename from the extension.
5. When a filename includes an extension, include the extension when used in conjunction with a OS/2 command (like COPY, TYPE, or ERASE).

WILD CARDS AND LITERALS Now that you understand filename rules, you should understand the use of two convenient tools: *wild cards* and *literals*.

Wild Cards In the card game poker, a wild card may be any card that the player chooses. For example, if deuces are "wild," a player can make three kings by using two kings and a deuce. In OS/2, an asterisk (*) character is "wild." The asterisk stands for one or more characters in a filename or extension, beginning with the asterisk position. If only an asterisk is used, it represents the entire filename.

A few examples are in order. If you wish to list a directory of all files having the extension COM, you can type the command DIR *.COM and press Return.

Every filename with the extension COM is listed. If you want to list a directory of every file beginning with the letter W, you can use the command DIR W*.*. Every filename beginning with W and having any extension is listed. The wild card lets you select a set of files based upon some common filename characteristic.

Literals The question mark (?) is used within filenames (and extensions) to represent any character. For example, the expression D???????.??? represents all filenames beginning with the character D. If you want to list a directory of filenames having four or less characters, you can use the command form DIR ????.???. You can also combine literals and wild cards to accomplish the same result by using the command form DIR ????.*.

For instance, to display the filenames DISKCOMP.COM and DISKCOPY.COM, you can use DIR DISKCO??.*.

USING DISK DRIVE DESIGNATORS WITH FILENAMES

Now that you know about filenames, you should also know that you can add the disk drive designator A: through G:, depending on the number of logical disk drives used by your system. For example, if you want to list a directory of all files on disk drive B beginning with the character D, use DIR B:D*.*.

Notice that the disk drive designator always includes a colon (:). Leaving the disk drive designator off of a filename causes OS/2 to "look" on the *logged* disk drive. That is, if the OS/2 prompt is [A:\], disk drive A is logged. If the [B:\] prompt is displayed, disk drive B is logged. Keep in mind that all OS/2 commands are directed to the logged disk drive unless a different disk drive designator is typed in the command. (Also see ASSIGN.)

You can change logged disk drives by simply typing the drive designator and pressing Return. To change from A to B, type B: and press Return. The [B:\] prompt is displayed.

USING PATHNAME DESIGNATORS WITH FILENAMES

Pathnames became available with the introduction of version 2.00 of OS/2. Pathnames let you subdivide a disk into separate directories (often called *subdirectories* or *file paths*). Every subdirectory has a pathname. This gives you the ability to collect similar kinds of information into separate directories, as you would collect files into a file cabinet and into file folders within the file cabinet. You can compare a pathname to the label on a file cabinet drawer or file folder. Module 18, which describes the DIR command, includes information about the creation, naming, and removal of subdirectories.

Pathnames use the same naming conventions as filenames. This is true with respect to:

- Legitimate characters
- Length of the pathname
- Optional extension name and length

However, attempting to use the same pathname and filename within a common directory is not permitted by OS/2.

For clarification, examine a complete filename. Include the disk drive, pathname, and filename designations. A file named MYDATA.DTA on drive C in the filepath \MASTER\SLAVE has the complete name C:\MASTER\SLAVE\MYDATA.DTA.

APPLICATIONS

A filename is an essential part of a file. As mentioned in the Description section of this module, meaningful filenames should be used if you are to know the use or contents of a file.

The wild card and literal characters give you expanded control in the way filenames are displayed, copied, or renamed. You can use wild cards and literals to restrict your operations to certain groups of filenames having common characteristics. For example, wild cards are often used to display a filename directory, or to copy, delete, and rename groups of files. Literals also are used for the same purpose, although to a lesser extent.

TYPICAL OPERATION

In this activity you use filenames, wild cards, and literals with the DIR command. Begin at the OS/2 prompt, [C:\].

1. Display a directory of all files beginning with the character D by typing **DIR D*.*** and pressing **Return**. Notice a display similar to the following:

```
[C:\]DIR D*.*

 The volume in drive C has no label
 Directory of  C:\

DISKCOPY COM     2576   3-17-87  12:00p
DISKCOPY COM     2188   3-17-87  12:00p
        2 File(s)     28672 bytes free

[C:\]
```

2. Display a directory of all files having the extension EXE by typing **DIR *.EXE** and pressing **Return**. Notice a display similar to the following:

```
[C:\]DIR D*.*

 The volume in drive C has no label
 Directory of  C:\

SORT       EXE     1408   3-17-87  12:00p
FIND       EXE     5888   3-17-87  12:00p
        2 File(s)     28672 bytes free

[C:\]
```

3. Display a directory of all files having four characters or less in the first part of the filename by typing **DIR ????.***. Notice a display similar to the following:

```
[C:\]DIR ????.*

 The volume in drive C has no label
 Directory of  C:\

SYS        EXE     1680   3-17-87  12:00p
COMP       EXE     2534   3-17-87  12:00p
TREE       COM     1513   3-17-87  12:00p
SORT       EXE     1408   3-17-87  12:00p
FIND       EXE     5888   3-17-87  12:00p
           8 File(s)     28672 bytes free

[C:\]
```

4. Turn to Module 19 to continue the learning sequence.

Module 33
FILTER COMMANDS

DESCRIPTION

The filter commands are used to intercept, rearrange, and output selected data. Three filter commands are SORT, FIND, and MORE. Each is described in the following paragraphs.

SORT The SORT command intercepts text data and organizes (or sorts) it in alphanumeric order. The general form of the SORT command is

SORT *source file >target file*

This command sorts each line in the source file and copies it to the target file in sorted order.

The normal SORT operation arranges data in ascending (0 - 9, A - Z) order. If you require a descending (or reverse) order sort, add /R to the end of the command line. This puts data in a Z - A, 9 - 0 order.

Another parameter (/ + n) is used to start the sort at a specific column within the specified source file. For example, you can start sorting on column 6 by typing / + 6 at the end of the SORT command line.

A few examples of how the SORT command is used are shown below. Some examples include piping commands. The greater than symbol (>) is a destination pipe; the less than symbol (<) is a source pipe.

DIR ¦SORT	This command alphabetizes the directory listing and then displays it on your screen.
DIR ¦SORT /R	This command is identical to the one above except that it places the directory in descending order. The /R option is used to reverse the order.
DIR ¦SORT >DIRFILE	This command alphabetizes the directory listing and directs (pipes) it to a file named DIRFILE.
SORT <FILE1 >FILE2	This command alphabetizes the lines of text in FILE1 and places it in FILE2.
SORT / + 10 <FILE1 >FILE2	This command is identical to the one above except that the sort begins with the tenth character in each line of text.
DIR ¦SORT >PRN	This command routes a sorted directory to the selected system printer.

FIND The FIND command is used to search a file for one or more designated characters (called a *text string*). Depending upon the form of the FIND command, each line having (or not having) the text string is sent to an output device, such as the display screen, a file, or the printer. The text string is always typed within quotes ("text string"). There are three parameters available with the FIND command:

/V Displays lines not having the designated text string.

/C Counts and displays the number of lines containing the text string.

/N Displays the relative line number in front of each line containing the text string.

A few examples of how the FIND command is used are shown below. Like SORT, piping commands are also available for use with the FIND command.

FIND "PN-1256" PARTFILE
Finds "PN-1256" in the file named PARTFILE and displays it on the screen.

FIND "PN-1256" PARTFILE.NY PARTFILE.DAL PARTFILE.LA
Finds "PN-1256" in the files named PARTFILE.NY, PARFILE.DAL, PARTFILE.LA and displays it on the screen.

FIND "Bob" TEX CAL
Finds "Bob" in the files TEX and CAL and displays it on the screen.

FIND "Bob" TEX /V
Displays the lines in the TEX file that do not contain the text string "Bob."

DIR ¦FIND "TXT"
Displays a directory of filenames having a "TXT" extension.

DIR ¦FIND "<DIR>" >FILE1
Places a directory of pathnames having a "<DIR>" in the directory listing in the file FILE1.

DIR ¦FIND "<DIR>" /N
Counts and displays the number of pathnames in a directory listing.

DIR ¦SORT ¦FIND "<DIR>"
Displays a sorted list of pathnames, where pathnames have <DIR> listed in the directory.

MORE The MORE command pauses the display screen; after each "screenful," the display pauses and the message "—More—" appears. Pressing any key displays the next screenful. A few examples of the MORE command lines follow.

MORE <FILE1.TXT
Displays the text file FILE1.TXT one screenful at a time. Pressing any character key displays the next screenful.

DIR ¦MORE
Pauses the directory display; similar to using the /P parameter of the DIR command.

APPLICATIONS

The filter commands are useful in many ways. The SORT command is excellent for alphabetizing large directories. If you wish, you can sort disk directories to your printer and then store the printed copy of the directory with the disk.

The FIND command also is used with the DIR command to find specific files or file types within a directory. As shown in one of the FIND examples, you can combine SORT with it to provide a sorted list of specified file types, such as pathnames having "<DIR>" entries.

The MORE command is frequently used with the TYPE command. When a large file is displayed using TYPE command, the MORE command conveniently pauses each screenful of the text. Without MORE, you have to use Ctrl-S to pause the display.

TYPICAL OPERATION

In this activity you use the SORT and FIND filter commands to find, sort, and display a specified group of filenames. Then you create a small file and use the FIND filter command to locate specified character strings. Begin at the OS/2 prompt, [C:\].

1. Type **DIR ¦SORT /R** and press **Return**; notice that your directory is listed and displayed in reverse alphabetical order.
2. Type **DIR C:\OS2 ¦FIND "EXE"** and press **Return**; notice that only those files having the EXE extension are listed.
3. Type **COPY CON TEST.TXT** and press **Return**.
4. Type the following five lines of text; press **Return** following each line. Press **Ctrl-C** and **Return** on the last line to end the copy.

```
Johnson, Bob
Taylor, Francis
Jones, Julia
Tanner, Fred
Joseph, Liz
^C
```

5. Type **FIND /N "Jo" TEST.TXT** and press **Return**; your display should resemble the following:

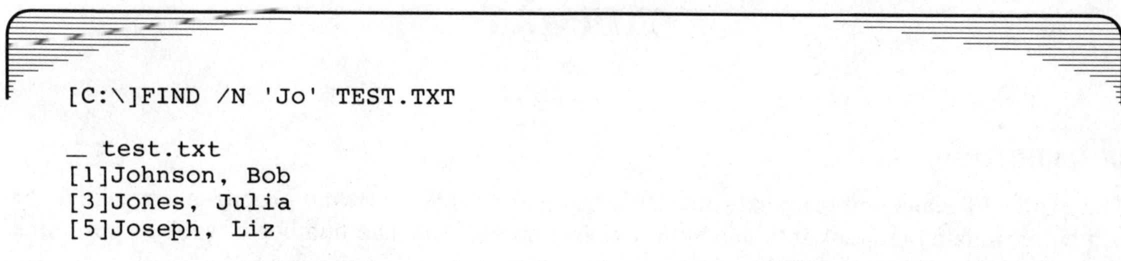

Notice that those lines containing the find string "Jo" are displayed. Also notice that the "/N" filter numbers the displayed lines.

6. Type **FIND /N /V "Jo" TEST.TXT** and press **Return**; your display should resemble the following:

```
[C:\]FIND /V 'Jo' TEST.TXT

_ test.txt
Taylor, Francis
Tanner, Fred
```

Notice that the "/V" parameter shows lines that do not contain the FIND text string.

7. This completes this activity. Use the DEL command to delete the TEST.TXT practice file from your disk.
8. Turn to Module 36 to continue the learning sequence.

Module 34

FORMAT

DESCRIPTION

The FORMAT command is an external OS/2 command. This command prepares a new disk for use by organizing the disk into magnetic tracks and sectors. The number of sectors per track varies with the size and density of the diskettte you use.

COMPATIBILITY WITH PC/MS-DOS DISKS

PC/MS-DOS versions prior to 2.00 use eight sectors per track, 40 tracks per side. Version 2.00 and later use nine sectors per track. PC/MS-DOS version 3.00 introduced a high-capacity formatting capability for the IBM PC-AT, which uses a high-capacity disk drive. PC/MS-DOS 3.30 introduced 3½ inch diskettes with 720KB and 1.44MB of storage.

When OS/2 is in use, files on the earlier PC/MS-DOS disks can be read and written. However, if your computer is using PC/MS-DOS 1.10 or 1.25, disks formatted with OS/2 or PC/MS-DOS 2.00 (or later) cannot be read.

With the introduction of PC/MS-DOS version 3.00's high-capacity disk format utility, the high-capacity drive (drive A) on the IBM PC-AT achieved 1.2 million bytes of storage. Like PC/MS-DOS 2.00 and later, the high-capacity disk can use data files and many programs on earlier PC/MS-DOS versions. However, earlier versions of PC/MS-DOS and standard disk drives cannot use PC/MS-DOS 3.00 high-capacity disks. On many AT-compatible machines, if you write a file to a 360KB diskette using the 1.2MB drive, you may render the diskette unusable in a 360KB drive. This is because the track width of 1.2MB drive is much narrower than that of 360KB drives. Even the file allocation table may be damaged, which keeps you from reading a directory on a 360KB drive.

FORMAT COMMAND FORMS

There are a number of FORMAT command forms. These are described in the following list.

CAUTION

Be aware that the FORMAT command erases all files from the disk being formatted. Many computer users have accidentally formatted the wrong disk. If you have programs or document files you wish to keep on a specific disk, do not format that disk!

FORMAT	Formats the disk in the default drive.
FORMAT B:	Formats the disk in drive B:.
FORMAT /S	Formats the disk in the default drive and transfers the OS/2 to it. (This places system files [OS/2 operating system] and some OS/2 utilities on the target disk.) If you plan to use the disk for data only, avoid using /S. The OS/2 files occupy valuable space. This option allows you to start (boot) OS/2 when the computer is turned on or rebooted with this formated disk in drive A:. Note that /S option is not available for 360KB and smaller diskettes. This copies all files listed in the file FORMATS.TBL to the newly formatted disk.
FORMAT B:/S	Formats the disk in drive B and copies the files listed in the file FORMATS.TBL to it.
FORMAT /V	Displays a prompt that asks for a one- to 11-character disk volume name.
FORMAT /S/V	Formats the disk, prompts for a volume name, and transfers the files in the file FORMATS.TBL to it.
FORMAT /4	Formats a 360KB diskette in a high-capacity (1.2MB) disk-drive (for operation of high-capacity drives like drive A: on the IBM PC-AT). Note that the capacity of the diskette is still 360KB even when formatted on the 1.2MB drive. **WARNING** 360KB diskettes formatted in a 1.2MB drive may not be reliablly read or written in a 360KB drive.
FORMAT /N:18 /T:80	Formats a 1.44MB 3½ inch double-sided diskette. the /N:18 parameter specifies nine sectors per track, while /T:80 specifies eighty tracks.
FORMAT /N:9 /T:80	Computers that use the 1.44MB 3½ inch double-sided diskettes, such as those used on the IBM Model 50 Personal System/2, can use and format 720KB diskettes. Use this command to format a 720KB diskette in a 1.44MB drive. The /N:9 parameter specifies nine sectors per track, while /T:80 specifies eighty tracks.

FORMAT COMMAND DIALOGUE When the FORMAT command is used, there is a built-in dialogue to help along the way. Following is a typical dialogue procedure, beginning with the FORMAT command:

```
[C:\]FORMAT B:                                     Remarks

Insert new diskette for drive B:       Insert the disk to be formatted
and strike any key when ready _        and press any key to start.

Head:   0 Cylinder:     39             Head and cylinder position
                                       displayed during format process.

Formatting has been completed.         Displayed upon completion of
                                       format.

Enter up to 11 characters for the volume label,
or press ENTER for no volume label._          Enter volume label name
                                       for this disk, or press Return
                                       for no label.

  xxxxxx bytes total disk space        Shows disk and memory status.
  xxxxxx bytes available on disk

Format another (Y/N)?_                 Type N to return to the system;
                                       type Y to format another disk.
```

OS/2 displays the cylinders and tracks during the formatting process. This display provides information about the location of defective tracks on your media.

FIXED DISK FORMATTING

You can use the FORMAT command to format a fixed (hard) disk. A factory-fresh fixed disk must undergo a low-level format before the FORMAT command is used. Low-level formatting, which organizes tracks and sectors, is accomplished using special utilities from the manufacturer (Advanced Diagnostics Disk from IBM) or the OS/2 DEBUG command. After the low-level process is completed, the OS/2 FDISK command (Module 31) is used to partition a fixed disk. After FDISK, then the OS/2 FORMAT command is used to format the OS/2 partition. You must format each partition on the hard disk with the corresponding operating system.

When you format the hard disk, FORMAT prompts you to verify the volume label. This is done to prevent you from formatting over a hard disk accidentally and permanently erasing all the data on the hard disk. When it prompts you for the hard disk volume label, enter the label. If the label is correct, then FORMAT will format the disk, otherwise, it will diplay an error message and quit. If you are formatting the partition for the first time, press RETURN at the volume label verify prompt. The FORMAT command then verifies that you really want to format the hard disk with the following prompt:

```
WARNING, ALL DATA ON NON-REMOVABLE DISK
DRIVE X: WILL BE LOST!
Proceed with Format (Y/N)?_
```

If you want to format the hard disk, type Y and press Return. If not, type N and press Return.

Just like with floppy disks, when the format is complete, it displays a message showing the total disk space, bytes used by the system, and the bytes available on the disk.

VOLUME NAMES

The /V parameter is handy for assigning a one- to 11-character name to a disk. Like filenames and pathnames, volume names should be meaningful. When FORMAT /V is used, the prompt

```
Volume label (11 characters, ENTER for none)? _
```

is displayed. In response, type a volume name of your choice and press Return (or Enter as it is sometimes called). The formatted disk is now tagged with the name you have chosen. The volume name is displayed when a directory is listed or when the VOL command is used. The VOL command is described in detail in Module 64. The LABEL command (Module 39) lets you create, change, or delete volume names.

FIXED DISK LOW-LEVEL FORMATTING

If your hard disk needs a low-level format, you may be able to low-level format your hard disk from the software contained on the disk controller card in your computer by calling it with the DEBUG program. Otherwise, you may have to purchase the Advanced Diagnostics Disk from IBM or your manufacturer to do the low-level format. Most microcomputer service centers can also perform this job for you for a nominal fee.

The DEBUG low-level format process for many computers is summarized in the following procedural steps. The precise procedure depends upon the number of disk drive heads and cylinders and the interleave factor recommended by the manufacturer of the drive and controller.

1. Insert the OS/2 diskette containing the DEBUG.COM file into drive A.
2. Type DEBUG and press Return; notice that a hyphen is displayed. This is DEBUG's way of prompting you for a command.
3. Type G = C800:5 and press Return to start the low-level process.
4. Respond to the prompts using values recommended by the disk drive and controller manufacturers.
5. Upon completion of the low-level format, use the OS/2 FDISK setup utility to specify the number of fixed disk partitions.
6. Lastly, use the OS/2 FORMAT command to format the OS/2 partition for use.

Because fixed disks are so large, formatting takes several minutes. Be sure to read Module 31 before formatting a fixed disk.

APPLICATIONS

The FORMAT command is essential in preparing new disks for use with your computer. It is also good for reformatting old disks and making them usable again. The /S parameter allows you to transfer OS/2 to the target disk. This transfers all internal commands such as COPY, DEL, DIR, REN, and TYPE, and makes the disk "bootable," which means it can be used to start your computer.

TYPICAL OPERATION

In this activity you use the FORMAT command to prepare a new disk in drive A. Use a high density diskette. Begin at the OS/2 prompt, [C:\].

1. Type **FORMAT A: /S** and press **Return**. Notice the following display:

```
[C:\]FORMAT A: /S

Insert new diskette in drive A:
and press ENTER when ready _
```

2. Insert the disk to be formatted and press **Return** to start the disk formatting process. The screen displays the Head and Cylinder location being formatted.
3. Wait until the following message is displayed:

```
Formatting has been completed.
System file transfer is in progress...
The System files have been transfered.

Enter up to 11 characters for the volume label,
or Press ENTER for no volume label._
```

4. Type **TESTDISK** and press **Return**.
5. Wait until the following message is displayed:

```
  1213952 bytes total disk space
   966144 bytes used by system files
   247808 bytes available on disk

Format another diskette (Y/N)? _
```

6. Type **N** and press **Return** to redisplay the system prompt.
7. Turn to Module 58 to continue the learning sequence.

Module 35

GRAFTABL

DESCRIPTION

The GRAFTABL command is a Dos Mode command that allows you to display an extended character set when in graphics mode. The extended character sets are associated with code-page switching. The form for the Graftabl command is

```
GRAFTABL XXX
```

where XXX is a valid code-page number. A list of valid code-pages are:

Value	*Code Page*
437	United States (default)
860	Portuguese
863	French-Canadian
865	Nordic

By entering

```
GRAFTABL /sta
```

you can display the active character set.

By entering

```
GRAFTABL ?
```

you can display the GRAFTABL options plus the active character set.

For more information, see Module 14 on code-page switching and Module 10 on the CHCP command.

Turn to Module 40 to continue the learning sequence.

Module 36

GROUPING COMMANDS

DESCRIPTION

The purpose of the GROUPING commands is to allow you to combine several OS/2 commands on the same command line. The grouping commands allow you to create logical statements in commands and batch files. For example, using the logical && (and) grouping command between to OS/2 commands, if the first OS/2 command or program completes successfully, then OS/2 executes the second command in the group, otherwise it is not executed.

The grouping commands are designed to work in conjunction with the redirection, piping, and filter commands. The grouping commands are the && symbol, the ¦¦ symbol, and the & symbol. Parentheses are used to combine combinations of the grouping, piping, redirection, and filter commands. Also available to you is the ^ character, which lets you use the special symbols as regular characters. With these commands you can create sophisticated and complex logical statements.

THE COMMAND SEPARATOR SYMBOL: &

The & symbol allows you to place multiple OS/2 commands on the command line, where all commands are executed from left to right. For example, if you enter the command

```
DIR C:\OS2 & TYPE C:\OS2\READ.ME
```

then OS/2 executes the DIR command, and then it executes the TYPE command; both commands are executed, the one on the left and then the one on the right.

THE AND SYMBOL: &&

The && symbol allows you to place multiple OS/2 commands on the command line; however, the command on the right does not execute if the command on the left does not execute properly. For example, if you enter the command

```
DIR ERRORS.DAT && TYPE ERRORS.DAT
```

then OS/2 first executes the DIR command. If the DIR command finds the ERRORS.DAT file, it executes the TYPE command. If the DIR command does not find the ERRORS.DAT file, the command on the right side of the && symbol is not executed. The command on the right only executes if the command on the left of the && symbol executes properly.

THE OR SYMBOL: ¦¦

The ¦¦ symbol allows you to place multiple OS/2 commands on the command line; however, if the command on the left executes properly then the command on the right does not execute. For example, if you enter the command

```
TYPE C:ERRORS.DAT || TYPE B:ERRORS.DAT
```

then OS/2 first attempts to execute the TYPE command on the left. If the type command finds the C:ERRORS.DAT file, it executes the TYPE C:ERRORS.DAT command and ends execution on this line. If the DIR command does not find the ERRORS.DAT file, the command on the right side of the || symbol is executed. The command on the right only executes if the command on the left of the || fails to execute properly.

THE GROUPER SYMBOLS: ( )

The ( ) symbols allow you to place parentheses around grouping commands to ensure that OS/2 executes them in the desired sequence. It also allows you to use a group of commands as a command in another group. For example, if you enter the command

```
DIR ERRORS.DAT && ( TYPE ERRORS.DAT | SORT >ERRORS.SRT )
```

then OS/2 executes the DIR command. If it executes, then OS/2 executes both the TYPE command and the SORT command.

If you enter the command

```
( TYPE PRODUCTS.NEW || TYPE PRODUCTS.OLD ) | SORT >PRODUCTS.SRT
```

then OS/2 attempts to type the PRODUCTS.NEW file. If it succeeds, then the output of this file is piped into the SORT program. If it fails, then the PRODUCTS.OLD file is typed and piped into the SORT program.

THE ESCAPE SYMBOL: ^

The ^ symbol allows you to use the special grouping and piping symbols as regular characters. For example, the command

```
ECHO  PAYROLL TOTALS FOR JAN. 1988 ^& FEB. 1988
```

will display: PAYROLL TOTALS FOR JAN. 1988 & FEB. 1988.

If the ^ symbol is not included in this command, then the command processor interprets this line as a line using the grouping command & and attempts to execute the program named Feb. after it completes the ECHO command.

APPLICATIONS

The grouping commands give you power, flexibility, and sophistication at the command prompt. Usually, the grouping commands are used with batch files, which are utilized heavily in the office environment during end-of-day, end-of-month, and end-of-year processing. The grouping commands offer greater control over the execution during batch procession and, therefore, simplify the computer operations since the operator is not required to make as many decisions in answering prompts.

TYPICAL OPERATION

In this activity you use grouping commands to combine two directories on disk and then sort and display the combined directories. Start at the OS/2 prompt, [C:\].

1. Type **(DIR C:\ & DIR C:\OS2) ¦ SORT ¦ MORE** and press **Return**.

This command line allows you to determine quickly if there are duplicate files in the two directories because the two directories are combined, sorted, and then displayed a screenful at a time.

2. Turn to Module 54 to continue the learning sequence.

Module 37

HELPMSG, HELP

DESCRIPTION

The HELPMSG command is an external OS/2 command. The purpose of the HELPMSG command is to provide you with additional information about an OS/2 error message or warning message.

The form for the HELPMSG command is

```
HELPMSG DOSmsg_nbr
```

where *DOSmsg nbr* is any OS/2 error or warning message you encounter. The HELPMSG is an on-line help utility to provide more information concerning errors and warnings and to offer some suggestions for a course of action to respond to each message.

If you enter

```
HELPMSG SYS1457
```

or

```
HELPMSG 1457
```

then the help message for error SYS1457 is displayed.

HELP HELP is a batch file. If you execute HELP with no parameters then HELP displays a help screen that tells you how to:

- Switch to the next session
- Switch to the program selector
- Turn help text on
- Turn help text off
- Display a HELPMSG message
- Exit a session

If you enter

```
HELP ON
```

a help line is displayed on the top line of the screen as part of the command prompt (Module 48). The help line on the top line of the screen reminds you how to return to the Program Selector Menu.

If you enter

```
HELP OFF
```

the help line is turned off.

If you receive an error message, you can use either HELPMSG or HELP to display the error message. If you enter

```
HELP 1457
```

then the help message for error DOS1457 is displayed. If you look at the HELP.CMD or HELP.BAT batch file, you can find out that it uses the HELPMSG command to display the error message.

APPLICATIONS

At some point you will receive an OS/2 message you are not quite sure how to respond to. The on-line help utility HELPMSG can assist you. For example, if you receive the following message, you may not know what to do first. You may end up trying many things and still not solving the problem, just wasting time and getting frustrated.

```
SYS1457: system is unable to transfer system files.
```

You can see that this message leaves a lot to be desired. It does not tell you what the cause of the problem is or how you can possibly solve it. Here are some of the possiblities you might think of:

1. You don't even know what a system file is, much less the cause.
2. You didn't even know you were wanting to transfer the system files.
3. You never received them.
4. Someone erased them.
5. The destination disk might be full.
6. The destination disk might be write protected.
7. Maybe you are using the wrong size diskette.
8. Maybe your disk is not formatted correctly.
9. Maybe your hard disk is having a read error.
10. Maybe you scratched the floppy disk when you wrote the label.
11. Maybe they are hidden and they must be unhidden to copy.
12. Maybe they are locked because your boss doesn't trust you.
13. Maybe they are write-only files.
14. Give up and try the on-line help command, HELPMSG.

The solution is presented in the next section of this module.

TYPICAL OPERATION

In this module you execute the HELPMSG command for the OS/2 error message of SYS1457. Start from the OS/2 prompt, [C:\].

1. Type **HELPMSG SYS1457** and press **Return**. The following message is displayed:

```
SYS1457: The system is unable to transfer system
files at this time.

EXPLANATION: There is an insufficient amount of
storage available to transfer the operating system files.
ACTION: Wait for another process to end and retry
the command.
```

Hopefully you have other processes running that you can wait to end. Otherwise, you may have to buy more memory.

2. Turn to Module 62 to continue the learning sequence.

Module 38

KEYB

DESCRIPTION

The KEYB command is an OS/2 protected command to support a variety of keyboard configurations conforming to different language requirements. The KEYB command is typically placed in the STARTUP.CMD file and loaded upon system turn on.

The general form of the KEYB command form is

```
KEYB xx
```

where xx is the keyboard code for the desired country.

A list of code-page and keyboard values are contained in the following table:

Country	*xx*	*code page*	*Country*	*xx*	*code page*
United States	US	001	Latin America	LA	003
Canada (Eng)	US	001	Australia	US	061
France	FR	033	Belgium	BE	032
Spain	SP	034	Canada (Fr)	CF	002
Italy	IT	039	Denmark	DK	045
United Kingdom	UK	044	Finland	SU	358
Germany	GR	049	Switzerland (Gr)	SG	041
Netherlands	NL	031	Norway	NO	047
Portugal	PO	351	Sweden	SV	046
Switzerland (Fr)	SF	041			

You can re-enter the KEYB command using new parameters to switch to a different code-page. For example, if you place the following statement:

```
DEVINFO=KBD,FR,KEYBOARD.DCP
```

in your config.sys file then you can switch to a French keyboard by entering:

```
KEYB FR
```

Some keyboard and code-page combinations are incompatible. Use of incompatible code page-keyboard combinations provides unpredictable results. The following table lists legitimate code-page and keyboard combinations:

Code Page	*437*	*850*	*860*	*863*	*865*
Keyboard	FR GR IT LA NL SP SV SU UK US	BE CF DK FR GR IT LA NL NO PO SF SG SF SP SV UK US	PO	CF	NO DK

APPLICATIONS

The KEYB command is normally used as a line within STARUP.CMD file, in conjunction with other code-page switching commands. The proper combination prepares your computer for use with the language of your choice. If you are using several different languages, you can type the desired KEYB command at the DOS prompt to change your keyboard setup. However, the corresponding code-page must have been prepared at boot time. To ensure proper printing and display, the appropriate device drivers must exist within your CONFIG.SYS file.

NOTE

The KEYB command can only be entered in an OS/2 session, but it still affects the Dos Mode session.

TYPICAL OPERATION

Because the KEYB command is used in conjunction with other commands, an activity is not presented here.

Turn to Module 10 to continue the learning sequence.

Module 39

LABEL

DESCRIPTION

LABEL is an external OS/2 command that creates and changes volume labels on a disk.

To create a new volume (disk) label where none exists, type

```
LABEL LABEL-NAME
```

where *LABEL-NAME* can be any name of your choosing up to 11 characters long. In this example, A: is assumed as the logged disk drive. The following prompt is displayed to help you:

```
The volume label in drive A is SCRATCH

Enter a volume label of up to 11 characters
or press Enter for no volume label update.
```

You can change a label name by typing:

```
LABEL A:
```

The following prompt is displayed:

```
The volume label in drive A is SCRATCH

Enter a volume label of up to 11 characters
or press Enter for no volume label update.
```

You can type the new name and press Return. For example, you may use something like DISK #001. Pressing Return without typing a new volume does not change the existing volume label.

APPLICATIONS

A volume label is assigned when formatting the disk with the /V parameter (see Module 34). The LABEL command lets you create and change label names, making it easy to maintain your disk organization system.

TYPICAL OPERATION

In this activity you use LABEL to create and then change a volume label on a scratch disk in drive A. Begin at the OS/2 prompt, [C:\].

1. Insert a scratch disk in drive A.
2. Type **LABEL A:NEWNAME** and press **Return**.
3. Check the new volume label name by typing **VOL A:** and pressing **Return**. Notice the display:

```
[C:\]VOL A:

The volume label in drive A is NEWNAME
```

4. Change the volume label by typing **LABEL A:** and pressing **Return**. Notice the prompt:

```
The volume label in drive A is NEWNAME

Enter a volume label of up to 11 characters
or press Enter for no volume label update.
```

5. Type **TESTLABEL** and press **Return**.
6. Check the new volume label name by typing **VOL A:** and pressing **Return**. Notice the display:

```
[C:\]VOL A:

The volume label in drive A is TESTLABEL

[C:\]
```

7. Turn to Module 32 to continue the learning sequence.

Module 40

LINK

DESCRIPTION

The LINK command is an external OS/2 command. This command normally is used only by programmers to:

- Combine (or link together) individual program modules that are in compiled (object) form;
- Incorporate program library modules that are referenced by the program being linked;
- Produce a display of the status and error messages encountered during the linking process;
- Produce a relocatable program load module.

After you have written a program and compiled it into an object file (with the extension .OBJ), it is ready to be linked. Depending upon the compiler (or assembler) you use, there may be one or more library files to include with the linking process. These have the extension .LIB and are specified by name during the linking process.

If you have an object file called MYPROG.OBJ, you can link it by typing the command

```
LINK
```

or

```
LINK MYPROG
```

or

```
LINK MYPROG,RUNFILE,MAPFILE,LIBFILE
```

Using the second form, a display similar to the following appears:

```
[C:\]LINK MYPROG

Microsoft (R) Segmented-Executable Linker Version 5.00
Copyright (C) Microsoft Corp 1984-1987. All rights reserved.

Run File [MYPROG.EXE]:
List File [NUL.MAP]:
Libraries &.LIB?:
```

You can enter filenames after each colon on the run file, list file, and libraries lines, or accept the defaults in brackets by pressing Return. The run file always has the extension .EXE. The list file is created only if you enter a filename. You can link multiple object (.OBJ) and library (.LIB) files by typing a plus sign (+) between the filenames. Placing two commas in place of the run and list files accepts default values. The following command line includes multiple object files, a run file, and two library files. The double comma accepts the default map file value.

```
LINK PROG1+PROG2+PROG3,PROG.EXE,,C1.LIB+C2.LIB
```

If you are using one or more libraries, you can specify library filenames on the libraries line. Like run files, use a plus sign between library filenames if more than one is used. If no libraries are used, press Return.

Several parameters for the LINK command exist. These parameters are placed at the end of the LINK command line. The possible parameters include:

/HELP	Linker to display list of options. Use without a filename.
/HI	Controls where the programs load in memory.
/L	Places line numbers in the list file.
/M	Lists all global symbols found in the object modules at the end of the list file.
/P	Pauses for a disk change before producing the run file.
/ST:n	Overrides the size of the stack produced by the Macro Assembler or compiler; n is a number between 0 and 65536.
/SE:n	Adjusts the total number of segments that an .EXE file can contain; n varies from 0 to 1024, where the default is 256. Controls the number of segments from all object files and libraries that an .EXE file can contain.
/I	Linker displays detailed information about the link process during the link.
/E	Instructs linker to pack the .EXE file.
/NOI	Instructs linker to distinguish between lower- and upper-case characters.
/NOD	Instructs linker to use only specified libraries, do not use default libraries.

If you have a Macro Assembler package, you can follow the activity in the Typical Operation section of this module. There a source file is created, compiled with the Macro Assembler, linked with LINK, and converted to a .COM file with EXE2BIN. EXE2BIN is described in Module 29. Even if you do not have a Macro Assembler, you may wish to review the compiling and linking steps as a matter of interest.

APPLICATIONS

Although the LINK command is used extensively by professional programmers, you may find that you never have a need for it unless you get into programming. If you are a typical microcomputer user, your interest is probably with computer applications programs rather than programming. However, it may be of interest to know what the LINK program does if you plan to broaden your knowledge of what goes on "behind the scenes" of microcomputing.

TYPICAL OPERATION

In this activity you use the LINK command to link a program that is assembled with the Macro Assembler. If you do not have the Macro Assembler, you may wish to follow the steps involved in creating a source file, assembling it, linking it, and then converting the resulting .EXE file into a .COM file with the EXE2BIN command. Begin at the OS/2 prompt, [C:\].

1. Create a source file with EDLIN in the Dos Mode (or your OS/2 editor in Protected Mode) with a name of NAME.ASM as follows:

   a. Type **EDLIN NAME.ASM** and press **Return**.
   b. Type **i** for insert and press **Return**.
   c. Type the following source file, ending each line with **Return**:

```
        title    display name on screen
code    segment  para public 'code'
        assume cs:code, ds:code
        org      100h
example proc
start:  push     cs
        pop      ds                     ; set DS equal to CS
        mov      dx , offset my_name ; DS:DX points to string to print
        mov      ax , 900h             ; print string function call
        int      21h                    ; DOS function call
        int      20h                    ; exit program back to DOS

my_name db       'Your Name Here$'     ; place $ at end of name
example endp                            ; $ will not print

code    ends
        end      start
```

   d. Press **Ctrl-C** on line 18 to return to the EDLIN prompt.
   e. Type **e** and press **Return** to save the file and quit EDLIN.
   f. Return to OS/2.

NOTE
The following step requires the Macro Assembler.

2. Type **MASM NAME,NAME,NAME;** and press **Return** to assemble the source file. Notice the following display:

```
[C:\]MASM NAME,NAME,NAME;
Microsoft (R) MACRO Assembler Version 4.50
Copyright (C) Microsoft Corp 1981, 1987. All rights reserved.


Warning Severe
Errors Errors
0       0

[C:\]
```

3. Type **LINK NAME;** and press **Return** to link the assembled program. Notice the following display:

```
[C:\]LINK NAME;
Microsoft (R) Segmented-Executable Linker Version 5.00
Copyright (C) Microsoft Corp 1984-1987. All rights reserved.


Warning: No STACK segment

There was 1 error detected                    (Ignore the error.)

[C:\]
```

4. Type **EXE2BIN NAME NAME.COM** and press **Return** to convert the .EXE file into a .COM file.
5. Type **NAME** and press **Return** to run your new program; notice that your name is displayed and the DOS prompt reappears.
6. This completes this practice activity. Save this program for the CODEVIEW module.
7. Turn to Module 29 to continue the learning sequence.

Module 41

MODE

DESCRIPTION

The MODE command is an external OS/2 utility. This module first describes the traditional uses of the MODE command.

TRADITIONAL MODE COMMAND USES

The MODE command is used to control several of the outputs of your computer including:

- DISPLAY OUTPUT
  - Width (40 or 80 characters per line)
  - Monochrome or color (Color commands require a color board.)
  - Horizontal alignment (shift left or right)
  - Test pattern display

Examples:

MODE 40	Displays 40 characters per line.
MODE 80	Displays 80 characters per line.
MODE BW40	Displays 40 characters per line in monochrome.
MODE BW80	Displays 80 characters per line in monochrome.
MODE CO40	Displays 40 characters per line in color.
MODE CO80	Displays 80 characters per line in color.
MODE CO80,43	Displays 80 characters per line in color, 43 lines.
MODE MONO	Switches display output to the monochrome board.

- PRINTER OUTPUT
  - LPT1:, LPT2:, or LPT3:
  - Print width (such as 80 or 132).
  - Automatic print retry (P)
  - Lines per inch (6 or 8)

Examples:

MODE LPT2:	Uses parallel printer 2.
MODE LPT1:,132,8	Uses parallel printer 1, 132 columns, 8 lines per inch.
MODE LPT1:,80,6	Uses parallel printer 1, 80 columns, 6 lines per inch.

NOTE

The redirection of parallel printer output to a serial printer is not supported by the MODE command but by the SPOOL command (Module 56).

- ASYNCHRONOUS COMMUNICATIONS OUTPUT
  - COM1, COM2, COM3, COM4, COM5, COM6, COM7, or COM8
  - Baud rate (speed)- 110, 150, 300, 600, 1200, 2400, 4800, or 9600
  - Parity (N = none, E = even, or O = odd)
  - Databits (7 or 8)
  - Stopbits (1 or 2)
  - Retries (P sets "retries" for interface to a serial printer)

Examples:

MODE COM1:12,N,8,1,P	Data output configured to 1200 baud, no parity, 8 databits, 1 stopbit; the P turns on automatic retry for printers.
MODE COM2:300,E,7,1	Data output configured to 300 baud, even parity, 7 databits, 1 stopbit, no printer retries.

NOTE

The use of MODE to set the com port is only allowed when the COM01.SYS device driver is installed. See Module 22 on device drivers for more information.

Other COM parameters in OS/2 Mode:

TO = X	X = OFF for normal timeout processing. (default) X = ON for infinite timeout processing.
XON = X	X = OFF to disable automatic transmit flow control. (default) X = ON to enable automatic transmit flow control.
IDSR = X	X = ON to enable input handshake using DSR. (default) X = OFF to disable input handshake using DSR.
ODSR = X	X = ON to enable output handshake using DSR. (default) X = OFF to disable output handshake using DSR.
OCTS = X	X = ON to enable output handshake using CTS. (default) X = OFF to disable output handshake using CTS.
DTR = X	X = ON to enable DTR. (default) X = OFF to disable DTR. X = HS to enable DTR handshaking.
RTS = X	X = ON to enable RTS. (default) X = OFF to disable RTS. X = HS to enable RTS handshaking. X = TOG to enable RTS toggling.

DISKETTE WRITE VERIFICATION

- Turn on diskette write verification
- Turn off diskette write verification
- Query the status of diskette write verification

MODE DSKT	to query status of diskette write verification
MODE DSKT VER = ON	to turn on diskette write verification
MODE DSKT VER = OFF	to turn off diskette write verification

APPLICATIONS

The MODE command has a number of important applications. It is used to control the width and color of your display. It is used to change from parallel to serial printer output or to change between printer output ports. Finally, it is used to establish communications *protocol* parameters, i.e., speed, parity, databits, and stopbits.

TYPICAL OPERATION

In this activity you use the MODE command to set your display width and then to setup a communications protocol. Begin at the DOS prompt, [REAL C:\].

1. Type **MODE 40** and press **Return.** Notice that your prompt looks twice as large in the 40 character mode.
2. Type **MODE 80** and press **Return** to return to the 80 character mode.

NOTE

If you have a serial output port on your computer (COM1:), perform the remaining steps. You also must have the DEVICE = COM01.SYS statement in the CONFIG.SYS file. Otherwise, go to Step 4.

3. Type **MODE COM1:1200,N,8,1,P** and press **Return.** Data output through COM1 (your serial port) is now setup as follows:

```
Baud rate - 1200
Parity - None
Databits - 8
Stopbits - 1
Automatic retry - On
```

4. Press **Ctrl-Esc** to return to Session Manager. Select OS/2 Command Prompt in the SWITCH TO A RUNNING PROGRAM window to return to OS/2 Mode.
5. Turn to Module 27 to continue the learning sequence.

Module 42

PATCH

DESCRIPTION

The PATCH command is an external OS/2 command. The purpose of the PATCH command is to make modifications to executable programs.

The form for the PATCH command is

```
PATCH filename.exe
```

where *filename.exe* is the name of the executable program you wish to patch. The PATCH command has two modes, Automatic and Interactive. Apply the /A parameter on the patch command line to enter Automatic mode, otherwise you are in Interactive mode. In Automatic mode, you are prompted for the filename of the file that contains the patches. In Interactive mode, you are prompted for the patches, for the offset and for the data. Always enter data in Hexidecimal.

NOTE

Always backup program being patched before applying any patches.

MANUAL MODE

PATCH prompts you for the offset to where the patch is to be made. Enter the offset and press Return. PATCH displays 16 bytes of data at the offset you entered. You can now enter the patch or quit. To enter data, just type the new data bytes in or press the Spacebar to leave the byte unchanged. The Backspace key can be used to move the cursor backwards to correct a mistake. Press Esc to have patch ignore any changes on the current line. If the cursor moves past the 16th byte, then 16 more bytes of data are displayed which you can change. Press Enter when patch has been made. You are prompted for other patches. If you enter Y, then you are prompted for the offset. If you enter N, then you are asked if you want to save the patched file to disk. If you enter Y, then the patched file is written to disk and PATCH terminates.

INTERACTIVE (AUTOMATIC) MODE

The /A option specifies automatic mode. This allows the PATCH command to get the patch information from a data file. Follow the instructions that accompany the patch. Cursor movement, changes, and prompts are as described above in MANUAL MODE.

APPLICATIONS

For large corporations with a large base of installed application programs, it is very expensive to mail a diskette to each user to correct a small programming bug or to provide an optional enhancement. An inexpensive solution to the problem is to publish the fixes/enhancements in a magazine and have the user apply the patches to the executable programs. The PATCH command is the command that allows you to patch executable programs.

Always follow the instructions exactly that you receive concerning patches. Only apply patches to the corresponding version of the program as specified in your instructions. Always backup before applying any patches. Never apply patches to your original diskettes.

Turn to Module 15 to continue the learning sequence.

Module 43
PATH

DESCRIPTION

The PATH command is an internal OS/2 command. It is used to provide access to external commands and programs located in other directory paths or other disks. The PATH command is usually entered as a line in the STARTUP.CMD or AUTOEXEC.BAT *batch* file, which most often contains one or more OS/2 commands. The STARTUP.CMD (AUTOEXEC.BAT in DOS Mode) file is automatically executed upon system turn on to establish desired parameters. Other batch files are executed upon command. When used, each command executes as it is encountered in the file. The creation and use of batch files is described in Module 8.

To illustrate the PATH command, assume you have a program named GATOR.COM that is located in a subdirectory. You are not sure if it is on disk C or disk A, so you want to search both disks and execute the command when found. To complicate matters, you are not sure if the program is in the SWAMP subdirectory or the MUD subdirectory.

Here is where the PATH command comes to your rescue. To set up a search for GATOR.COM, you can specify the disk and directories using the PATH command. While logged on disk C, assuming that you have a fixed disk system, type

```
PATH \SWAMP;\MUD;B:\SWAMP;B:\MUD
```

When you type GATOR to run your program, OS/2 first searches the C:\SWAMP subdirectory, then the C:\MUD subdirectory. Next, it searches the B:\SWAMP subdirectory. Finally, it searches the B:\MUD subdirectory where GATOR.COM is found and executed.

You also can use the PATH command to display the path setup. To do this, type PATH and press Return. A display similar to the following is displayed:

```
[C:\OS2]PATH

PATH=\SWAMP;\MUD;B:\SWAMP;B:\MUD
```

To cancel the path settings, type PATH; and press Return. The semicolon is the critical agent in this PATH command. Now when you check your paths with the PATH command, the message "No Path" is displayed.

APPLICATIONS

As you may suspect, a primary use of the PATH command is to provide access to programs located in multiple subdirectories. Experienced fixed disk users almost always provide a path to the subdirectory containing their OS/2 commands, in addition to other file utility directories.

For example, if you have three subdirectories on a fixed disk system that are frequently used with the pathnames C:\OS2, \SK, and \UTIL, a PATH command line is desirable in a batch file. Here is a practical way to create a batch file containing the desired PATH command line. Beginning at the root directory, perform the following procedure:

1. Type COPY CON: TBATCH.CMD and press Return.
2. Type the following lines of text ending each with Return. On the last line following the CLS (clear screen) command, press Ctrl-Z (represented by ^Z) and then press Return to save the file to disk.

```
ECHO OFF
PATH C:;C:\OS2;C:\SK;C:\UTIL
CLS^Z
```

3. Notice that the file is copied to your disk when you press Return.
4. Run the file by typing TBATCH and pressing Return.
5. Your paths are now established; the C:\, C:\OS2, C:\SK, and C:\UTIL subdirectories are automatically searched whenever you require access to a program.

TYPICAL OPERATION

In this activity you use the PATH command to establish a directory search and then use it to display the established routing. Next the paths are canceled. Finally, the path is restored. Begin at the OS/2 prompt, [C:\].

1. Type **PATH and press Return**. Write down the current path setting.
2. Type **PATH \SWAMP;\SWAMP\MUD** and press **Return**.
3. Type **PATH**, press **Return**, and notice the following display:

```
[C:\]PATH

PATH=\SWAMP;\SWAMP\MUD
```

4. Cancel the path by typing **PATH;** and pressing **Return**.
5. Type **PATH** and check for the following display:

```
[C:\]PATH
Path=
```

6. Re-enter the path saved in step 1 (like in step 2).
7. Turn to Module 26 to continue the learning sequence.

Module 44

PIPING COMMANDS

DESCRIPTION

OS/2 has a powerful internal utility that lets you redirect data input and output. This utility is called *piping*. Why piping? Because it is like redirecting the flow in a garden hose from one bucket to another. In more precise terms, data input and output are redirected to your computer's various devices. For example, you can pipe a screen display to a designated disk file or to your printer.

The greater than (>) and less than (<) symbols direct (or pipe) data input and output. One illustration of this is when you want to save a directory listing of the logged disk drive to a file named DIR.LST. This is achieved with the following command line:

```
DIR >DIR.LST
```

Listing a directory reveals the DIR.LST file, which contains a complete directory listing. You can alphabetize (or sort) the directory listing by including the SORT filter command. Use the command DIR ¦ SORT >DIR.LST to obtain a sorted directory file.

If you want to pipe the directory listing to your printer, use DIR >PRN. Be sure your printer is turned on and loaded with paper to avoid a printer error.

You can establish program control using pipes. The following example illustrates this capability. Here, EDLIN is used to create a list control file for displaying text on the screen. Once displayed, control returns to the command prompt. If you wish, you can perform the following steps:

1. Perform this example in Real Mode.
2. Type EDLIN LISTER and press Return.
3. Type i and press Return.
4. Type L on line 1 and press Return.
5. Type e on line 2 and press Return.
6. Press Ctrl-C on line 3; your file should resemble the following:

```
*i
     1: L
     2: e
     3: ^C
*
```

7. Type e and press Return to save the file and exit EDLIN.

8. Now type a sample text file (called "SAMPLE") as follows:
   a. Type EDLIN SAMPLE and press Return.
   b. Type i, press Return, and type the following two lines; end each line with Return.

      ```
      This is a sample file.
      It was prepared with EDLIN.
      ```

   c. Press Ctrl-C to stop text entry; then type e and press Return to save the file and exit EDLIN.
9. From the prompt, use piping with the LISTER file and EDLIN to display the SAMPLE file by typing the following command line:

   ```
   EDLIN SAMPLE <LISTER
   ```

10. Notice the following display:

```
*L
     1:*This is a sample file.
     2: It was prepared with EDLIN.
*e
[REAL A:\]
```

When piping is used in DOS Mode, OS/2 creates temporary piping files that contain the involved input and output data. These files appear on your directory as %PIPEx.$$$.

Filter commands, described in Module 33, are also used with the piping commands. For example, if you wish to print a sorted directory, you can type

```
DIR | SORT >PRN
```

If you want to place a sorted directory in a file named DIRFILE on the disk in drive A, you can type:

```
DIR | SORT >A:DIRFILE
```

Be sure to read about the filter commands in Module 33, as mixing piping and filter commands offers many powerful variations.

APPLICATIONS

You can use piping commands to save directories to files, send program output to your printer, control program operation with a prepared control file, or to add text from one file to the end of another.

One particularly useful command combines piping with the SORT filter to obtain an alphabetized list. For example, if you are preparing an index, you can type each entry and its page number using an ASCII word processor. Assume your index source file is named INDEX. It includes several hundred entries similar to the following:

```
Radiation, 24
Argon, 15
Lithium, 8
Mercury, 11
```

When the source file is saved, you can use the following command to alphabetize it and save the result to a file named INDEX.SRT:

```
SORT <INDEX >INDEX.SRT
```

If the file is large, give your computer time to complete the job. The sorting process occurs in memory and sometimes takes several seconds, depending upon the size of your source file.

TYPICAL OPERATION

In this activity you use piping commands to redirect output to files. Begin at the OS/2 prompt, [C:\].

1. Type **DIR >DIRFILE** and press **Return**.
2. Type **DIR** and press **Return**. Notice the filename DIRFILE is displayed. You have piped the directory listing to the file. (You may use TYPE DIRFILE to verify that it is a copy of the disk directory.)
3. If you have a printer, check to see that it is ready for printing.
4. Type **TYPE DIRFILE >PRN** and press **Return**. Notice that the file DIRFILE is directed to your printer.
5. Type **TYPE DIRFILE >NEWFILE** and press **Return**.
6. Type **DIR** and press **Return**. Notice that you have piped the screen output of the TYPE command to the file NEWFILE. (You can verify the contents of NEWFILE using the TYPE command.)
7. Delete the practice files DIRFILE and NEWFILE from your disk:

   Type **DEL DIRFILE** and press **Return**.
   Type **DEL NEWFILE** and press **Return**.
8. Turn to Module 33 to continue the learning sequence.

Module 45
PRESENTATION MANAGER

DESCRIPTION

The Presentation Manager provides the windowing functions for OS/2. The Presentation Manager provides multiple windows on the screen at the same time, pull-down menus, and dialog boxes. These features provide you with a consistent interface to the computer. Each program looks, feels, and operates the same. Once you learn how to operate one program, you quickly learn how to operate any other Presentation Manager program since you don't have to learn the user interface, only the application. You don't have to memorize program commands as the programs are menu driven.

The Presentation Manager provides the same functions as the Session Manager plus windowing. The features within the Presentation Manager include the following:

- The capability to display the output from several applications on the screen at the same time.
- The handling of mouse input and keyboard input into the proper application.
- A uniform method of user interface. All applications appear and operate similarly, therefore learning to run a new application is minimized.
- The capability of outputting alphanumeric and graphic data to a wide range of output devices, including video, printers, and plotters.
- An enhanced user interface, including icons, menu bars, captions, borders and scroll bars.

For an application to take advantage of the Presentation Manager functions, it must be programmed to do so. An application that is not programmed to take advantage of the Presentation Manager functions can still execute with the Presentation Manager, but it cannot be windowed on the screen with other applications. Applications that attempt to access the screen directly cannot be windowed with other applications, either. Applications which are not programmed to use the Presentation Manager are called non-Presentation Manager applications.

PRESENTATION MANAGER USER INTERFACE

The Presentation Manager provides the following user interface:

- Start a Program
  You are presented a list of the available programs that you can run. You choose one and it begins to execute. You can also choose the Command Processor to enter OS/2 commands.

- Switch to a Running Program
  You are presented with a list of executing programs and you choose which one to work with next. The lists include both Presentation Manager and non-Presentation Manager applications.

- Control the Size and Position of an Application Window
  You can change the size and the position of the window of an application that is executing.
- Control the Printing Function
  You are able to choose the appropriate printing functions for an application.
- Use of OS/2 File System
  You are able to perform file commands, such as copying, deleting, and renaming files.
- Control Presentation Manager Parameters
  You can change the Presentation Manager's default parameters.

PRESENTATION MANAGER SCREEN

When you begin an application it appears on the screen. A Presentation Manager application appears in a window and non-Presentation Manager applications are given the whole screen. The window for a Presentation Manager application is rectangular and may overlap another window, with only the top window being visible. Note that you can, as necessary, bring a window that is overlapped to the top so that it is completely visible.

An example of how a screen with windows may appear is:

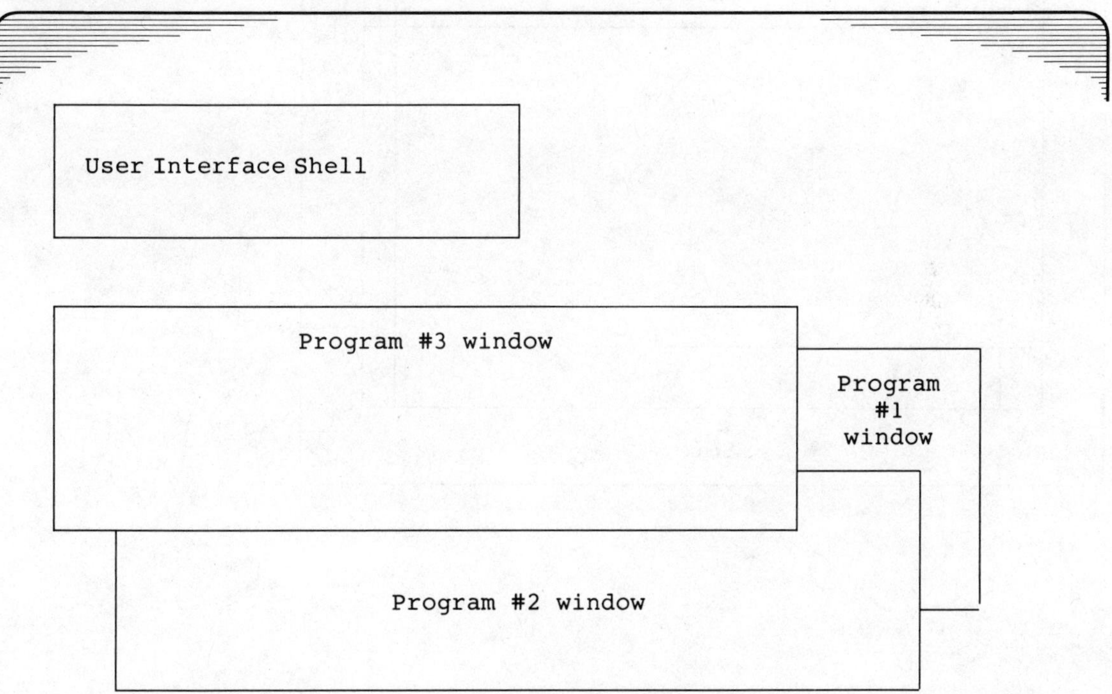

Windows

The windows displayed by the Presentation Manager are more than just rectangles. The inside of the window is called the client area. Around the border of the window, called the frame window, are a number of optional features. These features include the following:

- Borders
- Caption
- Scroll Bar
- Menu Bar
- System Icon
- Maximize and Minimize Icons

Description of Presentation Manager window:

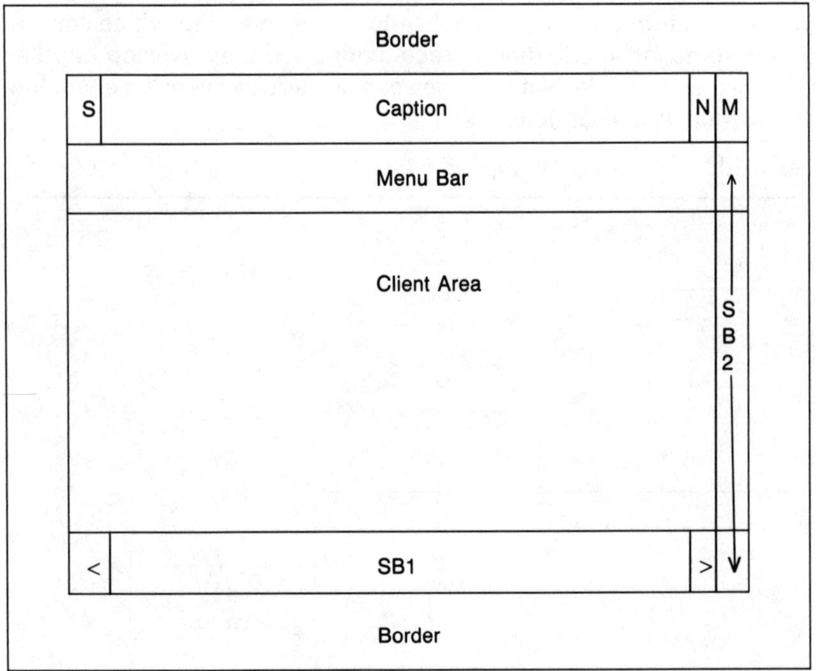

Where: S is the system icon
M is the maximize icon
N is the minimize icon
SB1 is the thumb mark for the horizontal scroll bar
SB2 is the thumb mark for the vertical scroll bar

Window Border	An application has four options for displaying the border: 1. Normal border 2. Heavy border 3. Thin border 4. No border
Caption	The caption to a window is called the window name. When you are interacting with a particular window, the caption bar of that window is highlighted.
Scroll Bars	There are two scroll bars. The vertical scroll bar is used to move the data within the window up and down. The horizontal scroll bar is used to move the data within the window right and left.
Menu Bar	An application places option that you can select on the menu bar. When you select an item on the menu bar, either a pull-down menu appears or a command is sent to the application.
System Icon	The system icon is an icon that you use to activate the system menu for a window. From the system menu you can move and size the window.
Maximize Icon	The maximize icon is an icon that you use to select the maximum size for a window for a particular application.
Minimize Icon	The minimize icon is an icon that you use to select the minimum size for a window for a particular application.

Menu Bar — User Controls

The Menu Bar with pull down menus provide you with a simple interface to the application you are running. Select the desired menu item and either a pull-down menu appears or a command is sent to the application. A pull-down menu example follows.

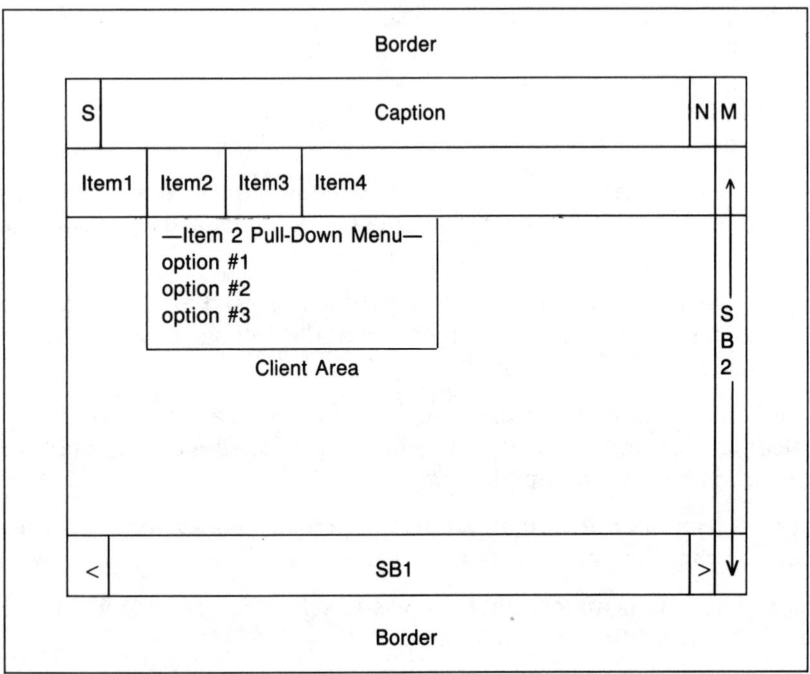

From within the pull-down window, you can select the desired option. Dialog boxes are also windows that prompt you for input, like a filename or confirmation for a particular program function.

The Presentation Manager is presented here in only a very brief summary. The Presentation Manager is so large that it requires a complete book to cover it satisfactory. However, this simple introduction should provide you with enough information to get started and experiment with a Presentation Manager application.

Turn to Module 13 to continue the learning sequence.

Module 46

PRINT

DESCRIPTION

The PRINT command is an external OS/2 command that prints a file on a printer or other output device. When used with the SPOOL command, PRINT can print one or more files while you are performing other operations. To print, the files must be standard text (or ASCII) files containing characters compatible with those used by your printer. The general form of the PRINT command is

```
PRINT /d:lpt1 FILENAME
```

where /d:lpt1 specifies that the output device is lpt1, and FILENAME specifies what file to print.

If you have the SPOOL command running in the background, the PRINT command spools the file to the spool-file and then returns immediately to the system prompt. Now while your document prints by the SPOOL command, you can perform other operations. This process is called *print spooling* or *concurrent printing*.

If you do not have the SPOOL command running in the background, then the PRINT command prints the file on the printer and does not return the system prompt until the file is completely printed. If you are not using the SPOOL command, then the PRINT command runs just like the following COPY command:

```
copy filename lpt1
```

The PRINT command lets you enter a list of filenames. For example, if you want to type NOTE1, MOMS.LTR, and a file on the disk in drive B called MYSTERY.TXT, the command is

```
PRINT /d:lpt1 NOTE1 MOMS.LTR B:MYSTERY.TXT
```

NOTE1 is printed first. When NOTE1 finishes printing, a form feed occurs at the end of the file and then MOMS.LTR starts printing at the top of a new page. As you might suspect, B:MYSTERY.TXT is printed last.

If you are not using the spooler, then only one OS/2 session can be printing at any one time. If you start two printing applications at the same time without the spooler, then the data being printed from the two applications is intermixed on the printer. If you have two or more printers, then you can be printing on more than one printer at the same time. Simply reroute the printer output in one session to LPT2, LPT3, or one of the COM ports if you have a serial printer.

The PRINT command offers several command options that work in conjunction with the SPOOL command. These are:

/B Indicates binary file. PRINT prints the entire file and does not interpret the Ctrl-Z characters as end-of-file characters.

/T Terminate all queued files. To clear out your print queue, use the command

```
PRINT /T
```

The print queue is emptied.

/C Cancel the named file(s) from the print queue. To cancel B:MYSTERY.TXT from your print queue, you can type the command

```
PRINT B:MYSTERY.TXT /C
```

The file b:mystery.txt is removed from the print queue. The /C parameter with no filename cancels the printing of the current spool file.

APPLICATIONS

The PRINT command is a time saving utility if you want to print one or more large text files while performing other computer operations. For example, if you want to print a long program listing while you work on an electronic spreadsheet, use PRINT with SPOOL. While the program is being listed on your printer, you can work with your spreadsheet program.

You also can queue up a large list of files for printing. While they are being printed, you can work on other things around the office or home. However, check that you have enough paper and ribbon in your printer before leaving printing unattended.

TYPICAL OPERATION

In this activity you use the PRINT command to queue up three files for printing. Begin at the OS/2 prompt, [C:\].

1. Check to see that your printer is on, unless you wish not to actually print the named files.
2. Create a practice file as follows:
   a. Type **COPY CON FILE1** and press **Return**.
   b. Type **This is a test file**, and press **Return**.
   c. Press **Ctrl-Z** and **Return**.
3. Copy the practice file to two other files with the following commands:
   a. Type **COPY FILE1 FILE2** and press **Return**.
   b. Type **COPY FILE1 FILE3** and press **Return**.
4. Type **PRINT /d:lpt1 FILE1 FILE2 FILE3** and press **Return**.
5. Notice that if the prompt does not return until all three files are printed, you do not have the spooler running. If the prompt does return before all three files are printed, then the spooler is loaded on your computer.
6. If the spooler is loaded, go on to Step 10.
7. Type **DETACH SPOOL C:\SPOOL /D:LPT1 /O:LPT1** and press **Return** to start the spooler.
8. Now repeat Steps 1 through 4 with the SPOOL command on. Notice the prompt returns as soon as the third file is spooled, such that you can be working while the files are printing. The SPOOL command is in Module 56.
9. Delete the practice files from your disk by typing **DEL FILE?** and pressing **Return**.
10. Turn to Module 21 to continue the learning sequence.

Module 47

PRINTING OPERATIONS

DESCRIPTION

OS/2 allows you print text-type (ASCII) files and the information displayed on a screen in several ways. You can:

1. Print displayed text by pressing Shift-PrtSc.
2. Display and print information concurrently by pressing Ctrl-P and:
   a. Using a command (like DIR) to display information.
   b. Using the TYPE command to display a text file on the screen.

   Concurrent printing is switched off by pressing Ctrl-P a second time.
3. Use the COPY command to copy a file to PRN, LPT1, LPT2, or LPT3 for parallel-type printers or COM1 through COM8 for serial-type printers.
4. Use the PRINT command followed by the printer device name and filename.
5. Use the OS/2 TYPE and piping commands to redirect the screen display to a printer device port.
6. OS/2 has a print spooler that you can optionally run. See Module 56 for complete details on the SPOOL command. The print spooler intercepts all output to the designated printer devices and writes it to a file and then prints the file. While you document prints, you can perform other operations. This process is called *print spooling* or *concurrent printing*.

USING THE PrtSc KEY The PrtSc key is used by OS/2 to send files to your printer. On most computers, you first press and hold Shift; then press PrtSc and whatever is displayed on the screen is sent to your printer.

USING Ctrl-P Pressing and holding the Ctrl key while typing P "toggles" OS/2's simultaneous print mode on. When on, lines of text are displayed and simultaneously printed. To stop simultaneous printing, just press Ctrl-P again. Assume that you want to make a hard copy of a file named NOTE on the disk in drive B:. You can type

`TYPE B:NOTE` (Don't press Return yet.)

press Ctrl-P; then press Return. Your file is displayed and printed at the same time. When printing is finished, the OS/2 prompt is redisplayed. Press Ctrl-P to turn off simultaneous printing.

You can also cause text that you type from the keyboard to be printed as you type. If you want to print a few lines on paper, such as an address or telephone number, press Ctrl-P, type ECHO, and then press Ctrl-J to force a line feed. Type the information ending each line with Ctrl-J. When you finish typing the note, press Ctrl-J several times to advance the paper. Finally, press Return to end the file. To turn off simultaneous printing, press Ctrl-P again.

USING THE SPOOL COMMAND The SPOOL command has several options that are described in detail in Module 56. For now, you should know that the SPOOL command lets you put one or more designated files into a list (or *print queue*). Once listed, the files are printed in the order listed as you perform other operations. Some people call this *print spooling*, while others call it *concurrent printing*. The SPOOL command takes printer output from all your applications, including printer output from the DOS Mode, simultaneously and separates each print job in the print queue so they don't intermix.

USING THE COPY COMMAND You can copy a text file from disk to your printer with the COPY command if you use a printer device name as a target name. To illustrate, assume that you want to copy your NOTE file from the disk in drive B to your printer. Just type COPY B:NOTE LPT1: and press Return to print the file.

USING THE PRINT COMMAND The PRINT command has several options that are described in detail in Module 46. The PRINT command lets you print a file to a designated printer or output device. Just type PRINT /d:LPT1 B:NOTE and press Return to print the file.

USING THE OS/2 TYPE AND PIPING COMMANDS OS/2 features piping commands that permit redirection of screen output to a device of your choice. This is described in detail in Module 44. To redirect screen output to your printer, the command TYPE *filename* >PRN redirects the typed file from screen output to printer output.

APPLICATIONS

Having all of the many OS/2 printing options available lets you print files and obtain paper copies (sometimes called *hard copy*) of display screens in a number of ways. You should know that many printing methods are available. Once you experiment with them, you should find the techniques that best satisfy your personal needs. Then, you can easily produce quick notes and reproduce displayed screens on paper.

TYPICAL OPERATION

In this activity you use the three different OS/2 printing techniques. Begin at the OS/2 prompt, [C:\].

1. Check to see that your printer is properly connected and turned on.
2. Type **ECHO test line advance**, and press **Ctrl-J** a few times to advance lines on the screen.
3. Press **Ctrl-P**, type **This is a note to myself.**, and then press **Ctrl-J** three times to advance the paper.
4. Press **Ctrl-P** to turn off printing.
5. Press **Return** to redisplay the OS/2 prompt and check the printed results on your printer.
6. Type **DIR** and press **Return** to display a disk directory.
7. Press **Shift-PrtSc**; notice that the displayed text is printed.
8. Type **DIR >PRN** and press **Return** for a hard copy of your directory.
9. Experiment with these and other print options to expand your familiarity with OS/2 printing operations.
10. Turn to Module 56 to continue the learning sequence.

Module 48

PROMPT

DESCRIPTION

The PROMPT command is an external OS/2 command. You can use this command to configure an OS/2 prompt to your liking. Many computer users want to display more information than a simple disk drive designator, such as A> or C>. People who are inexperienced in the use of an OS/2-based computer may be confused by this cryptic display. The PROMPT command gives you the ability to make the prompt more meaningful. For example, you may wish to display a prompt that says "Command?."

When entering the PROMPT command, it is followed by a space and either text or a dollar sign ($) followed by a special character. The dollar sign must precede the special character to have the desired effect. Special characters that are used with the dollar sign are contained in the following list:

$x	*Description*
$_	Moves the cursor to the next line (carriage return/line feed)
$$	Displays $ (dollar sign)
$a	Displays & character
$b	Displays ¦ (vertical bar)
$c	Displays (character
$d	Displays the system date
$e	The Escape character (∧[)
$f	Displays) character
$g	Displays > (greater than)
$h	Backspaces (and erases) the previous character
$i	Displays HELP line on top line of screen
$l	Displays < (less than)
$n	Displays the default drive letter
$p	Displays the default drive and directory pathname
$q	Displays = (equal sign)
$s	Displays a leading space
$t	Displays the system time
$v	Displays the OS/2 version number

The only way to appreciate what the PROMPT command does is to try a few examples. The following list illustrates commands and resulting prompts. Notice that examples are shown for subdirectories as well as main directories.

Command	*Displayed Results*
PROMPT Command?	Command?
PROMPT pq	
Main directory prompt	A:\=
WP subdirectory prompt	A:\WP=
PROMPT pg	
Main directory prompt	A:\>
DB subdirectory prompt	A:\DB>
PROMPT [$p] ; DEFAULT OS/2 PROMPT	
Main directory prompt	[A:\]
DB subdirectory prompt	[A:\DB]
PROMPT $p $d tg	
Main directory prompt	A:\ Fri 10-21-1988 11:05:32.09>
SS subdirectory prompt	A:\SS Fri 10-21-1988 11:06:16.74>
PROMPT lp$g	
Main directory prompt	<A:\>
DB subdirectory prompt	<A:\DB>
PROMPT $p:Command?	
Main directory prompt	A:\:Command?
123 subdirectory prompt	A:\123:Command?

If your terminal supports ANSI escape sequences and you have ANSI (see Module 4), you can use escape sequences in your prompt commands.

PROMPT $e[7m[$p]$e[m	
Main directory prompt	[A:\]
DB subdirectory prompt	[A:\DB]

- This prompt string displays the OS/2 default prompt in reverse video and returns to normal video for other text.

If the character following the $ is unrecognized, it is ignored and not displayed.

APPLICATIONS

Being able to design a prompt of your own is a convenient tool. Some experienced OS/2 users like to display the directory path ($p) and time ($t). Knowing the present subdirectory is particularly helpful when using a fixed disk system. It is easy to get lost in the subdirectory maze. However, by using the PROMPT $p command form, the subdirectory path designator is always displayed as part of the OS/2 prompt. The author uses PROMPT [$p] as a line in his STARTUP.CMD and HELP.CMD files, and PROMPT [REAL $p] in his AUTOEXEC.BAT and HELP.BAT files. Note that the author likes to know when he is in DOS Mode so he edited the HELP.BAT file furnished with OS/2 to reflect his "prompt" preference.

TYPICAL OPERATION

In this activity you use the PROMPT command to design a few prompts of your own. Begin at the OS/2 prompt, [C:\].

1. Type **PROMPT $P?** and press **Return**. Your prompt should look like this:

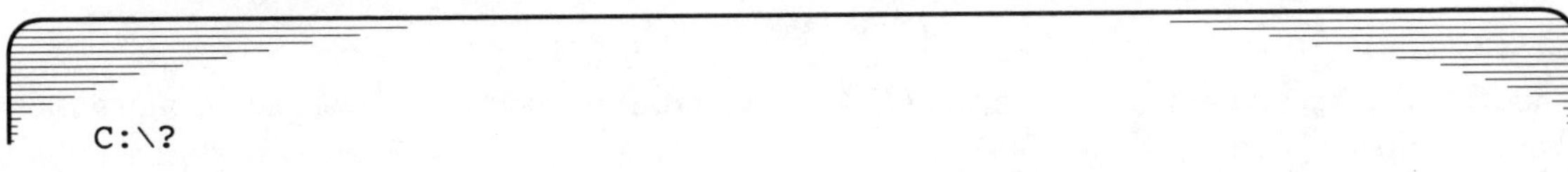

2. Type **PROMPT PD $T?** and press **Return**. Now check your prompt:

```
C:\Fri  10-21-88 19:25:05.31?
```

3. Type **PROMPT PG**, press **Return**, and check the resulting prompt:

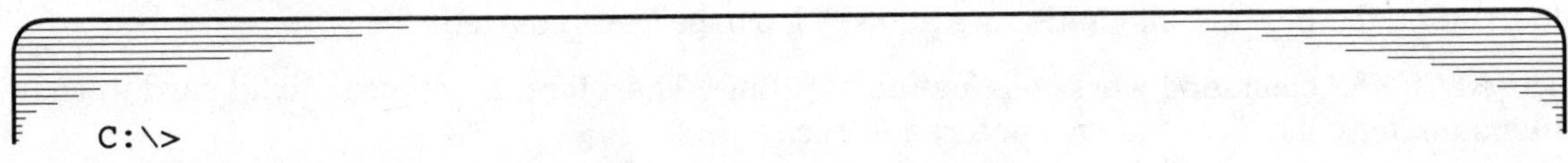

4. Type **PROMPT [$P]** and press **Return**. Your prompt now appears as it did when you started this module, like the following:

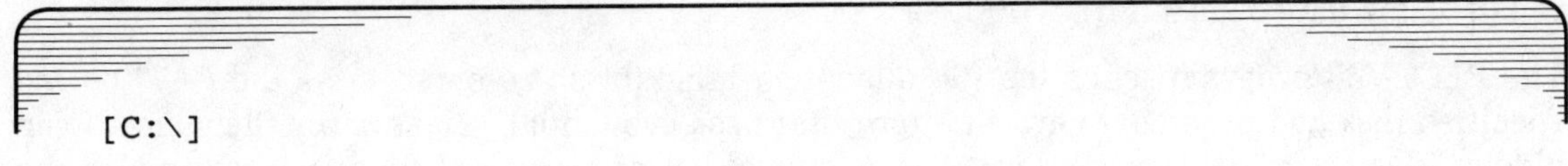

5. Turn to Module 19 to continue the learning sequence.

Module 49

RECOVER

DESCRIPTION

The RECOVER command is an external OS/2 command. It is used to recover one or more files from a defective disk.

FILES Use of RECOVER is best revealed through a common illustration of its use. Assume that you are experiencing problems reading or copying a file named LETTER.TXT in drive B:. You suspect data errors. You may be able to recover the file using the command RECOVER B:LETTER.TXT.

The bad data is often omitted by eliminating a bad disk sector from the file. If recovery is successful, you may be able to recreate the discarded data, which is preferable to having to recreate an entire file. You should be aware that recovered files often have extra data at the end. This sometimes can be deleted using a standard ASCII word processor. Be sure to check the end of the file and eliminate any added "garbage" as required.

The RECOVER command works on one file at a time. Therefore, if you use a wild card in your filename, only the first file encountered is recovered.

DIRECTORIES There are also times when a directory is damaged. The RECOVER program attempts to repair a damaged directory. Another illustration is in order. You suspect a bad directory on a disk in drive B. From your OS/2 directory (in either drive A: or C:), you may attempt repair using the command RECOVER B:.

The RECOVER program scans the file allocation table (often referred to as the *FAT*) on the specified disk and creates a new directory that uses sequential numbers for filenames. Even hidden files are placed in the directory. A typical list of recovered filenames resembles the following list. The REC file extension reveals the source of filename creation.

```
FILE0001.REC
FILE0002.REC
FILE0003.REC
FILE0004.REC
    :       :
```

NOTE

- The RECOVER command does not work on a network from a remote work station.
- The RECOVER command does not work on drives used in the SUBST or JOIN commands.

APPLICATIONS

The RECOVER command is a last resort when you have a problematic file. Before attempting to recover a file, you want to try to copy it to another disk. If the copy process encounters data errors, you are often given the opportunity to abort, retry, or ignore the problem. If you type I to ignore the data error, you may be able to copy most of the file. If you cannot copy the file, then you may wish to resort to the RECOVER command.

TYPICAL OPERATION

In this activity you use RECOVER to restructure the directory of a scratch disk. Begin at the OS/2 prompt, [C:\].

1. Place a scratch disk in drive A:.
2. Type **COPY C:\OS2\F*.* A:** and press **Return**.
3. Type **RECOVER B:** and press **Return**. Notice the following display:

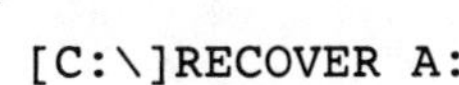

```
[C:\]RECOVER A:

Press ENTER to begin recovery of the
file[s] on drive A:
```

4. Press **Return** and notice the following message:

```
3 file(s) recovered
```

(Note that the number of files and the file sizes will vary between versions of OS/2.)

5. Type **DIR A:** and press **Return**; notice the filenames in the directory listing:

```
[C:\]DIR A:

 Volume in drive A has no label
 Directory of A:\

FILE0001 REC    5120    6-23-85    8:25p
FILE0002 REC   17408    6-23-85    8:25p
FILE0003 REC   18432    6-23-85    8:25p
3 File(s)   321536 bytes free

[C:\]
```

6. Delete the files on the disk in drive A: by typing **DEL A:*.REC** and pressing **Return**. The disk in drive A: is now blank.
7. Turn to Module 41 to continue the learning sequence.

Module 50

RENAME

DESCRIPTION

The RENAME command is an internal OS/2 command. It is used to change the name of one or more files. The RENAME command is straightforward and easy to use. The general form of the RENAME command is

```
REN OLDNAME.EXT NEWNAME.EXT
```

Either the entire word RENAME or the short form REN are permitted. Most users prefer the short form.

Several examples are provided to illustrate several forms of the RENAME command:

REN B:OL'NAME NEWNAME—This changes the file OL'NAME located on the disk in drive B to NEWNAME.

REN *.XYZ *.PRG—This changes the extension XYZ to PRG on all filenames located on the disk in the default drive.

REN LETTER *.FRM—This changes the filename LETTER to LETTER.FRM.

The following examples illustrate the use of pathnames with RENAME:

REN C:\WS\BOOK\CHAPT1.TXT CH1.BK—The filename CHAPT1.TXT in the second-level directory C:\WS\BOOK is changed to CH1.BK.

REN C:\DB*.DAT *.PRG—This changes the extension DAT to PRG on all filenames in the DB subdirectory of drive C.

APPLICATIONS

The RENAME command is a frequently used utility. It is called upon whenever you wish you had used a different name for a file. Although a long, descriptive name like "CHAPTER1.TXT" is easy to remember, you may regret having to type an eight-character filename every time you use it. It is both faster and less error prone to type something like "CH1." The RENAME command is helpful when a name change is called for.

The RENAME command is also useful when you want to change an entire series of filenames. A real-world example of this is when you rename batch files used with the PC/MS-DOS operating system files to OS/2 named batch files. The PC/MS-DOS extension for batch files is .BAT, while OS/2-based batch files use the extension .CMD. You can use the RENAME command to make the change from a .BAT to .CMD in a single pass. The command REN *.BAT *.CMD does the trick.

There are instances when you want to use several versions of the same program configured for different printers or help levels. You can use RENAME to provide descriptive names for each version of a program file. However, never modify the extensions .COM or .EXE, as this renders the file inoperable until it is changed back to a .COM or .EXE file, respectively.

TYPICAL OPERATION

In this activity you use the RENAME command to rename a file temporarily. You will check the directory to verify the change and then change it back again. Begin at the OS/2 prompt, [C:\].

1. List a directory of your OS/2 files by typing **DIR C:\OS2** and pressing **Return**. Notice the filename CHKDSK.COM in the following display:

```
[C:\]DIR C:\OS2

 Volume in drive C has no label
 Directory of  C:\OS2

FORMAT   COM      6912   3-17-87  12:00p
CHKDSK   COM      6400   3-17-87  12:00p
SYS      COM      1680   3-17-87  12:00p
FIND     EXE      5888   3-17-87  12:00p
   :        :        :        :          :
```

2. Rename the CHKDSK.COM file to CHK.COM by typing **REN C:\OS2\CHKDSK.COM CHK.COM** and pressing **Return**.
3. List the directory to verify the filename change by typing **DIR C:\OS2** and pressing **Return**. Notice the filename CHK.COM has replaced CHKDSK.COM in the following display:

```
[C:\]DIR C:\OS2

 Volume in drive C has no label
 Directory of  C:\OS2

FORMAT   COM      6912   3-17-87  12:00p
CHK      COM      6400   3-17-87  12:00p    <--- Changed from CHKDSK.COM
SYS      COM      1680   3-17-87  12:00p
FIND     EXE      5888   3-17-87  12:00p
   :        :        :        :          :
```

4. Change the name back to CHKDSK.COM by typing **REN C:\OS2\CHK.COM CHKDSK.COM** and pressing **Return**.
5. Turn to Module 12 to continue the learning sequence.

Module 51
REPLACE

DESCRIPTION

The REPLACE command is an external OS/2 command used selectively to replace files on the target disk with files having the same name on the source disk. The selection process is controlled by typing a switch, represented by /X in the following example. The command form is

```
REPLACE A:\PATHNAME C:\PATHNAME\FILENAME /X
```

The value of X controls the way REPLACE operates. Each of the available values are described in the following list:

/A Copies specified files that are not present on the target disk. This prevents overwriting files that exist on the target drive. The /A is never used with /S, described below.

/P Prompts you as each file is encountered on the target drive

```
Replace FILENAME? (Y/N)_
```

Answer the above prompt with a Y (for YES), else N (for NO), depending on whether you want to replace the file or not.

/R Replaces read-only and unprotected files on the target drive.

/S Searches all directories on the target drive for filenames that match those on the source drive.

/W Displays the prompt "Press any key to begin replacing file(s)." This option is used to let you insert a diskette before REPLACE begins its file search. If both /W and /A are used, the prompt takes the form "Press any key to begin adding file(s)."

The following REPLACE command examples are provided for clarification and for use as models:

REPLACE A:*.* B: Replaces all files on disk B: with those files on disk A: having the same filename.

REPLACE A:*.* B: /S Replaces all files in all subdirectories on disk B: with those files on disk A: having the same filename.

REPLACE A:*.DAT B: /S /P Replaces selected files in all subdirectories on disk B: with those files on disk A: having the same filename with the extension .DAT. Selection is made by typing Y or N in response to the (Y/N)? prompt.

APPLICATIONS

The REPLACE command is particularly valuable in ensuring that all files on one disk are copied to another. Any file or series of files that is updated can be copied from one disk to another without adding unwanted or unnecessary files to the target diskette. For example, if you wish to maintain a selection of text or data files on a backup diskette, you can use REPLACE to ensure that the latest versions of all files are copied from one disk to another. The REPLACE command eliminates the need for you to have to make a list of the selected filenames and copy them individually with the COPY command.

TYPICAL OPERATION

In this activity you copy two files to a destination diskette and then use REPLACE to see how the files are selectively copied. In addition, you use the /P option to display each filename before it is copied. Begin by formatting a floppy diskette for use as the destination disk. Place the destination disk in drive A:. The following procedure uses C: as the source disk and A: as the target disk. Start at the OS/2 prompt, [C:\].

1. Use the COPY command to copy the FORMAT.COM and DISKCOPY.COM files as follows:
   a. Type **COPY C:\OS2\FORMAT.COM A:** and press **Return.**
   b. Type **COPY C:\OS2\DISKCOPY.COM A:** and press **Return.**
2. Type **REPLACE C:\OS2*.* A: /P**. Notice that each of the two filenames are displayed and you are prompted for a copy decision. Type **Y** to copy each of the files.
3. You may experiment with other forms of the REPLACE command until you are satisfied that you understand its operation.
4. Turn to Module 65 to continue the learning sequence.

Module 52

RESTORE

DESCRIPTION

The RESTORE command is an external OS/2 command. RESTORE is usually used to copy files back to a fixed disk after they have been copied to floppy disks using BACKUP (Module 9).

Like the BACKUP command, RESTORE offers many options. It copies files from floppy disks to floppy disks, from fixed disk to floppy disks, from fixed disk to fixed disk, and floppy disks to a fixed disk. You can use RESTORE to copy one or more files from a single directory, all files within a directory, or all files in all directories.

Some forms of the RESTORE command are:

RESTORE A: C:\ /S—This command copies every file in every directory from the floppy disk(s) in drive A to the fixed disk (drive C). The /S designates all subdirectories. This command form normally means that you are restoring all files back to your fixed disk from several floppy disks.

RESTORE A: C:*.TXT—This command form copies all files having the extension TXT from the active directory to the fixed disk.

RESTORE A: C: /P—The /P parameter causes the program to prompt you before copying files that have changed since they were last backed up. You also are prompted if a file is marked "read only." The prompt allows you to selectively prevent files from being restored.

[C:\]RESTORE A: C:\PATH1\PATH2*.EXE—Here, the "[C:\]" represents the fixed disk OS/2 prompt and is not part of the command. This command causes the system to prompt you to insert the backup disk in drive A that contains the file(s) you want to restore. In this case, the files are those with the extension EXE. When the disk is inserted, pressing any key restores the files to the designated subdirectory.

RESTORE A: C:\WP\WS*.*—This command assumes a subdirectory WP for *word processing*, and one or more filenames within that subdirectory that begin with WS. These files are restored from the floppy disk in drive A to the fixed disk.

RESTORE A: C: /M—Restores only those files that have been modified since the last backup operation.

RESTORE A: C: /N—Restores only those files that no longer exist on the target disk.

RESTORE A: C: /A:07-01-88—Restores only the files that have been modified ON or AFTER the date of 07-01-88.

RESTORE A: C: /B:07-01-88—Restores only the files that have been modified ON or BEFORE the date of 07-01-88.

RESTORE A: C: /E:10:05:20—Restores only the files that have been modified ON or EARLIER than the time of 10:05:20.

RESTORE A: C: /L:10:05:20—Restores only the files that have been modified ON or LATER than the time of 10:05:20.

NOTE

The RESTORE command does not restore the system files (OS2BIO.COM, OS2DOS.COM, CMD.EXE, COMMAND.COM). The system files are not required to be backed up as they are large and are permanently backed up on your original OS/2 operating systems disks.

APPLICATIONS

The primary application of the RESTORE command is to restore backed-up files to a fixed disk. You can restore all files or selected files depending on the form of the command you use. Many OS/2 users choose to backup and restore individual directories rather than entire fixed disks because of the time it takes to restore several million characters to a large fixed disk.

TYPICAL OPERATION

In this activity you use RESTORE to restore selected files. The procedure assumes you have a fixed disk designated drive C:. If the drive is E:, then substitute E: for C:. Start at the OS/2 prompt, [C:\].

1. Place the backup disk created in Module 9 in drive A:.
2. Type **RESTORE A: C:*.EXE** and press **Return**.
3. Check for a prompt that resembles the following:

```
[C:\]RESTORE A: C:*.EXE

Insert backup diskette 01 in drive A:
Press Enter when ready.
```

4. Press **Return**; notice the message that displays the date that the files were backed up. Watch the filenames appear on the screen as they are copied.
5. Turn to Module 7 to continue the learning sequence.

Module 53

SESSION MANAGER (PROGRAM SELECTOR)

DESCRIPTION

The Session Manager is a menu driven facility that allows you to start the execution of a new program and to switch to any executing program from a menu. When you select a program to execute, it runs in the context of an OS/2 session. There can only be one DOS MODE session running at a time, but there can be many Protected Mode sessions running at any one time. All of this means that you can run many programs at the same time, and you can switch to any of them very easily through a menu.

The Session Manager manages the currently operating programs, called sessions. From the Session Manager you can select any active session. When you switch to a session, that session receives the keyboard input and mouse input and displays its output on the screen. From the Session Manager you can start programs in a new session. Note that with the START command (Module 57), you can also start a session which the Session Manager maintains for you.

When OS/2 boots and the Session Manager begins executing, the Session Manager displays the PROGRAM SELECTOR MENU. From the PROGRAM SELECTOR MENU you can:

- Start executing a new program
- Switch to a running program
- Update/change entries within the START A PROGRAM MENU
- Get Help

A summary of the Session Managers program selector selection options are:

Start a Program	A list of programs that can be started by the user by making a choice on the menu. The OS/2 command processor is one option.
Switch to a Running Program	A list of all currently executing programs. You can switch to any program by making a choice on the menu.
Update	Add, change, or delete entries in the start list.
Help	Display Help windows.

When you start executing a new program, the keyboard and monitor are switched to this program. If you switch to a running program, the keyboard and monitor are switched to the program and the last screen for the application is restored to the monitor. The keyboard and the monitor are attached to this application until you either switch to another application or back to the Session Manager. Within any application program, by entering Ctrl-Esc, you return to the PROGRAM SELECTOR MENU in the Session Manager; or by entering Alt-Esc, you switch to the next program in the Session Manager's executing program list.

When you return to the Session Manager and it displays the PROGRAM SELECTOR MENU, a screen similar to the following one appears:

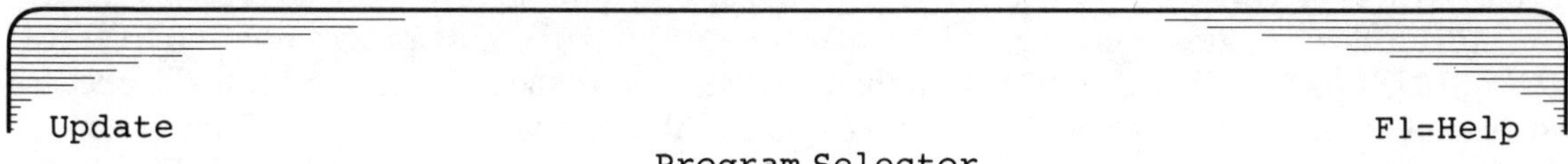

```
Update                                                             F1=Help
                            Program Selector

Use ← or → to move between Start a Program and Switch to Running Program.
Use ← or → to select, then press Enter.  F10 then Enter to Update lists.

        Start a Program                 Switch to a Running Program

    [ OS/2    Command Prompt            [  MS-DOS Command Prompt
    [ WPX     Word Processing           [  OS/2   Command Prompt
                                        [  WPX    Word Processing
```

From the PROGRAM SELECTOR MENU the following keys are active:

- Left and right arrow keys
- Up and down arrow keys
- Return key
- F1 function key
- F10 function key

The left and right arrow keys alternately select the START A PROGRAM or the SWITCH TO A RUNNING PROGRAM window. The up and down arrow keys allow you to go up and down the list of entries in the START A PROGRAM and the SWITCH TO A RUNNING PROGRAM windows. Pressing F10 selects the UPDATE MENU, pressing F1 selects HELP, and pressing Return selects the current highlighted program in either START A PROGRAM or the SWITCH TO A RUNNING PROGRAM window.

SWITCH TO A RUNNING PROGRAM

In the Switch to a Running Program window, by using the up and down arrow keys and pressing Return, you switch the keyboard and monitor to that process. Remember that OS/2 is a multitasking operating system, so all tasks shown in this window are executing; however, they may be suspended because they are waiting upon operator input. Also, remember that detached background tasks are NOT shown in this window. If you select the DOS Command Prompt entry, then the Session Manager transfers control to the program running in the DOS Mode (command.com). If you select the OS/2 Command Prompt entry, then the Session Manager transfers control to CMD.EXE in the Protected Mode. From either session, enter Ctrl-Esc and you return to the PROGRAM SELECTOR MENU in the Session Manager.

START A PROGRAM

In the START A PROGRAM WINDOW, by using the up and down arrow keys and pressing Return, you start a new program running. OS/2 makes an entry for the new program in the SWITCH TO A RUNNING PROGRAM window and then switches the keyboard and monitor to the process you selected. From the PROGRAM SELECTOR menu above, if you selected the OS/2 Command Prompt, then the Session Manager opens a new session and starts executing CMD.EXE in the new session. If you have a file named OS2INIT.CMD, the command processor executes it. The Session Manager also adds an entry for this session into the SWITCH TO A RUNNING PROGRAM window. If you return to the Session Manager, it displays the PROGRAM SELECTOR MENU and the following screen appears:

```
Update                                                            F1=Help
                            Program Selector

Use ← or → to move between Start a Program and Switch to Running Program.
Use ← or → to select, then press Enter.  F10 then Enter to Update lists.

        Start a Program                   Switch to a Running Program

   [ OS/2    Command Prompt              [ DOS     Command Prompt
   [ WPX     Word Processing             [ OS/2    Command Prompt
                                         [ WPX     Word Processing
                                         [ OS/2    Command Prompt 2
```

From the SWITCH TO A RUNNING PROGRAM window, you can select OS/2 Command Prompt session to execute OS/2 commands or application programs. Note that the first copy of the OS/2 Command Prompt is listed as CMD.EXE in the SWITCH TO A RUNNING PROGRAM window.

UPDATE OPTION

From the PROGRAM SELECTOR menu, by pressing F10 and pressing Return, you select the Update option. From the Update option, you can add, delete, or change entries in the START A PROGRAM WINDOW. Use the up and down arrow keys to make your selection and press Return to perform your selection.

Your options are:

Add a program	Add a program to the Session Managers list.
Delete a program	Delete a program for the list.
Change a program	Change the information for a program.
Refresh	Update the switch list to reflect the current Session Manager's list. This includes any terminations or start in sessions that were active when you selected the update option.

When you select the ADD option on the Update window, an Add a Program Title window appears. Enter the program title, the optional pathname, and the optional program parameters. When you have completed this, OS/2 makes an entry for this program in the Start A Program window. The program title is the name you want displayed in the Start A Program window. The pathname includes the drive, directory, and filename of the program to execute when the program title is selected. The program parameters are any optional parameters that the program requires each time it begins execution. If the parameter field must be input by the operator each time the program is selected, then place a question mark (?) in this field and the system will prompt you for the parameters each time you select this program.

When you select the DELETE option on the Update window, a Delete a Program Title window appears. Use the up and down arrow keys to select the program to delete and press Return. A Verification window appears and requires confirmation before the program title is deleted from the Start a Program window.

When you select the CHANGE option on the Update window, a Change a Program window appears. Use the up and down arrow keys to select the program to change and press Return. Now the program title, the pathname, and the programs parameters are displayed and you can add or change them as you need to. Press Return when you have made the needed changes. Next time this program is selected, the new pathname and/or parameters is used. Note that the pathname and the program parameters fields are actually 64 characters in length even though you can only view 30 at one time. These two fields can be scrolled left or right to completely view the fields. See the list below for editing key definitions.

Up arrow	Move to previous field
Down arrow	Move to next field
Left arrow	Move cursor left one character
Right arrow	Move cursor right one character
Home	Beginning of fields window
End	End of fields window
Ins	Toggle insert mode
Del	Delete character under cursor
Ctrl-Left arrow	Beginning of field
Ctrl-Right arrow	End of data in field
Ctrl-Home	Move to first field in window
Ctrl-End	Move to last field in window
Alt-F7	Erase to end of field
F1	Help for this field

NOTE

For the inquiring mind, the Session Manager maintains the selection list in two files, Shell11f.aii and Shell11f.aif. These files are saved so that all adds, changes, and deletes are maintained and are reflected each time you boot your computer.

HELP OPTION

Pressing F1 in the PROGRAM SELECTOR window selects Help, and a Help window appears. From the Help window, you can receive more Help by pressing F1, you can get the Help index by pressing F5, and by pressing F9, you can get the Help window on Function Keys.

When you press F9 the following window is displayed:

```
   Help  -  Function Keys

            F1=Help
            F2=Switch to "Update"
            F5=Help Index
            F9=Key Assignments
           ESC=Cancel
         Enter=Read Screen /Display Next
        Alt+F6=Switch between Help
               and Panel
       Alt+Esc=Switch Task
      Ctrl+Esc=Display Program Selector
     Ctrl+Home=Beginning of Field
      Ctrl+End=End of Field

 Esc=Cancel     F1=Help
```

APPLICATIONS

The Session Manager is one way for you to begin execution of another application program or to transfer control to a running program. You need to know how to use the Session Manager in order to run multiple programs at the same time and how to move from one executing program to another. You also need to know how to start a program and how to add, change, and delete programs in the Start a Program window. You also need to know how to use the Help options.

Turn to Module 45 to continue the learning sequence.

Module 54

SET

DESCRIPTION

The SET command is an internal command. When SET is typed as a command without following text, in the form

```
SET
```

the SET command displays the current OS/2 "environment." For example, typing SET and pressing Return displays a screen similiar to the following:

```
[C:\OS2]SET
PATH=C:;C:\OS2
DPATH=C:\DATA;C:\OS2BOOK
PROMPT=[$P]
COMSPEC=C:\CMD.EXE
```

You can use SET to insert strings used by the OS/2 command processor that affect established system parameters. For example, if you want to change the command processor specification (COMSPEC) to another (this is not recommended for non-programmers) you can type

```
SET COMSPEC=PROC1.COM
```

where PROC1.COM is another command processor that performs functions similar to OS/2's standard CMD.EXE command processor.

You can set a parameter using a command similar to

```
SET PATH=C:\DB
```

When you use the SET command to display OS/2 environment settings, PATH = C:\DB is displayed. To cancel the path setting, type

```
SET PATH=
```

Displaying the settings now shows PATH = . Of course, the path setting can be changed using the PATH command itself.

```
[C:\OS2]SET PATH=
PATH=
DPATH=C:\DATA;C:\OS2BOOK
PROMPT=[$P]
COMSPEC=C:\CMD.EXE
```

APPLICATIONS

One of the most convenient uses of the SET command is reviewing the setup of the OS/2 environment. If you wish to view the current active directory paths and the PROMPT command form, you can use the SET command to see all of the OS/2 settings in a single display.

TYPICAL OPERATION

In this activity you use the SET command to view the OS/2 environment, to change the prompt parameters, and then to cancel the prompt parameters. Begin at the OS/2 prompt, [C:\].

1. Type **SET** and press **Return**. Check for a display similar to the following illustration. Note that the PATH and COMSPEC may be different and that other entries may be present. If you have an entry for the PROMPT command, write it down so that you can re-enter it in Step 6.

```
[C:\]SET
PATH=C:\OS2;C:\
COMSPEC=C:\CMD.EXE
PROMPT=[$P]
```

2. Type **SET PROMPT = $P:** and press **Return**.
3. Check the OS/2 environment again by typing **SET** and pressing **Return**. Notice that the new PROMPT command form is displayed.

```
[C:\]SET
PATH=C:\OS2;C:\
COMSPEC=C:\CMD.EXE
PROMPT=$P:
```

4. Cancel the prompt setting by typing **SET PROMPT =** and press **Return**.
5. Type **SET** and press **Return** again to check the OS/2 environment; notice that the canceled PROMPT setting is no longer displayed.

```
[C:\]SET
PATH=C:\OS2;C:\
COMSPEC=C:\CMD.EXE
```

6. If in Step 1 you saved the prompt entry, then do this step: Re-enter your prompt entry with the following command, but substituting your saved prompt command for the question mark:

   Type **SET PROMPT = ?** and press **Return**.
7. Turn to Module 8 to continue the learning sequence.

Module 55

SETCOM40

DESCRIPTION

The SETCOM40 command is an external OS/2 command that allows some DOS Mode programs to use a COM port that will not run with the OS/2 COM.SYS device driver. Note that some DOS Mode programs still may not run, even with the SETCOM40 command.

To set the COM1 address for a DOS Mode program to use the serial port enter

```
SETCOM40 COM1=ON
```

To remove the COM1 from the DOS Mode enter

```
SETCOM40 COM1=OFF
```

Before using a serial port with the SETCOM40 command, make sure no OS/2 session is using the same serial port. Note that the SETCOM40 command does not change the baud rate or initialize the serial port.

APPLICATIONS

Some DOS Mode programs access the BIOS to determine if a serial port is available before the program tries to access it directly. The SETCOM40 command places the serial port address into the BIOS to satisfy this type of program. The SETCOM40 command removes the serial port address from the BIOS when the OFF parameter is specified. If a DOS Mode program does not work with a serial port, then try executing the SETCOM40 program and then retry the DOS Mode program. The program may or may not work.

TYPICAL OPERATION

In this operation you enable COM1 serial port availability to a DOS Mode program. You then disable the COM1 serial port availability to the DOS Mode. Note that the DEVICE = COM01.SYS statement must be in the CONFIG.SYS file for this operation to work. Start at the DOS prompt.

1. Type **SETCOM40 COM1 = ON** and press **Return** to make the COM1 serial port available to the DOS Mode.
2. Type **SETCOM40 COM1 = OFF** and press **Return** to make the COM1 serial port not available to the DOS Mode.
3. Press **Ctrl-Esc** to return to Session Manager. Select OS/2 Command Prompt in the SWITCH TO A RUNNING PROGRAM window to return to OS/2 Mode.
4. Turn to Module 40 to continue the learning sequence.

Module 56

SPOOL

DESCRIPTION

The SPOOL command is an external OS/2 command that provides background printing while you are performing other operations. The print spooler (SPOOL command) intercepts all output to the designated print device and writes the data to a temporary spool file. Printer output captured includes output from the PRINT command, the print screen function, and from your application programs. The data is written to disk and then printed in the background while you perform other operations. This process is called *print spooling* or *concurrent printing*.

The form of the SPOOL command is

```
SPOOL PATHNAME /d:lpt1 /o:lpt1
```

where /d:lpt1 specifies lpt1 as the port connected with the print device, /o:lpt1 specifies that the output device is lpt1, and PATHNAME specifies in what directory to place the temporary spool file. The PATHNAME is optional. The default pathname is \SPOOL. The allowable output devices are LPT1, LPT2, LPT3, PRN, and COM1 through COM8. If you are using the serial ports, you must load the COM01.SYS device driver (Module 22).

The PRINT command offers several command options that work in conjunction with the SPOOL command. These are:

/T — Terminate all queued files. To clear out your print queue, use the command

```
PRINT /T
```

The spooler queue is emptied.

/C — Cancel the named file(s) from the print spooler queue. To cancel B:MYSTERY.TXT from your print queue, you can type the command

```
PRINT B:MYSTERY.TXT /C
```

The file b:mystery.txt is removed from the spooler queue.

```
PRINT /C
```

The file currently printing is cancelled and the next file in the spool queue is started printing.

The SPOOL command is normally placed in the CONFIG.SYS file. For example, to start the two spoolers, you can enter the following commands in the CONFIG.SYS file:

```
RUN=SPOOL C:\SPOOL /D:LPT1 /O:LPT1
RUN=SPOOL C:\SPOOL /D:LPT2 /O:LPT2
```

The SPOOL command can be placed in the STARTUP.CMD file. For example, to start two spoolers, you can enter the following commands in the STARTUP.CMD file (or the command prompt):

```
START SPOOL C:\SPOOL /D:LPT1 /O:LPT1
START SPOOL C:\SPOOL /D:LPT2 /O:LPT2
```

The SPOOL command can also be started with the DETACH command; for example,

```
DETACH SPOOL C:\SPOOL /D:LPT1 /O:LPT1
```

If the COM01.SYS device driver is loaded, any of the following commands print the output of LPT2 on the printer connected to COM2:

```
RUN=SPOOL C:\SPOOL /D:LPT2 /O:COM2
START SPOOL C:\SPOOL /D:LPT2 /O:COM2
DETACH SPOOL C:\SPOOL /D:LPT2 /O:COM2
```

APPLICATIONS

The SPOOL command is a time saving utility if you want to print while performing other computer operations. For example, if you want to print a long program listing while you work on an electronic spreadsheet, use the SPOOL command. While the program is being listed on your printer, you can work with your spreadsheet program.

You also can queue up a large list of files for printing. While they are being printed, you can work on other things around the office or home. However, check that you have enough paper and ribbon in your printer before leaving printing unattended.

TYPICAL OPERATION

Since the SPOOL command is so inter-related with the PRINT command, the typical operation of this module is combined with the PRINT command, which is the next module in your learning sequence.

Turn to Module 46 to continue the learning sequence.

Module 57
START

DESCRIPTION

The START command is an internal OS/2 command. The START command lets you begin another OS/2 session with a command and without going through the Session Manager or the Presentation Manager.

The form for the START command is

```
START "SESSION-NAME" PROGRAM program-arguments
```

where *PROGRAM* is your application program, batch (.cmd) file, or an OS/2 command you want to execute in another session. The session is added to the list of running programs that is maintained by the Session Manager.

To start another session and just have the CMD.EXE command processor running, enter the following:

```
START "SESSION2"
```

You can access this session through the Session Manager by selecting the entry called "SESSION2."

To start a process for end-of-day part1, you would enter the following:

```
START "EOD Part1" EOD-1
```

This command starts the EOD-1.CMD batch file. When the batch file ends, the session is at a CMD.EXE prompt as the session is still active. You can access this session through the Session Manager.

When you START a program, you can add parameters, input/output redirection, and piping functions. To start a process to sort your OS/2 commands directory and place the output into a file on drive A named OS2-SORT.DIR, enter the following command:

```
START "dir-sort" /c "DIR C:\OS2 ¦ C:\OS2\SORT >A:OS2-SORT.DIR"
```

When this sequence of commands completes, this session is exited and control is returned to the Session Manager because you added the /c option. Notice that the command to execute is in quotes. It is in quotes because of the redirection. For example, to start a process to sort your OS/2 commands directory and display the output on the screen but place the output of the START command in a file on drive A called OS2START.DIR, enter

```
START "dir-sort" /c DIR C:\OS2 ¦ C:\OS2\SORT >A:OS2START.DIR
```

Here the redirection is for the START command, not the DIR ¦ SORT commands.

The START command differs from the DETACH command (Module 21) in that the START command begins the execution of programs in the foreground, where DETACH begins programs in the background. Foreground programs have access to the video and keyboard since they can be selected through the Session Manager; background programs do not have access to the video or keyboard and cannot be accessed through the Session Manager. the START command functions just like the RUN command in the CONFIG.SYS file (Module 18).

APPLICATIONS

The primary uses of the START command is to start OS/2 programs automatically when you start your computer by placing START commands in your STARTUP.CMD file. Another use of the START command is to start programs that you have not yet entered into the Session Manager through the UPDATE function. The START function is also a handy means to get directory listings while you perform some other function. To do this, use the procedure in the Typical Operation section except route the output to the desired printer.

TYPICAL OPERATION

In this activity you use the START command to produce an alphabetical listing of your OS/2 directory and place the output on a floppy disk in drive A:. Begin at the OS/2 prompt, [C:\].

1. Insert a work floppy disk into drive A:.
2. Type **START "sort-dir" "DIR C:\OS2 ¦ C:\OS2\SORT > A:OS2-SORT.DIR"** and press **Return.**
3. Type **DIR** and press **Return**. Notice that while the directory of drive C: is listing, the light on drive A: is blinking as the output of the SORT command is being written to the diskette in drive A: in the newly started OS/2 session.
4. Type **TYPE A:OS2-SORT.DIR**. Notice that the output is an alphabetical list of the directory C:\OS2.
5. Type **DEL A:OS2-SORT.DIR** and press **Return** to delete the file OS2-SORT.DIR from drive A:.
6. Press **Ctrl-Esc** to select the Session Manager.
7. Notice the entry for "sort-dir." Select this entry with the arrow keys and press **Return.**
8. Type **EXIT** and press **Return** to terminate the newly started session.
9. Turn to Module 24 to continue the learning sequence.

Module 58
SYS

DESCRIPTION

The SYS command is an external OS/2 command. This command transfers the OS/2 system files OS2BIO.COM and OS2DOS.COM (IBMBIO and IBMDOS for IBM) to a specified target disk. Note that these file are hidden.

The SYS command has this form

```
SYS B:
```

When OS/2 is successfully transferred, the message "System transferred." is displayed. In this example, the system files are transferred to drive A:. The command processor is not transferred so you must copy it yourself.

In addition, to copy the files listed in the file FORMATS.TBL when you transfer the OS/2 system files, enter the following command:

```
SYS A: /S
```

The /S option informs the SYS command to also copy the files listed in the file FORMATS.TBL.

APPLICATIONS

The SYS command is normally used to update OS/2 on your computer with a new version of OS/2. The SYS command can also be used to place the system file on to a floppy disk, so that you can optionally boot from a floppy disk. It is necessary at times for some users to configure their OS/2 differently than the normal daily operation. For example, this can occur when one shares a computer with a programmer, say at night, or when the computer network is down.

TYPICAL OPERATION

In this activity you use the FORMAT and SYS commands to format a new (or used) disk and transfer the system. Begin at the OS/2 prompt, [C:\].

NOTE

In the following step, a *scratch* disk is one that you can use for practice. It should either be a new, blank disk or an old one containing obsolete data files that you no longer want.

1. Place a scratch disk in drive A and close the load lever.
2. Type **FORMAT A:** and press **Return**.
3. Once the disk is formatted, type **N** and press **Return** in response to the "Format another (Y/N)?" prompt.
4. Type **SYS A:** and press **Return**. When OS/2 is transferred, check the display:

```
[C:\]SYS A:

The system files have been transferred.

[C:\]
```

5. Turn to Module 64 to continue the learning sequence.

Module 59

TIME

DESCRIPTION

Like the DATE command, the TIME command is also one of OS/2's internal commands and is not seen when a directory of disk files is displayed. You can run the TIME command by typing TIME and pressing Return from the OS/2 prompt. The following screen is displayed:

```
[C:\]TIME
The current time is: 11:01:35.87
Enter the new time: _
```

The time expression is given in:

hours:minutes:seconds.hundredths of a second

Type the current hour and minute in the form 10:45 and press Return. The time is recorded by OS/2. The time input sets the time known to the computer and also the computer's clock. If the time is not important to you, you can respond to the TIME prompt by pressing Return, but this sets the time to 0:0.

You can also type TIME, the current time notation, and press Return to set the time. This command form inputs the date without displaying the OS/2 time prompt.

NOTE

You can change the TIME command format by changing the country command in the config.sys file. See Code Page Switching (Module 14) for more information.

APPLICATIONS

As in the DATE command, it is much easier to press the Return key than to enter the time notation. However, files that are saved to disk are tagged with the time and date. This lets you examine a directory to determine which files are most current. Therefore, it is best to set the clock to the current time. Some programs use the system time to display a clock on the screen.

Although it may seem like a lot of trouble to enter the time every time you turn on your computer, it is recommended for these reasons.

If entering the time becomes a nuisance, you can obtain a clock-calendar option board to eliminate the need to type the date and time every time you turn on your computer. Many computers come equipped from the manufacturer with a clock-calendar. These boards use a battery to maintain clock and calendar operation. Even when the computer is turned off or disconnected from the wall outlet, the clock and calendar continue to operate.

TYPICAL OPERATION

In this activity you use the TIME command to enter the current time. Check to see that your computer is properly connected. Begin at the OS/2 prompt, [C:\].

1. Type **TIME** and press **Return**; notice the TIME prompt.

```
[C:\]TIME
The current time is: 11:01:35.87
Enter the new time: _
```

2. Type the current time in the indicated form (separate the hour and minute with a colon) and press **Return**.
3. The current time is now recorded. To verify the current time, you can repeat Step 1. If you do not want to change the time, press **Return** to redisplay the OS/2 prompt. Pressing Return leaves the system time unchanged.
4. Turn to Module 37 to continue the learning sequence.

Module 60

TREE

DESCRIPTION

The TREE command is an external OS/2 command that displays all directory pathnames on the specified disk. For example, if you wish to view all directories contained on drive C:, you can type

```
TREE C:
```

A screen similar to the following is displayed:

```
[C:\]TREE C:

Directory Path Listing

Path: \BILL
Sub-directories:  LILBILL
                  WMJR

Path: \BILL\LILBILL
Sub-directories:  None

Path: \BILL\WMJR
Sub-directories:  None

Path: \TOM
Sub-directories:  None

Path: \MARY
Sub-directories:  None

Path: \JOAN
Sub-directories:  None
```

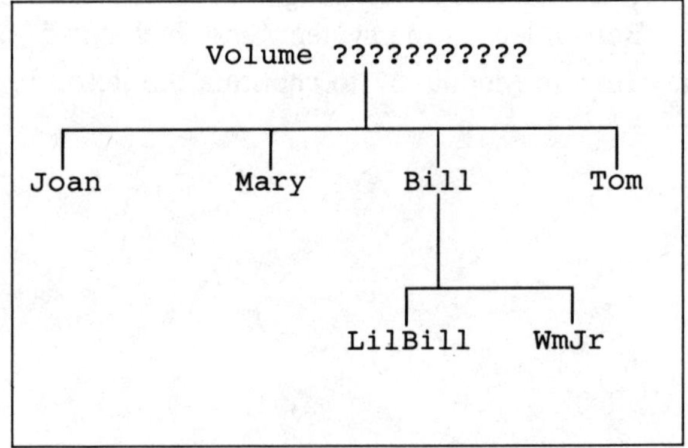

You can pause the display by pressing Ctrl-S. To resume the display, press any key. Another way to pause the display automatically is to add the MORE filter to the TREE command line by typing

```
TREE C: |MORE
```

If you want to view all of the filenames within each directory, you can type the TREE command followed by /F in the form

```
TREE C:/F          (or TREE C:/F ¦MORE)
```

A screen similar to the following is displayed:

```
[C:\]TREE C:

Directory Path Listing

Path: \BILL
Sub-directories:  LILBILL
                  WMJR

Files:            EDLIN .COM

Path: \BILL\LILBILL
Sub-directories:  None

Files:            None

Path: \BILL\WMJR
Sub-directories:  None

Files:            None

Path: \TOM
Sub-directories:  None

Files:            None

Path: \MARY
Sub-directories:  None

Files:            MEMO    .BAK
                  MEMO    .#01

Path: \JOAN
Sub-directories:  None

Files:            DEPT    .LTR
```

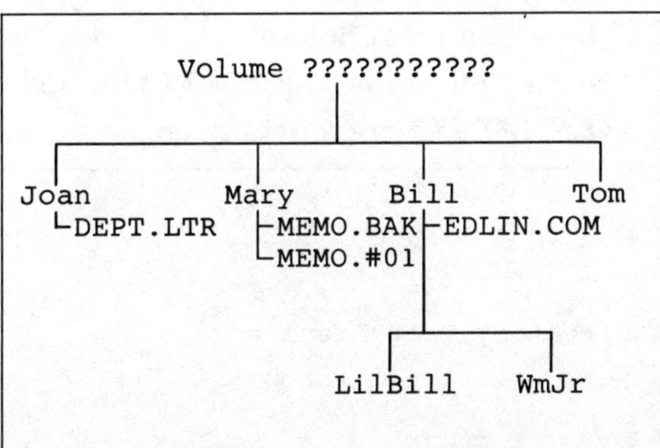

To print the above list on your printer, type the following:

```
TREE C: /F >prn
```

APPLICATIONS

It is often important to know all pathnames and filenames within file paths. The TREE command is an indispensable tool for determining the organization of your disk, particularly if it is a large fixed disk.

TYPICAL OPERATION

In this activity you use the TREE command to determine which pathnames and filenames exist on an OS/2 disk. Begin at the OS/2 prompt, [C:\].

1. Insert a scratch disk into drive A:.
2. Type **A:** and press **Return**.
3. Make a directory by typing **MD FANG** and pressing **Return**.
4. Type **TREE** and press **Return**; notice a display like the following:

```
[A:\]TREE

Directory Path Listing


Path: \FANG

Sub-directories:  None
```

5. Remove the FANG pathname by typing **RD FANG** and pressing **Return**.
6. Type **C:** and press **Return** to return to drive C:.
7. Turn to Module 48 to continue the learning sequence.

Module 61

TYPE

DESCRIPTION

The TYPE command is an internal OS/2 command. This command displays the contents of standard text (ASCII) files on your screen. The general form of the TYPE command is

```
TYPE filename
```

The named file is displayed on the screen. If it is longer than the screen, it scrolls upward until the last line of the file is displayed. Then the OS/2 prompt is redisplayed. The *typed* (or displayed) file moves upward so rapidly it is difficult to read. However, you can stop the movement by pressing Ctrl-S. When you are ready, press any key to resume scrolling.

The OS/2 Mode form of the TYPE command is

```
TYPE filename filename
```

so you can type more than one file with one TYPE command. Also in OS/2 Mode wild card characters (* and ?) are permitted. For example, if CHAP1.OS2 and CHAP1.BAK exist and you enter the following command:

```
TYPE CHAP1.*
```

then both files CHAP1.OS2 and CHAP1.BAK are typed. To list the first nine chapters in this book I can type:

```
TYPE CHAP?.OS2
```

and CHAP1.OS2, CHAP2.OS2, CHAP3.OS2, CHAP4.OS2, CHAP5.OS2, CHAP6.OS2, CHAP7.OS2, CHAP8.OS2, and CHAP9.OS2 are typed.

You can use the MORE filter command to freeze each screen full of information. Using TYPE LETTER.001 ¦MORE freezes each screen full of information and prompts you to strike a key to display the next screen full. See Module 33 for more information about filter commands.

If you want to display and print a file simultaneously, you can press Ctrl-P (or Ctrl-PrtSc) prior to pressing Return at the end of the TYPE command line. You should also check your printer for proper connection and power before you press Return.

The OS/2 piping commands (Module 44) also provide a means to route a typed file to your printer. Look at the following illustration:

```
TYPE filename >PRN
```

This command routes (or pipes) the named file to your printer.

APPLICATIONS

The TYPE command offers a convenient way to examine files by displaying them on your screen. For example, if you are trying to find a certain file and cannot remember what name you used, the TYPE command can come to your rescue. Just TYPE the suspect files to the screen until you recognize the one you need.

As mentioned above, TYPE also offers a quick way to print a file. By turning on printing (with Ctrl-P), you can dump a file to your printer to obtain a fast paper copy. You can also use the piping or filter commands described above. These operations eliminate the need to use word processing software to print a standard text file. Be aware, however, that you cannot TYPE (and print) binary or other non-ASCII format files; if you try, only garbage is displayed. This is because your printer is unable to process non-printable characters.

TYPICAL OPERATION

In this activity you use the TYPE command to display a file on your screen. Begin at the OS/2 prompt, [C:\].

1. Create a temporary file using the COPY command as follows:
   a. Insert a scratch diskette into drive A:.
   b. Type **COPY CON: A:TESTFILE** and press **Return.**
   c. Type **This is a test file.** and press **Return.**
   d. Press **Ctrl-Z**; then press **Return** to write the file to disk. (Ctrl-Z inserts an end-of-file marker.)
2. Type **TYPE A:TESTFILE**, press **Return**, and notice the following display:

```
[C:\]TYPE A:TESTFILE
This is a test file.

[C:\]
```

3. Type **DEL A:TESTFILE** and press **Return** to delete the file from your disk.
4. Turn to Module 11 to continue the learning sequence.

Module 62

VER

DESCRIPTION

The VER command is an internal OS/2 command that displays the version of OS/2 you are using. To run the VER program, type VER and press Return. The screen displays a message similar to the following:

```
[C:\]VER

MS OS/2 Version 10.00

[C:\]
```

APPLICATIONS

Because several different versions of OS/2 are available, you may wish to determine which version you are using. This is accomplished with the VER command. Knowing the installed OS/2 version is important, since different versions of OS/2 have different command forms. In addition, some programs are specifically designed to operate with specific versions of OS/2.

TYPICAL OPERATION

In this activity you use the VER command to see which version of OS/2 you are using. Begin at the OS/2 prompt, [C:\].

1. Type **VER** and press **Return.**
2. Notice the following screen illustration:

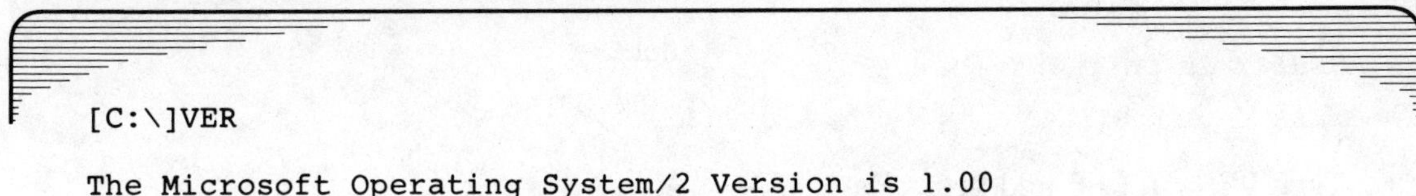

3. Turn to Module 34 to continue the learning sequence.

Module 63

VERIFY

DESCRIPTION

The VERIFY command is an internal OS/2 command. The command verifies that data is recorded properly when written to a disk, hard or floppy. The default setting is for VERIFY to be off. To turn VERIFY on, type VERIFY ON and press Return. When on, all disk write operations are verified for accuracy. To determine whether or not VERIFY is on, you can type VERIFY and press Return. The message "VERIFY is on" is displayed when it is active. When VERIFY is on, file operations take slightly longer because of the extra time it takes to check the data as it is written.

To turn VERIFY off, type VERIFY OFF and press Return. Now when you type VERIFY and press Return, the message "VERIFY is off" is displayed.

APPLICATIONS

You can use the VERIFY command when the integrity of data transfer is critical. In addition, turning on the VERIFY function eliminates the need to use the /V parameter during file copying operations (see Module 19).

TYPICAL OPERATION

In this activity you use the VERIFY command to turn on verification, then examine the VERIFY status, and finally, turn VERIFY off. Begin at the OS/2 prompt, [C:\].

1. Type **VERIFY ON** and press **Return.**
2. Type **VERIFY** and press **Return**; notice the display:

```
[C:\]VERIFY
VERIFY is on

[C:\]
```

3. Type **VERIFY OFF** and press **Return.**
4. Type **VERIFY** and press **Return**; notice the display:

```
[C:\]VERIFY
VERIFY is off

[C:\]
```

5. Turn to Module 43 to continue the learning sequence.

Module 64

VOL

DESCRIPTION

The VOL command is an internal OS/2 command that displays the volume label (or name) of the specified disk. You may recall from Module 34, which describes the FORMAT command, that an optional one- to 11-character volume name may be assigned to a disk by typing the FORMAT command with the /V parameter. The VOL command is used to check the name of a volume.

Typing VOL C: and pressing Return displays a message similar to the following:

```
[C:\]VOL C:
The volume label in drive C is DRIVE-C

[C:\]
```

The LABEL command (Module 39) lets you assign or change a volume name after a disk has been formatted.

In OS/2 MODE, typing VOL A: C: and pressing Return displays a message similar to the following:

```
[C:\]VOL A: C:
The volume label in drive A is SCRATCH

The volume label in drive C is DRIVE-C

[C:\]
```

APPLICATIONS

It is sometimes a good idea to assign volume names to disks for identification purposes. By giving a disk a meaningful volume name, you can examine the volume name to determine disk contents. Even if the paper label is separated from the disk, having an embedded, meaningful volume name lets you identify the disk quickly.

TYPICAL OPERATION

In this activity you use the FORMAT /V and VOL commands to assign and then check the volume name of the disk in drive B. Begin at the OS/2 prompt, [C:\].

1. Place a scratch disk in drive A: and close the load lever.
2. Type **FORMAT A:/V** and press **Return**.
3. Once the disk is formatted, notice the following prompt:

```
Enter up to 11 characters for the volume label,
or press ENTER for no volume label._
```

4. Type **SCRATCH** and press **Return**.
5. Type **N** in response to the "Format another (Y/N)?" prompt.
6. Type **VOL A:** and press **Return**; notice the following display:

```
[C:\]VOL A:
The volume label in drive A is SCRATCH

[C:\]
```

7. Turn to Module 39 to continue the learning sequence.

Module 65
XCOPY

DESCRIPTION

The XCOPY command is an external command. It is used to selectively copy files from one disk to another or to copy those files that have been created or modified since the last backup. The general form of the XCOPY command is

```
XCOPY A: C:\path\filename
```

This form of the command operates like the COPY command. There are a number of options that are added after the target filename to control file selection. The option letters, represented by /x in the following command line example, are quite useful.

```
XCOPY A: C:\path\filename /x
```

The value of /x controls the way XCOPY operates. Each of the available values is described in the following list:

/A — Copies files that have the archive bit, which is set with the BACKUP and ATTRIB commands, set to a value of one.

/D — Copies all files that are the same or later than a specified date. The date is added to the command as shown:

```
XCOPY A: C:/D:06-21-88
```

Note that the date format mm-dd-yy varies according to the country code.

/E — Creates subdirectories on the target disk even if the new subdirectories are empty. This happens when the command option used prevents the transfer of files within the subdirectory because they do not meet selection criteria.

/M — Copies files having an archive bit value of one. When copied, the archive bit is reset to zero on the source file. This lets you use XCOPY in backup operations. An archive bit value of one indicates that the file was created or modified since the last BACKUP or XCOPY /M operation.

/P — Displays a (Y/N)? prompt before copying a file to allow selection.

/S — Copies files from the source disk that are within and subordinate to the active (or *logged*) directory. This can include a number of directory paths, as XCOPY searches through the directory tree. This option does not create new directory paths on the target disk unless the /E option is also used. If /S is omitted, XCOPY works only within the named directory.

/V — As in COPY, this option verifies that data is written properly. As in the COPY command, the /V option slows the copy process.

A few important XCOPY features include:

- The default value of filenames is *.*.
- XCOPY creates file paths on the target diskette if they do not exist.
- You can specify target filenames as with COPY.
- XCOPY creates file paths on the target diskette if they do not exist.
- You can specify target filenames as with COPY.
- The maximum number of characters for a disk, path, and filename is 63.
- XCOPY does not copy hidden or deny-read files.

The following XCOPY command examples are provided for clarification and should serve as models:

```
XCOPY C:\ E:\ /S
```

— Copies all files from drive C:\ to drive E:\ including all files in subordinate directory paths. Drive E: may be another disk or a tape device.

```
XCOPY C:\ E:\ /S /P
```

— This command form performs the same operation as the preceding example except that each filename is displayed and you are prompted for a copy decision.

```
XCOPY C:\WP E:\ /S
```

— Copies all files from the C:\WP file path to the E:\WP file path. Any file paths that are subordinate to \WP are also copied from drive C: to drive E:.

```
XCOPY C:\ E:\ /S /M
```

— Copies all files in all subdirectories from drive C:\ to drive E:\. The /M option resets the archive bit of the source files to zero. The value zero indicates that the file has been modified (or created) since the last backup operation. This lets you substitute XCOPY for the BACKUP command.

NOTE

The XCOPY command may prompt you to specify if the target is a file or a directory. If you don't want to receive this prompt and have the program determine if the target is a file or not, you can copy the XCOPY program and name it MCOPY (like the following example):

```
copy /b xcopy.exe mcopy.exe
```

The MCOPY program is the same program except that it does not prompt you for the source type but uses the following rules in determining whether the target is a file or a directory:

- If the source is a directory, then the target is a directory.
- If the target ends in a backslash (\), then the target is a directory.
- If the source includes multiple files, then the target is a directory.

APPLICATIONS

The XCOPY command provides a convenient way to copy multiple files without having to copy each individually. The available options let you copy only those files that were created or modified after: 1) the last backup operation, or 2) a specified date. It also gives you an alternate way to perform a backup procedure without using the BACKUP command.

You can also use XCOPY to reset file attributes within a selected directory. This provides an alternate to the ATTRIB command.

The /P option displays a (Y/N)? prompt before a file is copied. This is a convenient way to copy several files from a directory without having to type the filename of each.

TYPICAL OPERATION

In this activity you use XCOPY selectively to copy files with the filename extension COM in all subdirectories. In addition, you use the /P option to display each filename before it is copied. Place a formatted diskette in drive A:. The following procedure uses C: as the source disk and A: as the target disk. Start at the OS/2 prompt, [C:\].

NOTE

In the following step, select three files to copy. Omit the rest by typing **N** in response to the (Y/N)? prompt. This will keep you from exceeding the capacity of the target diskette.

1. Type **XCOPY C:\OS2*.COM A: /S/P** and press **Return**. Notice that a filename is displayed and you are prompted for a copy decision.
2. Type **Y** to copy some files and **N** to omit others.
3. You may experiment with other forms of the XCOPY command until you are satisfied that you understand its operation.
4. Turn to Module 49 to continue the learning sequence.

Appendix A

TERMS AND DEFINITIONS

Term	*Definition*
Active program	A program that is running, either interactive or non-interactive.
ASCII file	A file consisting of characters that conform to the American Standard Code for Information Interchange. This is the standard code used by most computer systems. It is comprised of a 7-bit code that represents 128 characters and control codes.
Applications program	A computer program designed to perform a common application such as word processing, accounting, or database management.
Assembler	A program used to convert a file containing instructions recognizable by programmers into machine language recognizable by the microprocessor in use.
Assembly language	An instruction set comprised of mnemonics that are recognizable by an assembler program such as the IBM Macro Assembler.
Asynchronous	A communications format that is independent of instructions (or synchronization) from another computer with which it is communicating.
Binary file	A file made up of binary digits (bits) that is more space efficient than the 7-bit ASCII code.
Bisynchronous	A computer communications format that relies on interaction (or synchronization) with another computer with which it is communicating.
Bit	Binary digit; its value is either 1 or 0.
Branching	A decision point or *branch* in the flow of a program, process, or structure.
Breakpoint	A forced interruption within a computer program at a predetermined location or event.
Byte	A computer character made up of eight binary digits.
Calls	A program instruction that either fetches or sends one or more control codes or characters to a device or memory location within the computer.
Chains	A sequence of location pointers that connect (or *chain together*) the parts of a disk file.
Child process	A process that is started by another process.
Command	An instruction that is recognized by a computer program.
Compiler	A computer program used to convert a program written in a high-level programming language, such as FORTRAN or Pascal, into machine-recognizable code.
Concatenate	To collect separate elements into one. An example is when separate files are combined into one.

Term	*Definition*
Cursor	A flashing rectangle or bar that designates where characters are entered on a computer's display screen.
DOS	The acronym for Disk Operating System.
Diagnostic	A program used to evaluate the condition of a computer or computer device.
Directory	A list of filenames contained on a disk.
Dummy device	A device name used to simulate program operations.
Extension	One to three optional characters that can be added to the end of a filename for added clarity.
File	A program of data file residing on disk.
File allocation table	Part of the DOS directory in which statistical information about each file is kept.
File control block	A file control block exists for each file on a disk. Here, information about the file's name, location, and size is maintained.
Filename	A 1- to 8-character name used to identify a computer file; an optional 1- to 3-character extension may be used.
Flag	A digit used to indicate an occurrence or state.
Format	The way in which media (usually a disk) is organized.
Global	Applies to an entire file or disk.
Handshaking	The interaction between two devices, as in bisynchronous communications, where two computers are interdependent.
Hexadecimal	The base 16 number system consisting of the digits 0 1 2 3 4 5 6 7 8 9 A B C D E F.
I/O device	A computer input/output device. Your keyboard is an input device; your display screen and printer are output devices. Your disk drive is both an input and output device.
Inactive program	Program that is running but currently suspended.
Initialization	Setting a device to its beginning (or initial) state.
Interactive program	Program that can own the keyboard, display, and mouse.
Interface	The interconnection between two devices.
Interprocess communication	The exchange of information between programs (processes).
Landscape mode	A wide presentation. In printing, this refers to printing so that the printout is sideways on the paper.
Library	A collection of utility programs used by certain high-level programming languages. Having a library of common utilities eliminates the need for programmers to write commonly used routines.
Logged disk	The active (or default) disk drive.

Term	*Definition*
Logical device	A portion of memory or disk that is named and treated by software (or a program) as a physical device.
Macro assembler	An assembler that interprets an instruction set made up of mnemonics (abbreviated instructions) and converts them into machine language.
Multiprogramming	The concurrent processing of two or more programs.
Multitasking	The virtually simultaneous processing of more than one task by the operating system.
Multiuser	The virtually simultaneous processing of more than one user by the operating system on one computer.
Noninteractive program	An active program but cannot get input from a keyboard or mouse or output to a display.
Object file	A file created by an assembler.
Operating system files	Files that contain the operating system, OS2BIO.COM and OS2DOS.COM.
Overhead	Extra space used by system files.
Parallel	A computer connection scheme in which data elements are transmitted simultaneously (or in *parallel*) over multiple paths.
Parent directory	The top level directory for a specified directory path. Can be the top level (or *root*) directory but usually refers to a pathname one level below the root directory.
Parent process	A process that creates another process called a child process.
Partition	A portion of a fixed disk that is reserved for a group of files that operate under control of a common operating system, like CP/M-86.
Pathname	The name of a directory path within a tree-structured directory system. Used with DOS version 2.00 and higher.
Portrait mode	The vertical (or normal) printout mode.
Ports	Input/output connectors on a computer.
Process	A collection of system resources including one or more threads.
Prompts	A message displayed by a computer program to encourage a user response.
Protocol	A computer communication specification defining software and hardware requirements.
Queue	A list of events waiting to be executed.
RAM	Random access memory; a memory structure that allows the direct access of any part of computer memory, regardless of physical location.
ROM	Read-only memory; a preprogrammed device that cannot be altered.
Refresh	Update the screen with the latest information.

Term	Definition
Register	A storage location within a digital computer device designed to store data, instructions, or location or status information.
Root directory	The top-level or main directory within a tree-structured directory system.
Scratch disk	A working disk normally used for experimentation or practice.
Scroll	The vertical or horizontal movement of characters on a computer screen.
Serial	A computer connection scheme in which data elements are transmitted in a sequential stream (or in *serial*) over an electrical conductor.
Session	Refers to the group of processes associated with an application.
Spooler	A program that stores printer output on disk until it can print the output.
Starvation	A situation in which a process cannot complete its task because it does not get enough processor time.
Strings	A continuous series (or *string*) of characters. A text string can be any unique sequence of letters.
Swapping	A method of temporarily moving out of memory to disk some information that is not currently utilized.
System	Often used as a short form for Disk Operating System.
Task	The basic unit of work to be accomplished by the computer. A program running in the computer.
Thread	The smallest unit of processing within a process.
Time-critical process	A high-priority process that must be run ahead of other processes.
Time slice	The designated interval of time allocated for processing a task.
Utilities	A program that performs a commonly used task.
Volume name	The name (or label) given to a disk when it is formatted. With DOS version 3.00, the LABEL command lets you create, change, or delete a volume name.
Warm boot	Reinitialization of the computer and disk operating system without turning the power off. With DOS, this is achieved by simultaneously pressing Ctrl-Alt-Del.

Appendix B

OS/2 EXERCISES

1. About This Book
   a. Describe the purpose of an operating system.
   b. What is an OS/2 command?
   c. How is the Recommended Learning Sequence used?
   d. What does <cr> mean?
2. A Sample Session With OS/2
   a. How are disk drives designated?
   b. What is the left-hand disk drive normally designated?
   c. What is the difference between a floppy disk and a hard (or fixed) disk?
   d. List five ways to damage a floppy disk.
   e. What is the purpose of the write-protect notch?
   f. What is a distribution disk?
   g. What is a working copy?
   h. What is a prompt?
3. System Overview
   a. List five things that OS/2 can do for you.
   b. Draw a diagram of a disk showing tracks and sectors.
   c. What is a computer term for character?
   d. What does the term boot strap a computer mean?
   e. What is the difference between an internal and external program?
   f. What is a device?
   g. What keys are pressed to reset your computer?
4. ANSI
   a. List five extended display functions provided by the ANSI command.
   b. List two extended keyboard functions provided by the ANSI command.
   c. What command is used to enable ANSI functions in DOS Mode?
5. APPEND
   a. What is the function of the APPEND command?
   b. What is the OS/2 command to accompish the same function in OS/2 Mode?
   c. What is the purpose of keeping APPEND commands in the environment?
6. ASSIGN
   a. Write the command line for redirecting drive A: commands to drive B:.
   b. Write the command line that disables the ASSIGN command.

   JOIN
   a. What is the first step in using the JOIN command?
   b. What directory may not be used with the JOIN command?

c. What five commands are avoided when JOIN is in use?
d. When JOIN is in use, what is displayed when you type JOIN and press Return?

SUBST
a. What is the function of the SUBST command?
b. Describe the operation of the command SUBST E: C:\DOS\UTIL.
c. How can you display the current status of the SUBST command?

7. ATTRIB
   a. What is the purpose of the ATTRIB command?
   b. Write the command that makes MYPROG.COM a read-only file.
   c. Write the command to verify that MYPROG.COM is a read-only file.
   d. Write the command that returns the file to read/write.

8. Automatic File Execution (Batch Commands)
   a. What is a batch file?
   b. In what order are commands within a batch file executed?
   c. What key sequence is pressed to stop batch file operation?
   d. Why might you use the REM command?
   e. Give two good reasons for creating and using automatic batch files.

9. BACKUP
   a. What is the purpose of the BACKUP command?
   b. What is the command to backup all files in all directories from disk drive C: to disk drive A:?
   c. What is the command to backup those files in the WP subdirectory on drive C: to a disk in drive A:?
   d. What is the command to backup only those files that have been modified since the last time BACKUP was used?
   e. What does the command BACKUP C: A: /S /D:10-21-84 accomplish?

10. CHCP
   a. Is CHCP an external or interal DOS command?
   b. What does the CHCP command change?
   c. What command must be used before CHCP takes effect?

11. CHKDSK
   a. What is the purpose of the CHKDSK command?
   b. Why might you use the /F parameter with CHKDSK?
   c. What is meant by the message "Contains 2 non-contiguous blocks"?

12. Clear Screen (CLS)
   a. Why might you use the CLS command?
   b. Where is the prompt displayed after the CLS command is used?

13. CMD (OS/2 command processor)
   a. When you begin another command processor, what, if any thing, is in the new sessions environment?

b. What parameter informs CMD.EXE not to remain resident in memory after it has executed the specified command?
c. Why can't you change the environment variables of the previous command processor?

14. Code Page Switching
a. What is the primary purpose of code-page switching?
b. Describe how the CONFIG.SYS and AUTOEXEC.BAT files are used with code-page switching.
c. Describe the use of the MODE command in the preparation of code-page switching.
d. Write the MODE command that prepares your system for use with an EGA display.
e. Write the COUNTRY command that prepares your system for use with the Spanish language.

15. Codeview
a. Who usually uses the Codeview utility?
b. What command line is used to debug the file MYPROG.COM with Codeview?
c. How do you move Codeview's pointer to a specific memory address?
d. What command displays (or dumps) the contents of memory address 3C4?
e. Memory address 0105 contains 31 hex and you wish to replace it with 39 hex. What command lets you enter 39 hex in place of 31?
f. What command is used to quit the Codeview program?

16. COMMAND (DOS Mode command processor)
a. What are two reasons for starting another command processor?
b. How do you make the next command processor permanent in memory?
c. What is the maximum environment size?

17. COMP
a. What is the COMP command used for?
b. You want to compare a:file1 to b:file1. Give the command line.
c. If the files are different in size, what message is displayed?

18. Configuration Commands (The CONFIG.SYS File)
a. What is the filename of a configuration file?
b. How can a configuration file be created?
c. What effect does BREAK = ON have on DOS operation?
d. What does the command FILES = 20 do?
e. Describe a buffer.

19. COPY
a. Give four uses of the COPY command.
b. What does the term concatenate mean?
c. Define sourcefile and targetfile.
d. What is the result of the command COPY FILE1 + FILE2 FILE3?
e. What does the command COPY CON: MYFILE do?
f. What does Ctrl-Z do relative to the above question?

20. DATE
   a. Show how the date is typed in response to the date prompt.
   b. How can you bypass your response to the date prompt?
   c. Why is it important to type the date?

21. DETACH
   a. What kind of programs can be detached?
   b. How do you cancel a detached program? Why?
   c. Can DOS Mode programs be detached? Why or why not?

22. Device Drivers
   a. Why are device drivers necessary?
   b. Name five standard device drivers standard on all OS/2 systems.
   c. How are device drivers loaded?

23. Directory Commands
   a. What is the purpose of the DIR command?
   b. Describe two ways to pause the directory display.
   c. How are subdirectories created?
   d. Describe the directory "tree" structure.
   e. What must be done before a subdirectory can be removed from disk?
   f. Describe the purpose of MD, CD, and RD.

24. DISKCOMP
   a. Describe the purpose of the DISKCOMP command.
   b. Write the command to compare disk A: to disk B:.
   c. Write the command to compare an 8-sector disk to a 9-sector disk.
   d. What message is displayed if the disk comparison is okay?

25. DISKCOPY
   a. Describe the purpose of the DISKCOPY command.
   b. Write the command to copy the contents of disk A: to disk B:.
   c. What might be a problem when using DISKCOPY?
   d. Write the command to copy all files on disk A: to disk B: using the COPY command instead of the DISKCOPY command.

26. DPATH
   a. What is the purpose of the DPATH command?
   b. Where is the DPATH value stored?
   c. Write a DPATH command to access files on drive B: in the NEWDATA directory.

27. EDLIN
   a. How does EDLIN differ from a full-screen editor?
   b. What are some uses of EDLIN?
   c. Write the command to create a file named MY.BAT using EDLIN.
   d. How do you start entering text into MY.BAT?
   e. Once several lines are typed, how do you return to the EDLIN prompt?
   f. How is the file displayed (or listed) to the screen?

g. What does the command 5i do?
h. What does the command 4,6,1m do?
i. What command is used to save the file and return to DOS?

28. ERASE (or DELETE)
a. Describe uses for the DEL command.
b. Write the command to delete all files having the extension DAT.
c. How can all files on a disk be simultaneously deleted?

29. EXE2BIN
a. Where did this command get its name?
b. Write the EXE2BIN command for converting PROG.EXE to PROG.COM.

30. EXIT
a. What is the purpose of the EXIT command?
b. When does the EXIT command have no effect?
c. Can the last OS/2 command processor be removed by EXIT? Why?

31. FDISK
a. Describe the purpose of the FDISK command.
b. After a fixed disk is partitioned, what must be done?
c. Write the command to format hard disk drive C: and simultaneously transfer the operating system.

32. Filenames
a. What is the purpose of a filename?
b. What kind of filenames should you use?
c. What is an extension?
d. How many characters can you have in a filename? In an extension?
e. What do the extensions EXE and COM normally indicate?
f. What is a wild card?
g. Write the command to list all filenames beginning with "G."

33. Filter Commands
a. Describe the concept of filtering a command.
b. Give a use for the SORT filter.
c. What can the FIND filter be used for?
d. When might you use the MORE filter?

34. FORMAT
a. What does the FORMAT command do to a new disk?
b. What happens if you format a disk containing files?
c. Write the command to format the disk in drive B: with a system.
d. How do you assign a volume name to a disk when it is formatted?
e. Can you format a 360KB disk in a 1.2MB drive? If you can, how much storage does it have? Why?

35. GRAFTABL
   a. What characters are accessed using GRAFTABL?
   b. What is a common use for these characters?
   c. Write the command form for displaying the GRAFTABL status.

36. Grouping Commands
   a. List and define the purpose of each grouping command.
   b. Write a grouping statement that will only execute PROG2.EXE if PROG1.EXE terminates normally.

37. HELPMSG
   a. Write two ways a HELPMSG command will display the help screen for the SYS1490 error message.

   HELP
   a. How do you turn the Help line displayed at the top of the screen on and off?
   b. Which OS/2 command actually controls the Help line on the top of the screen?
   c. Is the HELP command an internal or external command? Why?

38. KEYB
   a. What is the purpose of the KEYB command?
   b. Where is the KEYB command normally found?
   c. What are the keyboard and country codes for Germany, Denmark, and the Netherlands?

39. LABEL
   a. What is the purpose of the LABEL command?
   b. Write the command to change an existing label to DISK #1.
   c. Write the command to change DISK #1 to DISK #2.

40. LINK
   a. List four functions performed by the LINK command.
   b. Who normally uses the LINK command?
   c. How is the file VM.TMP created?
   d. What is meant by compiling and linking?

41. MODE
   a. What outputs are controlled with the MODE command?
   b. Write the command to redirect printing from LPT1 to LPT2.
   c. Write the command to set the following communications parameters:
      Output port - COM1
      Transfer speed - 1200 baud
      Parity - None
      Data bits - 8
      Stop bits - 1

42. PATCH
    a. What should always be done before PATCH is run?
    b. What is the purpose of the PATCH command?
    c. When do you make patches?

43. PATH
    a. What does the PATH command achieve?
    b. Write the PATH command to access program files in the root (main) directory from a subdirectory.
    c. How are established directory paths canceled?

44. Piping Commands
    a. What is meant by piping?
    b. Write the command to pipe a directory to the file B:NAMES.LST.
    c. Write the command to pipe a directory listing to your printer.

45. Presentation Manager
    a. What does the Presentation Manager provide for OS/2?
    b. What programs take advantage of the Program Manager?
    c. What is meant by the term "client area"?

46. PRINT
    a. Describe the purpose of the PRINT command.
    b. What do the terms concurrent printing or print spooling mean?
    c. Write the command to print MYFILE.TXT with the PRINT command.
    d. Write the command to add the file DADS.LTR to the print queue.
    e. Write the command to terminate printing of all queued files.

47. Printing Operations
    a. How can you print text that is displayed on the screen?
    b. How can lines of text be simultaneously printed as they are displayed?
    c. Write the COPY command to print A:MYFILE.TXT.
    d. Write the piping command to print A:MYFILE.TXT on your printer.

48. PROMPT
    a. Why might you use the PROMPT command?
    b. Write the command to display the time as part of the DOS prompt.
    c. Write the command to display the pathname as part of the DOS prompt.

49. RECOVER
    a. Describe the purpose of the RECOVER command.
    b. Write the command to recover the file A:MYTEXT.DAT.
    c. What may exist at the end of a recovered file?
    d. What is the filename FILE0001.REC?

50. RENAME
    a. Why might you wish to rename a file?
    b. Write the command to rename all files with the extension CMD to PRG.

51. REPLACE
    a. What is the purpose of the REPLACE command?
    b. What is the purpose of the /A option?
    c. What is the purpose of the /P option?
    d. Describe the operation of the command REPLACE A: B: /S/P.
52. RESTORE
    a. What is the purpose of the RESTORE command?
    b. Write the command to restore all files from floppy disks in drive A: to a hard disk in drive C:.
    c. Write the command to restore all files with the extension TXT from floppy disks in drive A: to a hard disk designated drive C:.
53. Session Manager (Program Selector)
    a. What are the three main functions available with the Session Manager?
    b. What features does the Update function provide?
    c. How do you return to the Session Manager (Program Selector) from an OS/2 session? The DOS Mode?
    d. How do you indicate to the Session Manager to prompt for the parameters when you start a program?
54. SET
    a. What is displayed when SET is typed from the DOS prompt?
    b. Write the command to cancel path settings.
55. SETCOM40
    a. What is the purpose of the SETCOM40 command?
    b. Can you change the baud rate with SETCOM40?
    c. Does SETCOM40 allow you to share a COM port with an active OS/2 session?
56. SPOOL
    a. What is the default spool directory?
    b. Write the SPOOL command to use LPT1 output to be printed on COM1.
    c. What device driver must be loaded before the spooler can output to a com port?
    d. What command cancels the current file being printed by the print spooler?
57. START
    a. When is the START command normally used?
    b. Can the START command be used to start background programs? Why?
58. SYS
    a. Describe the purpose of the SYS command.
    b. Why might SYS not work on a disk containing files?
59. TIME
    a. Show how the time is typed in response to the time prompt.
    b. How can you bypass your response to the time prompt?
    c. Why is it important to type the time?

60. TREE
    a. Describe the use of the TREE command.
    b. How can you pause the display when using the TREE command?
    c. Write the command for displaying all files within directories.

61. TYPE
    a. Describe the purpose of the TYPE command.
    b. What is meant by scrolling?
    c. How can you pause and resume scrolling?
    d. How can you type and print a file simultaneously?

62. VER
    a. Describe the purpose of the VER command.
    b. Write the command to display the version of your OS/2 system.

63. VERIFY
    a. Describe the purpose of the VERIFY command.
    b. What is the default state of the VERIFY command?
    c. How is automatic verification turned on?

64. VOL
    a. Describe the purpose of the VOL command.
    b. How is a volume name initially created?
    c. How many characters are allowed within a volume name?
    d. Write the command to display the volume name of the logged disk.

65. XCOPY
    a. Compare the XCOPY and REPLACE commands.
    b. Which files are copied from one disk to another using the command XCOPY C:*.PRG A:/D:10-21-88?
    c. What is the effect of the command XCOPY A: B:/P?
    d. Describe the XCOPY /M and /W options.
    e. What two file types are not copied with the XCOPY command?

Index